Movie Moguls Speak

Movie Moguls Speak

Interviews with
Top Film Producers

STEVEN PRIGGÉ

McFarland & Company, Inc., Publishers
Jefferson, North Carolina, and London

LIBRARY OF CONGRESS CATALOGUING-IN-PUBLICATION DATA

Movie moguls speak : interviews with top film producers / Steven E. Priggé.
p.   cm.
Includes index.

ISBN 0-7864-1929-6 (softcover : 50# alkaline paper) ∞

1. Motion picture producers and directors — United States — Interviews.
I. Priggé, Steven, 1975–
PN1998.2.M72   2004   791.4302'32'092273 — dc22   2004014718

British Library cataloguing data are available

Cover photograph ©2004 Corbis Images

Manufactured in the United States of America

*McFarland & Company, Inc., Publishers
Box 611, Jefferson, North Carolina 28640
www.mcfarlandpub.com*

To my father,
Alan Priggé,
who shares this passionate love of movies with me

"Thousands and thousands of details go into the making of a movie. It is the sum total of all these things that either makes a great picture or destroys it. So, this is our mission as producers — to oversee it, to guide it, to give it birth."

— David O. Selznick,
producer of *Gone with the Wind*

Acknowledgments

It is time to share my gratitude with the many wonderful people who helped make my dream of writing this book a reality.

A very special thanks to the producers who were extremely generous with their time and thoughts and so kind to allow me to interview them. It was a sincere honor and pleasure to spend time with each and every one of you. You are all great producers but, more importantly, great people.

My appreciation to my father, Alan Priggé, who is not only a great dad, but one of my best friends. Without his tireless help with editing this book, the project would have never come to fruition. Thanks also to Lina Hansson for all of her genuine love and support; Lou Massaia, a true friend who has always supported me in my life and my work; my mother, Deanna Priggé; my sister, Dana Priggé; Robert Shoblock, Susan Prigge, Jules Mignonac, Burt Young, Chris Bregman, Keya Morgan, Jeanine Lobell, Anthony Edwards, Tom Weaver, Diane Kachmar, Carol Higgins Clark, Jerry Ohlinger, Egizio Panetti and Richard Hart, who supported me with their love and assistance. I tip my hat to you all!

Appreciation to Anne Bennett at Eon Productions; Roberta Shintani at the Dino De Laurentiis Company; Sarah Feinberg at Cappa Productions; Charles Pugliese at Killer Films; Kathy Liska at The Donners' Company; Annett Wolf at Wolf/Kasteler; Lori Imbler Vernon at Chartoff Productions; Cody Zwieg at Craven/Maddalena Films; Grady Lee, Gunnar Clancey, Tricia Gregory and Darren Miller at Cruise/Wagner Productions; Michael Milton and Monique Bell at The Producer Circle; Kathy Day and Ryan Patterson at Mace Neufeld Productions; Christina Stiegelmeyer at Miracle Pictures; Amy Noble at View Askew Productions.

Also, thanks to the many coffee shops in New York City, New Jersey and Los Angeles that allowed me to park myself at their tables for hours and hours with my computer.

Thank you, God, for giving me the strength to do this book.

Once again, my deepest gratitude to all of these valued companions that helped me on this journey called writing a book.

Contents

Introduction

Here's your front row seat to the most exciting, talked-about and profitable business of this or the past century—the making of motion pictures. Go behind the scenes with the deal makers, the creative visionaries, the financial packagers—the movie moguls who are the dynamic men and women producing our greatest films.

Certainly, the movie producers of today owe a debt to the producers of yesteryear, whose imagination and determination built an entire industry. Although I am writing this book in New Jersey, some 3,000 miles from Hollywood, I don't feel removed from the American film industry, since one of the first movies, *The Great Train Robbery* (1903), produced by Thomas Edison, was shot in nearby Fort Lee and West Orange. But, of course, someone said, "Go west, young man!"—and then Hollywood was built. It was the pioneering producers who built Tinseltown. They had the imagination and guts to sink their dollars into a risky dream that could have easily sunk. It was the legendary producers like Samuel Goldwyn, David O. Selznick, Jack Warner, Carl Laemmle, Irving Thalberg, Louis B. Mayer, Walt Disney, Darryl F. Zanuck and Adolph Zukor who made it all happen. Their magical names literally jumped off the silver screen at movie audiences sitting in the darkened theaters of a bygone era. In fact, my own sense of these pioneering producers was brought home when my father fueled my childhood fantasies by describing the one-hundredth birthday party of Adolph Zukor, which he attended at the Beverly Hilton Hotel in 1973. Zukor's Paramount Studios gave us a wide array of quality films like *The Ten Commandments, Shane, Psycho* and many, many more. My father reflected on the truly monumental evening by describing the hundreds of famous Hollywood stars who streamed in to salute this true pioneer producer who conquered all odds to make movies that mattered. Who couldn't be inspired by the guest list which included Bob Hope, Bing Crosby, Grace Kelly, Frank Sinatra, John Wayne, Katharine Hepburn, Warren Beatty, Robert Redford, Faye Dunaway and many more giants of the industry. They all paid homage to a dreamer who had the stuff to make dreams come true—the producer!

Somehow in the intervening years, with the decline of the studio system, the concept of the movie producer was not lost, but definitely took a back seat to the dynamics that brought the director and star to the forefront. Therefore, the public today is largely unaware of the three-dimensional contribution that a producer makes to their favorite motion pictures. Today, I feel that producers are, in fact, "unsung heroes"

1

because they are involved so totally in a project from the beginning — finding the script, attaching the director, attaching the talent, finding the money, getting the distribution — and yet, they do not get the credit they deserve. As always, the producer's task begins long before the start of production and doesn't end until long after the movie's final wrap. In the film world today, there is extraordinary attention paid to actors, actresses and directors, but what about the producers who gave them their first breaks? What about the producers who helped mold their careers? As you will learn throughout this book, the producers featured have given early opportunities to actors and actresses like Al Pacino and Demi Moore, film directors like Steven Spielberg and Todd Haynes and writers like Aaron Sorkin. We might never have heard of these legends if it wasn't for these monumental producers' behind-the-scenes insight and the ability to recognize talent.

The title of "motion picture producer" has become one of the biggest mysteries to come out of Hollywood. When you look at the on-screen credits on a film today, the proliferation of titles like "executive producer," "producer" and "associate producer" (with five names listed under each title) is baffling to audiences and film industry insiders alike. Obviously, it doesn't take fifteen producers to make a movie, so probably there *weren't* that many in reality. Professors teaching college and university film courses across the world have an increasingly difficult time explaining this phenomenon to their students. To quote producer Barbara De Fina, "The title of producer has become a big controversy. In fact, it has gotten out of control!" The Academy Awards Committee made a new ruling that only three producers on a movie could receive an Oscar. Doesn't that tell you something? In this book, I tackle the very important question "What does a producer really do?" I also bring to the forefront their major contributions to the biggest motion pictures of our time.

So, come join me as I talk intimately with the most successful movie producers in the world today — visionaries who have translated scripts, directors, actors and actresses into billions of dollars in box office profits, defying recessions and all economic downturns. I interview producers like Martin Richards (*Chicago, The Shining*), Michael Phillips (*Taxi Driver, Close Encounters of the Third Kind*), Barbara Broccoli and Michael Wilson (*GoldenEye, Die Another Day*), David Brown (*Jaws, A Few Good Men*), Martin Bregman (*Dog Day Afternoon, Scarface*), Lauren Shuler Donner (*You've Got Mail, X-Men*), Robert Chartoff (*Rocky, Raging Bull*), Dino De Laurentiis (*La Strada, Hannibal, Red Dragon*), Paula Wagner (*Vanilla Sky, Mission: Impossible*) and many, many more. Hear them answer questions, including: How did they break into what seems to be the impenetrable motion picture industry? What attracts them to a script that can ultimately make people line up around the block at theaters across the world on opening day? How do they handle a temperamental actor or actress who threatens to walk off the set halfway through production? How do you convince a studio or bank executive to give you $100 million or more to make celluloid dreams come true? In this book I will reveal who the "real" movie moguls of Hollywood are. Find out more about the "movers and shakers" who are there from the conceptual stage to the final edit of your favorite films: the producers.

David Brown

Born in 1916 in New York City, David Brown never had any desire to enter the film business. After graduating from Stanford University, he went on to a career in journalism and worked on such popular publications as Women's Wear Daily, Good Housekeeping *and* Cosmopolitan. *During Brown's time at* Cosmopolitan, *the head of 20th Century-Fox, Darryl F. Zanuck, had a vision to re-shape his studio. He wanted to run it like a national magazine and wanted what he called "the best editor in New York City, David Brown." David had no interest in entering the film business, but because of a nasty divorce, he took the opportunity to, as he recalls, "get a new life, a new wife and get the hell out of town." While working for several productive years at Fox, he became friends with Darryl's son Richard Zanuck. David and Richard decided to join forces, which would turn out to be one of the most prolific producing partnerships in film history. For their first film they chose* Sugarland Express *and decided to hire a first-time film director by the name of Steven Spielberg. David Brown has gone on to produce the classic films* Jaws, The Verdict, Cocoon, Deep Impact, A Few Good Men, The Player *and* Chocolat. *David is a recipient of the coveted Irving Thalberg Award. At 87 years old, he is currently busy with new projects and lives in New York City with his wife Helen Gurley Brown, editor-in-chief of* Cosmopolitan.

As far as my life goes, I can't give you the story of a passionate man who wanted to be involved in films and that was all he wanted to do. During the early years in my life, I had no interest in film. Movies were never my passion. It was never the passion of my generation during the '20s and '30s. My generation was a literary generation. I was in born in New York. I am a fourth generation New Yorker. I grew up in Long Island and on Southhampton. I remember my Long Island childhood as a time when I could find Indian arrowheads in my backyard. This was after the first World War when Long Island was being built up to be a suburban community. I enjoyed playing outdoors instead of sitting in a movie theater. I was a Boy Scout and camped out often. It was a rural childhood within the sight of the towers of Manhattan. I do remember the first movie I have ever seen. It was Charlie Chaplin in *The Gold Rush*. I remember the scene with the cabin teetering on the edge of the snow bank. Once again movies were never my passion. I was more interested in journalism. That was my first love and my first career. I got into the movie industry by sheer accident.

Where did you attend college?

I went to college at Stanford University. My major there was social sciences and journalism. I went from New York to San Francisco by ship to attend Stanford. The route I traveled was from New York to Havana, Cuba, to Kingston, Jamaica, through the Panama Canal up the West Coast of Central America, pausing briefly in Costa Rica to go to a theater in the jungle where I saw Mae West for the first time in a movie with Cary Grant, *She Done Him Wrong*, where she uttered that memorable line, "Come see me again some time." Then I was back on the ship up to San Pedro, which is the port of Los Angeles, then on to San Francisco where, at the age of 17, I got a train and went down to Stanford University and became a freshman in the class of 1936. I did college in three years because the summer courses counted and I did not want to travel back East. I attended college during the midst of the worldwide Depression, which makes this current economy look like a boom. Everyone was out of work. I was lucky to have an affluent father who worked for J.P. Morgan. When I graduated Stanford, I again left by ship to New York. I went to graduate school at Columbia University where I got a master's degree in journalism.

After graduating from Columbia University, did you immediately work in the field of journalism?

For my first full-time job, I was second-string drama critic and night editor for *Women's Wear Daily*. The magazine was not the trendsetter back then that it is today. We worked in an old building at 8 East 13th Street in Greenwich Village. During the same period, a very close friend of mine, Ernest Lehman, now an established Hollywood screenwriter who wrote *The King and I*, *North by Northwest*, *The Sound of Music*, *Who's Afraid of Virginia Woolf* and so on, was then a financial writer for a doomed publication called *Dealer's Commentator*. Ernest and I quit our jobs, partnered up and became freelance writers. We decided to specialize in show business articles. Our first article was about an old vaudeville star named Ted Lewis. Surprisingly, we wound up selling it to *Collier's*, the nation's second largest weekly magazine, for $400, a very decent amount of money for those days. We then went on to write and sell numerous articles about show business. After we wrote a freelance piece about Eddie Cantor, a huge Ziegfeld star and a movie star for Samuel Goldwyn, he invited us to write for his radio show. So, we became comedy writers as a result of becoming freelance magazine writers. Eddie wanted us to write a screenplay for a novel he bought the rights to, entitled *The Flying Yorkshireman*, by Eric Knight. It was a pre–Superman story about a man who had the supernatural power of flying. We were going to go to Hollywood, but the deal fell through. So, we had to wait a few years before Darryl F. Zanuck summoned me to Hollywood and I summoned Ernest Lehman to Hollywood.

Why did the head of 20th Century-Fox, Darryl F. Zanuck, summon you, a magazine editor, to Hollywood to make movies?

I got into the movies by sheer accident. I was a well-known journalist in New York and one of the reigning movie moguls of the time, Darryl F. Zanuck, the head of 20th, asked me if I was interested in working for him. Zanuck wanted to make some changes at 20th and wanted the best editor in New York to work for him. That was me, he said. I was the editor of several magazines, including my position as managing editor of *Cosmopolitan*, ages before my wife, Helen Gurley Brown, made it a worldwide publishing phenomenon. In any case, Zanuck wanted to fashion 20th Century-Fox like a national magazine. So I got offered the job and I took it. During that time in my life, I was going through a personal crisis, a very stressful divorce. That was the only reason I got into movies. I saw this as an opportunity to get a new life, get a new wife and get the hell out of town. I didn't even like movies, I had to go through a crash course of seeing them when I got the job. I was more interested in theater. I was interested in journalism and literature, as I still am now. Well, to make a long story short, the

David Brown. Photograph by David Derex.

next thing I knew, I was on a train called the Super Chief on my way to Los Angeles to become head of the story department at 20th Century-Fox.

What did your job duties consist of in this new position at 20th Century-Fox?

Story editors in those days were probably the number two job at the studios. It was a highly elevated position. I was one of the few people who had access to the head of production, Darryl F. Zanuck. My job consisted of finding the material to make movies. We didn't have development executives. We didn't have business affairs executives. I would buy the stories which 20th Century-Fox based their movies on. I was closer to Zanuck, I think, than most of his employees because I was a story man, and as far as he was concerned, stories were the single most important thing in making a movie. Richard Zanuck, the son of Darryl F. Zanuck, and I bonded during the bad days at 20th Century-Fox. Dick Zanuck and I became best friends, which we still are today. We got fired because there was a very odd situation involving his father, Darryl Zanuck. He was paranoid about us. Darryl thought we were trying to replace him at 20th. He felt that we were going to take over the empire. The fact was that he was losing his mind. He was putting his girlfriend in the movies and it wasn't working out. We felt for him, though. Finally, Dick and I were thrown out of 20th Century-Fox.

How did you make the transition to producer on your first film, *Sugarland Express*?

Immediately after our departure, Warner Brothers hired Dick Zanuck and me as executives. At first, the jobs satisfied our egos, but it wasn't what we really wanted to do. What we wanted to do was produce movies. Dick and I gave up our Warner Brothers contract and began looking for scripts to produce into major motion pictures. One of the first scripts that landed on our desk was a wonderful story called *Sugarland Express* with a young director attached by the name of Steven Spielberg. We had this particular script at 20th, but we were thrown out before we could do anything about it. We went to Universal as producers and Spielberg, Dick and I made *Sugarland Express,* which later led to our enticing him to direct *Jaws.* That was the beginning of Spielberg's success story and ours. I felt *Sugarland Express* was a wonderful movie. It is a true story about a woman who convinces her husband to escape from prison so they can attempt to kidnap their own child, who was placed with foster parents. Goldie Hawn was exceptional in the role of Lou Jean Poplin. I felt she should have won an Oscar for her performance. *Sugarland Express* went on to win a big award at the Cannes Film Festival. It did not turn out to be a commercial success, but it was artistically celebrated. I am very proud of that film.

Was it hard to pitch this film to Universal, you being a first-time producer and Steven Spielberg being a first-time feature film director?

Don't forget, we were experienced movie executives. Nobody thought we couldn't produce. Producing was a cinch compared to being an executive. When Dick Zanuck and I were at 20th Century–Fox, we were producing most of the films even though our names weren't credited. We selected the directors, actors and producers who back then were called supervisors. So, there was no problem with us being first-time producers. We were seasoned in that world. Steven Spielberg was a successful TV director, prior. As a very young man he directed a segment for a TV show called *Night Gallery,* with Joan Crawford and Tom Bosley. Then, he went on to direct a very successful television movie called *Duel* with Dennis Weaver, who played a business commuter pursued on the highway by a psychotic driver of a massive tractor-trailer truck. So, it wasn't as if Spielberg didn't know where to put the camera. It wasn't a very tough sell.

Can you tell me how *Jaws* came to your attention?

My wife, Helen, who was the head of *Cosmopolitan,* used to bring home 8x10 filing cards of the fiction that was being submitted to the magazine's fiction department and one of them had a small synopsis of the novel by Peter Benchley entitled, *Jaws.* The last comment on the card said, "Might make a good movie." Meanwhile, Richard Zanuck, who was on the opposite coast, heard about the same book and together we pursued it. If we had read the book twice, we would have never made the movie because *Jaws* had production problems that had never been solved up to that point in time. For instance, how do you create a shark that will swallow people, swim and do all those things, but be an artificial shark and still look real enough to scare people? Keep in mind that this was before the creation of CGI, computer generated images.

What was the prep like for a film of the magnitude of *Jaws*?

The preparation was to first get a script written. Several people ended up working on it. The writers involved were Peter Benchley, who originally wrote the book,

Jaws (1975, Universal Studios). Matt Hooper (Richard Dreyfuss), a young ichthyologist, and Chief of Police Martin Brody (Roy Scheider) are relieved when a tiger shark, believed to be the sea monster that has attacked swimmers, is caught by bounty hunters.

Carl Gottlieb and a playwright named Howard Sackler, who won a Pulitzer Prize for his play *The Great White Hope*. Through these talented writers, we came up with a script. During pre-production, there was a threat of an actors' strike which meant the picture had to be completed by a certain date, or we wouldn't start at all. So, we fudged it and promised to get the picture started and we finished in that time frame. Then, there was a huge search for a location. We went all over the country to find the right spot. We needed a vacation area that was lower middle class enough so that an appearance of a shark would destroy the tourist business. In Southampton, they would pay you to have a shark to keep the tourists out. So, that was not going to be the spot. We searched eastern Long Island and found it was too grand. So, we settled on Martha's Vineyard.

How many days did it take to film *Jaws* and how grueling was the shooting process for you, Spielberg and the rest of the crew?

For a total of 159 long days, we shot the movie *Jaws*. It was a tough shoot. We had several imitation sharks. We had numerous shark components. We created separate bodies, fins, heads, and it was a very difficult technically because there never was a real live shark. We had to invent one. Joseph Alves, our production designer, was told by everyone that it was impossible to invent a realistic-looking shark. We had to hire a man, Robert Mattey, to come out of retirement, who in his career created the giant squid in *20,000 Leagues Under the Sea* for Disney. He encouraged us to believe that we could create this shark. It was like building an entirely new device and we had to know about the temperature of the water, the depth of the water currents and the effect of salt water on the electrical equipment. It was a big engineering feat. As I mentioned, this was before the days of computer generated images. Everything you saw in the film actually took place. I remembered watching the first shark test and seeing the shark sink to the bottom of Nantucket Sound and we felt that our career in motion pictures had just sunk with it. Everything that could have gone wrong with the shark had gone wrong. We were literally [dead] in the water. There were no special effects on *Jaws*. We had no idea if the picture would work until we showed it to our cast and crew, who were around through all the failures and sometimes laughed, thinking this film would never work. They were so startled, they actually jumped out of their seats, even though they knew all the flaws and off-camera glitches.

How did the executives at Universal react to the first preview screenings of *Jaws*?

The studio was exhilarated and pumped up. There were two previews and they were both big successes. The first one was in a shopping mall in Dallas, Texas, and the second was at a theater in Long Beach, California. In those days, we circulated cards to get the audiences' reactions. We did not have focus or research groups. Just preview cards. I still remember one of the cards. It said, "This is a great picture, now don't fuck it up." Basically, after a preview, you started tinkering with the picture. We fixed only one shot that was not in the first preview screening. Steven Spielberg was not satisfied with the initial shot of the fisherman's head. Steven felt he didn't time it right and that is why nobody screamed. So we re-shot it in our editor Verna Fields' swimming pool in the San Fernando Valley. Steven changed it so that Richard Dreyfuss is underwater and the fisherman's head pops out of the hole of the sunken ship. The head floated into the frame of the camera instead of the camera finding the head. Steven was right because that produced the desired scream. Those first screams were the beginning of the legend of *Jaws* and the beginning of the "summer blockbuster" tradition.

What was the budget of *Jaws* compared to *Jaws 2*?

The budget for the first *Jaws* was $4 million and the picture wound up costing $9 million. *Jaws 2* wound up costing $30 million. We didn't budget it at all, because Universal would never have given a green light to a $30 million budget in those days.

After the tremendous success of *Jaws*, did the studio give you more freedom during the making of *Jaws 2*?

Nobody gives you freedom in the movie business. The studio controls the money, so they have the final word. Universal really wanted to make *Jaws 2*. Spielberg felt he had already made the definitive shark movie and thought a sequel would be a big mistake for him. Dick Zanuck and I decided to produce the film and it turned out to be highly successful. Howard Sackler wrote *Jaws 2*. It took a total of eight long months to shoot. It was a much more difficult picture to produce than *Jaws* because we had 13 children in it. We also had a navy of 18 sailboats which had to be anchored each time they were photographed and many more production obstacles.

Jaws (1975, Universal Studios). Quint (Robert Shaw) desperately fights to reel in the killer shark while Chief of Police Martin Brody (Roy Scheider) intently watches.

In a youth-driven market, especially today, I felt it was a pretty daring move to produce a movie about senior citizens. What attracted you to the script for *Cocoon*?

Cocoon was produced during a period where studio heads could still exercise their passions without calling up a research department to see what the demographics were for attendance. During *Cocoon*, Dick and I were helped by Lili Fini Zanuck, Dick's wife, who discovered the script. We developed *Cocoon* at 20th Century-Fox. We didn't think about old people or young people. We just thought it was a damn good story. So there were no discussions about a youth-driven market, and it ultimately worked. We weren't looking for the youth market or any particular market. We were just looking for a good movie. Today, it would be harder to convince a studio to fund a film like *Cocoon*.

Driving Miss Daisy (1989, Warner Brothers). A promotional shot of Daisy Werthan (Jessica Tandy) and her driver Hoke Colburn (Morgan Freeman).

You went through many struggles in getting the Pulitzer Prize–winning play *Driving Miss Daisy* from the stage to the big screen. Is that true?

That was produced by Dick Zanuck and his wife, Lili Fini Zanuck, and I was the executive producer. Obtaining the rights to Alfred Uhry's Pulitzer Prize–winning play, *Driving Miss Daisy*, was a battle. I had to telephone Alfred's agent, Flora Roberts, hourly. Over many meals, I entreated Alfred to favor the Zanuck/Brown Company. The film barely got made. It only got made because producer Lili Fini Zanuck had a lot to do with it. Warner Brothers only put up $4 million. We had an outside investor who bought the British rights and that turned out to be instrumental funding in getting the film made. It was extremely tough to get *Driving Miss Daisy* financed.

How did it feel to win the Academy Award for *Driving Miss Daisy*, a picture that no one wanted to originally finance?

It was standard. It had happened before.

Many people in the movie business always say, "Don't make a film about the movie business." Why did you go against that mold and produce a film like *The Player*?

I have been an avid magazine reader ever since I began as a magazine editor. There was a magazine I was reading called *Manhattan Inc.* and inside there was a little story called "The Player," which was an excerpt from a novella. I read it and felt that the author, Michael Tolkin, really knew what he was talking about in relation to Hollywood. I had read many stories, spent decades in Hollywood and I felt that this was the real stuff. Unfortunately, I felt it was impossible to make because of all the internal monologue of the character. I hadn't given it any further thought until I had lunch with a publisher at Time Books who said, "We are publishing a little book that might interest you called *The Player*." I said, "I read an excerpt on it." He said, "Maybe I should send you a copy for your own amusement." I said, "Sure, I'd love to read it." I read it and thought, "it won't make a movie, but what the hell, I'll offer him $2,500 and option it." Michael Tolkin took the $2,500 and his agent was angry and released Tolkin for selling it so cheap. I bought it so cheap because nobody else was interested in producing it. I made Michael Tolkin a partner and I told him to write the screenplay. He wrote the screenplay, and when I passed it around, we got idiotic responses by Hollywood. One person said, "Why Hollywood? Why not the steel business?" One day, Robert Altman called me and said, "You own a property that I was born to direct called *The Player*." I said, "Wonderful. Let's meet." We met and had breakfast at the Westbury Hotel in New York. Afterward, we decided to go with Altman. Originally, Chevy Chase was interested in starring in the lead role. His father published the book, but Warner Brothers would not let Chevy Chase appear in it. So we ultimately went with Tim Robbins, who was fantastic. Carrie Brokaw, who was the head of Avenue Pictures, expressed an interest in financing the development. We thought we had enough money to finance the picture without a studio by working with Avenue Pictures. Well, we didn't. By the time we finished *The Player,* the picture belonged to the Dawai Bank of Tokyo. We had so little money, we sometimes couldn't bail out our dailies from the lab. When *The Player* came out, it was an immediate success. An instant hit! It portrayed Hollywood in a way that Hollywood found amusing. It is a Valentine to Hollywood. But to be honest, Hollywood is much more bizarre than what we portrayed it to be in *The Player*.

How did you get 65 cameos with the likes of Jack Lemmon, Nick Nolte, Julia Roberts, Burt Reynolds, Bruce Willis and others, considering the very low budget on *The Player*?

Director Robert Altman attracts every actor in the world. Everybody wants to work with him. Altman is a great talent. It wasn't tough at all to get the 65 cameos. Altman could have gotten 165 cameos if he wanted to. He is that admired and respected as a director by the world's top actors and actresses.

The majority of your movies are based on either books or plays. What do you look for in a book or play when considering producing it into a major motion picture?

I don't care how I get a script as long as it's good. I honestly couldn't care less if it came from an original script, play or book. Obviously, if you have a script that is viable, you save a lot of time and money. When I read a piece of literature, I look to be moved. It is important to be emotionally touched. I need to cry, laugh and feel. I meant what I said at the beginning of our interview. At first, I did not have a passion for film, but I now have the same passion for films as I do for plays because of being involved with them. My entire career has been built on the written word. Starting with being a freelance writer for magazines and as a judge of short stories for the Benjamin Franklin Awards at the University of Illinois, words have been the key. It has always been words and stories that have moved me. When I am moved by a story written by anyone, that is my thrill. I think I've leaned towards plays during my producing career because when I was an executive at 20th Century-Fox, one of my jobs was to buy the film rights to plays all over the world. I bought the rights to plays like *The King and I* and *The Sound of Music*, so I was very familiar with the theater. I scouted plays all the time. So, it was a natural thing. I have always loved plays. I loved them as a child. I wanted to produce for the theater. I have produced seven shows and I am preparing for another right now. We, most recently, had an artistic triumph, but a commercial failure in *Sweet Smell of Success*. I was very proud of that musical. John Lithgow won a Tony Award for his role. I also produced a play called *Truth*. Years ago, I produced a fabulous play called *A Few Good Men* on Broadway, before I made it into a major motion picture.

Could you tell the story how you discovered someone who has evolved as one of the greatest writers in film and television, Aaron Sorkin, and his play, *A Few Good Men*?

The way *A Few Good Men* came about was basically this. I read a tiny article in *The New York Times* about a little one-act play called *Making Movies* by a guy named Aaron Sorkin. It intrigued me. I asked one of my associates to find out more about the writer Aaron Sorkin. We found out he had written a play called *A Few Good Men* and they were having readings off–Broadway. I went there with my theater partner, Louis Allen, and his wife, and we acquired the rights and produced it for Broadway. Later, when I was developing movies for Tri-Star, I presented this script to them. Mike Medavoy said, "It is an interesting play, but we would not be interested in funding it unless you have a star director and a star actor or actress already attached." I said, "We don't have that." He said, "Sorry, I can't help you." Later, I got a call from a man at Castle Rock named Alan Horn, who is now with Warner Brothers. He said, "We are interested in making a movie of a play you produced called *A Few Good Men*." I said, "We don't have any stars." Alan said, "I don't give a damn if you don't have any stars. We'll make it anyway." I met with Alan Horn and we made a deal. Lo and behold, Tom Cruise came to New York, saw the play and said, "I want to be in this." Then Rob Reiner, who was one of the partners at Castle Rock, said, "*A Few Good Men* is going to be my next picture that I'm going to direct." Jack Nicholson and Demi Moore heard about it and they wanted in. The company that wouldn't buy it lost out to the company which would buy it under any conditions and, in the end, got the stars anyway. That is how I produced the film *A Few Good Men*. Subsequently, that is how Aaron Sorkin started his career in television as well.

You have worked with Hollywood's most talented directors, like Steven Spielberg, Robert Altman, George Roy Hill, Ron Howard and so many others. Is there any one director that stands out from the rest of the pack?

Well, they are all different. I worked with Alan Parker, who directed *Angela's Ashes*, and produced it along with my associate, Kit Golden. It is a picture that I am very proud of. I like the style of director Phillip Noyce. We did *The Saint* together in Moscow and

Top: A Few Good Men (1992, Castle Rock). Col. Nathan R. Jessep (Jack Nicholson), in full uniform, stares down the courtroom. *Bottom: A Few Good Men* (1992, Castle Rock). In the story of a peacetime military coverup, Navy lawyers played by Demi Moore and Tom Cruise confer about the pending case.

England. The director for *Chocolat*, Lasse Hallstrom, is so very talented. Sydney Lumet, who directed one of my favorite movies that I have ever produced, *The Verdict*, with Paul Newman, is one of the best directors in the business. All the great directors that I have had the pleasure of working with stand out for different reasons. Steven Spielberg possesses one style, while Billy Friedkin has another style. They all are different, but I am honored to have worked with every one of them.

You have worked with many great actors and actresses, ranging from Paul Newman, Robert Redford and Tom Cruise to Jessica Tandy, Demi Moore and so many others. What guidance can you give to an aspiring actor or actress?

You have to have talent, God-given talent. You also have to study. If you can get a shot at the theater, I think it is the best training for acting in movies. Naturally, there are big differences between stage acting and film acting. Stage actors project their voices, while movie actors whisper. Jack Nicholson can be dangerous and incredibly effective with a whisper. George Lang, who played one of the lead roles in the Broadway production of *A Few Good Men*, projected beautifully on stage, but it was too much for film. Obviously, he was not going to work for the movie. We actually read all the actors from that show, but they were too strong for us. There are exceptions, though. Morgan Freeman originally came from the theater. The first time I saw him act was in the off–Broadway production of *Driving Miss Daisy*. Morgan told me he thought he never had a shot at the movie. I said, "Morgan, like the New York Lottery says — hey, you never know." And look, he got the part and he was great! But there is a difference between film and stage and if you accommodate that difference, theater has the tremendous power to submerge yourself in a role and make you stand out. The acting world can be quite a bit of luck. I have personally gotten breaks because of luck in my own life. The luck of the draw was that Darryl F. Zanuck was looking for a story editor and I was going through a divorce and wanted to get out of New York. Now, that was luck. If I hadn't had been lucky enough to get that call, I wouldn't have gone to Hollywood, and I wouldn't have met my wonderful wife, Helen.

How important is the musical score for a movie?

In the case of *Jaws*, it practically made the movie. We first screened *Jaws* with the studio executives without any music. When the lights turned on, nobody said anything. I turned to Sid Sheinberg, who was then the head of Universal, and said, "What do you think of the film?" Sid replied, "It's okay." When composer John Williams put the *Bum, Bum, Bum, Bum* in the movie, the imagination took over and we had one powerful film. It changed the whole feel of the picture. Steven Spielberg is quoted as saying that the score of *Jaws* is clearly responsible for half the success of the movie. Music is as powerful as anything else in a film.

The definition of the title of producer has become one of the big mysteries in Hollywood. Can you define what you do as a producer?

Richard Zanuck and I are proud to be among the group of true producers. We both agree that there are not many real producers left. A producer is someone, man or woman, who has a vision of a movie, having found a literary property, a script, a novel, a poem, a play, and the belief that it can become a movie. The producer has to be capable and willing to go through the long process of bringing this vision to the screen. That means finding a writer who can adapt it, finding someone who will finance the writer and then finding a director. You have to find the right director who will attract the right actors to make this a reality. A producer has to be able to deal with handling a budget and, of course, has to be able to guide the marketing of the film. But, primarily, the main thrust of the job is identifying the property on which the movie is based and shepherding it through development, assembling a crew, principal photography, post-production and finally on to the marketing of the film. All those things are what a producer is supposed to do, but very few do, especially today.

There have been so many stories about producers romancing actors and actresses to keep them happy during the production of a film, such as buying Elizabeth Taylor a diamond necklace or giving Frank Sinatra an automobile. Have you had to do a lot of that during your producing career?

That might have existed during another era. However, I feel it is more important to comment positively on an actor's or actress' work during production. You also have to protect them from obsessed fans. Genuine care and involvement are also very important. I have always made it a point to go to dinner with each member of the cast and key members of the crew during production. Due to all the hours you spend working on a movie, it is important to make the film set feel like a family atmosphere. To answer your question more precisely, there are no lavish gifts given out today like the old days of cinema. The best gift you can give an actor or actress is a great script and a picture that has the potential to be a hit.

You and Dick Zanuck have had one of the most powerful and successful producing partnerships in film history. Can you tell me about your relationship?

Dick Zanuck and I bonded in the early days of 20th Century-Fox's falling apart. We became lifelong friends. Our partnership is a real collaboration. We can finish each other's sentences. I have enjoyed every moment working with him. He is like a brother. Now I have a brilliant young woman, Kit Golden, who is president of my company, the Manhattan Project. Kit has brought me *Angela's Ashes*, *Chocolat*, and I have made her a producer as well. Partnerships are like marriages. You fight, but together you each bring something to the table that the other does not necessarily have.

Did you ever consider directing?

No, you have to wake up way too early in the morning.

Being a former successful journalist, did you ever consider writing a screenplay?

I am not good enough. Dramatic writing is a whole different world from writing a piece of prose. Dramatic writing is a specialty. You have to be gifted. Many novelists want to be dramatists, but no dramatists want to be novelists. That was told to me by a famous writer, James Michener, who wrote *South Pacific*, *Hawaii* and *The Bridges at Toko-Ri*, among other things.

How do you think the business has changed since you started your producing career?

The movie business has gotten a lot duller. Today, it is run by multi-national corporations, rather than by entrepreneurs who have a true passion for it and the risk-taking spirit to possibly fail, in order to do something that they believe in. It is all about money and marketing now. It is not nearly as much fun.

Are there any real studio heads left in the film business?

Harvey Weinstein and Sherry Lansing come to mind.

What interests you beyond all your successful career achievements?

Well, my wife Helen and I enjoy traveling to uncomfortable places. We go on elephant safaris and travel to places like Turkey, China and Indonesia. We are planning on going to the South Pole next year. We just got back from an amazing trip to Cambodia. My wife and I share a passion for adventure and discovery.

What does the future hold for Mr. David Brown?

I am now 87 years old. I hope the future holds a few more years of productive life. I have four Broadway shows in various stages of development. I have four movies in development as well. I am also currently writing a book. So, I have various projects in the works.

David Brown Filmography

Framed (Rob Lowe) 2001, TV — executive producer; *Along Came a Spider* (Morgan Freeman) 2001— producer; *Enigma* (Kate Winslet) 2001— co-producer; *Chocolat* (Juliette Binoche, Johnny Depp) 2000— producer; *Angela's Ashes* (Emily Watson, Robert Carlyle) 1999 — producer; *Deep Impact* (Robert Duvall, Tea Leoni, Morgan Freeman) 1998 — producer; *Kiss the Girls* (Morgan Freeman, Ashley Judd) 1997 — producer; *The Saint* (Val Kilmer, Elisabeth Shue) 1997 — producer; *A Season in Purgatory* (Patrick Dempsey) 1996, TV miniseries — executive producer; *Canadian Bacon* (John Candy, Alan Alda) 1995 — producer; *Watch It* (Peter Gallagher, Tom Sizemore) 1993 — executive producer; *Rich in Love* (Albert Finney, Ethan Hawke) 1993 — co-producer; *The Cemetery Club* (Ellen Burstyn, Danny Aiello) 1993 — producer; *A Few Good Men* (Tom Cruise, Demi Moore, Jack Nicholson) 1992 — producer; *The Player* (Tim Robbins, Whoopi Goldberg) 1992 — producer; *Women & Men 2: In Love There Are No Rules* (Juliette Binoche) 1991, TV — producer; *Driving Miss Daisy* (Morgan Freeman, Jessica Tandy) 1989 — executive producer; *Cocoon: The Return* (Don Ameche, Wilford Brimley) 1988 — producer; *Target* (Gene Hackman, Matt Dillon) 1985 — producer; *Cocoon* (Don Ameche, Wilford Brimley) 1985 — producer; *The Verdict* (Paul Newman) 1982 — producer; *Neighbors* (John Belushi, Dan Aykroyd) 1981— producer; *The Island* (Michael Caine) 1980— producer; *Jaws 2* (Roy Scheider, Lorraine Gary) 1978 — producer; *Jaws* (Roy Scheider, Robert Shaw, Richard Dreyfuss) 1975 — producer; *The Eiger Sanction* (Clint Eastwood) 1975 — executive producer; *The Girl from Petrovka* (Goldie Hawn, Anthony Hopkins) 1974 — producer; *Willie Dynamite* (Roscoe Orman, Diana Sands) 1974 — producer; *The Black Windmill* (Michael Caine) 1974 — executive producer; *The Sugarland Express* (Goldie Hawn, Ben Johnson) 1974 — producer; *SSSSSSS* (Dirk Benedict) 1973 — executive producer

Barbara Broccoli
and Michael G. Wilson

Michael G. Wilson was born in New York City. After attending Stanford Law School and working as a lawyer for eight years, his creative juices prompted him to leave that field and enter the movie industry. Being the stepson of legendary James Bond producer Albert "Cubby" Broccoli, Wilson had early experiences with the movie industry. His first producer credit came in 1979 on the James Bond film Moonraker. *He then acted as a co-screenwriter (with Richard Maibaum), writing such classic 007 films as* For Your Eyes Only, Octopussy *and* A View to a Kill. *In 1995, he began a producing partnership with his sister, Barbara Broccoli. Their first three films (*GoldenEye, Tomorrow Never Dies *and* The World Is Not Enough) *have made a staggering $1.1 billion at the box office. Michael G. Wilson has made major contributions toward making the series of James Bond movies the longest-running franchise in film history.*

Barbara Broccoli was born in London, England. Being the daughter of legendary Bond producer Albert "Cubby" Broccoli, she was introduced to the film business at a very young age. After graduating from Loyola Marymount College in California with a major in communications, she immediately went into the film industry. Barbara worked her way up through the ranks of various Bond films. She went from being an assistant director on Octopussy *to an associate producer on* The Living Daylights. *In 1995, on the hit movie* GoldenEye, *Barbara began her producing partnership with her brother, Michael G. Wilson. Their latest Bond film,* Die Another Day, *resulted in the biggest 007 opening ever with $46.3 million in box office revenue in the U.S. alone, proving that, thanks to Broccoli and Wilson, the James Bond franchise is bigger and better than ever.*

MW: Every kid from my generation, because I'm 61 years old, spent Saturday afternoons watching movies at the cinema. I was brought up on Westerns. I also enjoyed comedies and my favorite comedy teams were Abbott and Costello and Dean Martin and Jerry Lewis. As far as the pictures that I saw that affected me and are relative to the James Bond films I am producing today, they are *North by Northwest* and *The Guns of Navarone*. These two movies came before the James Bond franchise, but at the time, definitely showed new direction for film.

BB: I was born in 1960, so I grew up in London during the '60s. I used to go and see all of director David Lean's pictures. I liked his big epic films like *Dr. Zhivago* and

Left: Michael G. Wilson. Photograph courtesy of Eon Productions. *Right:* Barbara Broccoli. Photograph courtesy of Eon Productions.

Lawrence of Arabia. When I saw those pictures as a little kid, I was very impressed. I also enjoyed watching old movies on television. But looking back, I think the big epic dramas were what really impressed me and started my love for cinema.

Where were you both educated?

MW: I went to a science and engineering college. After graduation, I attended Stanford Law School and, ultimately, became a lawyer. I practiced law for eight years, part of which I was a partner in a law firm. In college I didn't take any courses related to film.

BB: I went to Loyola Marymount College in California and studied film communications. I had already had some practical film experience from working with my father on his James Bond films during summer breaks. It was basically a four-year college with filmmaking courses. After I graduated, I went straight into working in film.

Since this film franchise has been in your family almost your whole lives, what is your earliest recollection of being on a James Bond movie set?

BB: One of my earliest memories is being on the set in Japan when my father was making *You Only Live Twice.* I was about seven or eight years old at the time. I have a very vivid memory of seeing this exotic tea ceremony. I don't think I quite understood what went into making a film. I think I was more impressed with the beautiful costumes, beautiful setting and the very talented actors and actresses. I remember Japan as being this exotic world. It was great to see all of these people I knew and cared about from London in this beautiful exotic setting. I remember feeling very comfortable there.

As a child, I also remember going to Pinewood Studios just outside London quite a lot. My sister and I used to go on Friday afternoons after school. We didn't hang out on the set too often and were more apt to be in my father's office. Actually, being in my father's office was great too, because I got to see him at work first hand. So, I began my learning process of producing at a young age.

MW: My first recollection of stepping foot on a Bond set was on *Dr. No* in 1962. They were shooting at Pinewood and were reconstructing a beach scene. That was where I first met Sean Connery.

Can you tell me about your first paid job on a Bond film?

BB: My first job was on *The Spy Who Loved Me*. I worked in the publicity department. My job duties consisted of mostly logging stills and doing captions for those stills. I thought the job was a lot of fun.

MW: My entry into working on a Bond film happened on *Goldfinger*. I was on the Fort Knox shoot. I went over with Cubby, our director Guy Hamilton, production designer Ken Adams, our cameraman and our first assistant director. That was the only crew we took from the U.K. to the United States. I was on summer holiday during law school and was basically a third assistant. We only had a crew of 20 on this shoot. It was a great learning experience.

On which Bond film did you begin your producing partnership?

BB: Well, Cubby and Michael produced together for years. Then, I became an associate producer on *The Living Daylights*. I was credited with Michael for the first time as a producer on *GoldenEye*.

MW: I have to say that even when Barbara was an associate producer, she was very involved. We have actually been working together since *Octopussy*, where she was the third assistant. She has worked her way up on various Bond films. Then, Barbara became an associate producer and now a producer, and my partner. We have worked together for a long time, besides knowing each other all of our lives, since we are brother and sister.

When you were putting together *GoldenEye* and looking for a new Bond, was Pierce Brosnan always in the forefront of your thinking?

BB: The decision to have Pierce play James Bond was conceived very early on. Cubby was always very much a part of that decision-making process.

MW: We really wanted Pierce. He was an extremely enthusiastic choice to play James Bond.

When *Tomorrow Never Dies* was released, it was up against *Titanic* at the box office. How important as a producer is it to solidify the right release date for your film? Can it make or break the ultimate success of a picture?

BB: I don't know how you can predict what a good release date is. In that particular case, and now it sounds ludicrous, but everyone at the time thought *Titanic* was going to be a big disaster. Very few people thought it was going to do well. We didn't have any idea how successful the film was going to be, but we did know it was a big

James Bond (Sean Connery) and Pussy Galore (Honor Blackman) in *Goldfinger. Goldfinger* ©
1964 Danjaq LLC and United Artists Corporation. All rights reserved.

picture and going head-to-head was a bit risky. As it turned out, I think it was a good
release date for us. Our guiding philosophy has always been that if there is a good
group of movies out there, the audience will support them all. Good movies are good
for overall business. It turned out that *Titanic* was a huge success and that was terrific.
We were number two at the box office and trailed right behind it. We benefited because

some moviegoers were saying, " Let's see *Tomorrow Never Dies*," while others said "Let's see *Titanic*," and in the end, they wound up seeing both of them. We did very well with *Tomorrow Never Dies*. Back in 1981 when we opened up against *Raiders of the Lost Ark* with *For Your Eyes Only*, nobody knew anything about *Raiders*. To the movie's credit, Steven Spielberg was well-known at the time. But, I don't think, in general, that you can let other pictures dictate what you do. We are in a fortunate situation here. We have the longest-running series in film history. People know what Bond is. We never shy away from a date because of another picture.

MW: We let other people give us breathing room. On the other hand, in the case of *Die Another Day*, we were up against two really big pictures, *Lord of the Rings* and *Harry Potter*. They were on either side of us. As it turned out, we all did really well at the box office.

BB: When there aren't any really good films in the theater, then people begin to be negative and wind up not going to the movies. I feel they are afraid of being disappointed, or perhaps were just disappointed the weekend before.

MW: I agree, because I feel that when viewers have gone to a movie the previous weekend and enjoyed it, I think they want to repeat that experience the very next weekend.

Since James Bond has been an ongoing, successful series for 40 years strong, do you feel you have to top yourself with every next picture?

MW: It is extremely hard when you are doing a series because you have a pre-existing fan base, eagerly anticipating every film you make. There are different ways you can top yourself. We like to do it with a more interesting storyline, with a new and exciting situation for Bond, rather than with a bigger "bang," if you know what I mean. I think the action sequences and the exciting car chases have been a hallmark of the James Bond films since *Thunderball*. The unique stunts, gadgets, gorgeous women and exotic settings are all the things that the viewer comes to expect when paying to see a new Bond film. We just try to offer those same elements at a level that keeps it fresh and exciting for the audience.

BB: I think when you have a successful film series, there are certain parameters that you have to follow. We do try to make it different so that we can send Bond and the audience on a new and different journey. We try our very best to not make the Bond films all the same. Some films are more dramatic, some are more adventurous and some are more exotic. I think the goal is to create a new story and see where it takes you. The other most important factor is the choice of director. The director can shape the picture and within certain parameters take it in very different directions. I think our latest director Lee Tamahori [*Die Another Day*] very much wanted to make it a bigger and more elaborate type of film. So, I think his vision had a lot to do with it.

MW: In *Die Another Day*, I think our having James Bond captured at the end of the opening sequence, instead of his usual neat getaway followed by a kiss with the beautiful girl, was a welcome change. Instead, we have Bond dragged off to a prison and beaten. That is a real departure, taking Bond into that situation. However, I think it was fresh, exciting and extremely well-received.

James Bond (Pierce Brosnan) and Wai Lin (Michelle Yeoh) during a dramatic motorbike chase through the crowded streets of Saigon in *Tomorrow Never Dies*. *Tomorrow Never Dies* © 1997 Danjaq LLC and United Artists Corporation. All rights reserved.

As evidenced by *Die Another Day,* your films have had one of the most elaborate product placement programs of any film in history. Do the product placement and the cooperative advertising from manufacturers help the budget and bottom line of your film?

BB: I think one of the biggest fallacies of product placement in films is that you get fees for putting products in your movie. We have received fees maybe once or twice, but we do not generally take fees for a product. It comes out as promotion activities for support of the film's release. The interesting thing is that if you go back and read the Ian Fleming books, you will see the way he describes Bond's world. Fleming describes the types of clothes Bond wore, that his cigarettes were hand rolled, the types of cars he drove and so on. These were the ways to describe a man who has particular tastes in luxury items that he enjoys using. Since it was always a major part of the books, it has become a major part of the films. I also think that when you show the luxurious world he inhabits, the audience wants to inhabit that world too. I think these fun things like his impeccably stylish suit that doesn't wrinkle, even from an explosion, makes the audience part of the experience. These product exposures help support the release of the film when we need it.

MW: Actually, some things are hard for us to do without the support of these companies, especially regarding to the automobiles we use. During the filming of *Tomorrow Never Dies*, we did a car chase in a garage in Germany. We had so many gadgets on the car, with so many different things that each gadget did that we wound up needing 19 of the same BMWs for the scene. Each car had different amounts of damage done, and they all had different functions on them. Even though it was the same model

Pierce Brosnan and Halle Berry at the start of a production press conference for *Die Another Day*, held at Pinewood Studios. *Die Another Day* © 2002 Danjaq LLC and United Artists Corporation. All rights reserved.

of car, each car was unique. Since we had to modify the cars and all the work was done by computer, we had to have factory engineers on site. We had two BMW engineers there to keep the cars operating because they operated far beyond spec. So, in a situation like that, we couldn't have done that scene without the full cooperation of the manufacturer.

BB: On the film *Diamonds Are Forever,* the film that Cubby made in 1971, I think you'll notice that Ford Motor Company got very well-deserved credit on that film because of the huge car chase all through Las Vegas. We needed support with those cars, so Ford did it for the credit. I think a lot of films have licensing partners. Because we are a continuing series, we get involved with solid on-screen images that become traditions. Over the years, we have had good relations with wonderful marketing people and their products and we like to keep them going. I think that if you don't have Bond drinking Bollinger Champagne, the audience would say, "What's happening?"

What was the budget on *Die Another Day*? Some reports are that is was well over $100 million.
BB: Let's just say it was a lot!
MW: Actually, I'd have to check with the studio before I could reveal the exact numbers.

What percentage would you say went to the bottom line?
MW: Twenty-five percent of the total budget.

What percentage went to the editing, CGI and the dynamic visual effects that seemed to surpass any previous Bond film?
BB: With post-production, I'd have to say ten percent of the total budget.

Do you both get involved heavily in the post-production of your films?
MW: Barbara and I are totally involved, from soup to nuts.

I had read that on *Die Another Day*, you had a thousand-person crew, all filming and working simultaneously. Is that employee figure accurate?
BB: If you count the construction crew, then that figure is probably right.
MW: Some days, we also had a lot of extras. But, if you're just talking about shooting crews, we had about 600 construction employees alone when we were at full blast.
BB: We have multiple units on our films. The first unit crew is about 140 people and our second unit is about the same. Then, we have other smaller units that consist of underwater and aerial shooting. Also, we have other departments like art and editing. So, we do have a very big crew.

As producers, how do you keep the film organized and move consistently forward with that many people on staff?
MW: We have a very professional production office team that supports us in handling that part of the film. They deserve a great deal of credit.

James Bond (Roger Moore) and Anya Amasova (Barbara Bach) in *The Spy Who Loved Me. The Spy Who Loved Me* © 1977 Danjaq LLC and United Artists Corporation. All rights reserved.

BB: We also have great department heads. When you are producing a movie, it is key to hire the right department heads. These people do an amazing job. They oversee exactly what is going on and if there is a major problem that they can't handle, they then report it to us.

MW: The administrative part of the production process is a facet that Barbara handles and oversees more than I do. She is more experienced from being an associate producer on previous Bond films. Barbara is great with the budget and scheduling. I think for both of us, the real work we do is keeping the picture moving from an artistic point of view. There are always issues of casting and script changes. Since we have such a large second unit crew, one of us has to go out with them and make sure they are moving along on schedule. We communicate consistently between the director, the assistant director and editors to make sure we are getting the footage that we ultimately need. So, it is that kind of intense and organized supervision from a producer's point of view that really counts.

BB: Michael and I have to make sure we are shooting the script in an orderly fashion and keeping our time frame on target, so we can deliver the final product on the release date. We also have to make sure we are keeping the film within its budget requirements. Sometimes we have to make decisions during production like cutting out a sequence because we are going over budget. We are basically like train engineers keeping the train on the track.

MW: We are usually not more than five percent over budget. Most of the time, we are right on budget.

All 007 fans see Pierce Brosnan on the screen as the smooth actor who plays the consummate agent, James Bond. In reality, what does he bring to the table behind the scenes for you, his fellow cast members and the crew?

BB: Pierce is such a lovely, giving guy. He is so professional and hard-working. He brings his enthusiasm, energy and spirit to the set. He is never late, never a problem or a prima donna. Pierce is completely up for it and pleased to come to work. I think that is a very important influence for everybody else.

MW: Here is a perfect example of Pierce. In the middle of shooting *Die Another Day*, he injured his knee. He daringly hobbled along for a couple of weeks until he couldn't take the pain any more. We closed the picture down for seven days while Pierce went to California to have specialists attend to his knee. We re-scheduled the whole picture. Pierce came back and never had a day off. Through his diligent physical therapy regimen, his knee gradually healed so he could do the action scenes. Throughout this rigorous process, Pierce never complained once about it. He has been fantastic! Pierce would say to Barbara and me, "I really hope I didn't screw things up for you guys...." He is a totally unselfish kind of person.

Your Bond girls are always good-looking and popular, but never the high profile type like Academy Award winner Halle Berry. How did you wind up casting Berry in the *Die Another Day* role of "Jinx"?

BB: Halle wasn't an Academy Award winner when we signed her to play "Jinx" in Bond. But it was to our good fortune that she became one.

MW: In fact, she hadn't have even been nominated for an Oscar yet.

BB: Halle is a fantastic actress, absolutely drop-dead-gorgeous and perfect for the role of "Jinx." The character was written for a hot, sexy, sassy agent who could be Bond's equal.

MW: It is important to remember that it was not written as a black role and was just written as a role for a woman. We weren't trying to cast anyone with a particular ethnicity. She just brought her own chemistry and was fantastic.

BB: Halle is another absolute professional and she is happy to come to work, always smiling and friendly with the crew. She and Pierce got along very, very well. So we were lucky. These pictures shoot for a very long period of time. Six months straight. We are all off in difficult locations with all types of weather conditions. So, people can soon get tired and cranky, but not Pierce and Halle. It says a lot about them and how professional they are.

With popular adventure films like *The Matrix*, *X-Men* and *Spider-Man* proliferating, do you feel that your films today should contain more action and fewer love scenes?

BB: I think we like to have a little bit of everything. People who come to see a James Bond film expect a lot of action and stunts and things like that. However, I also think they expect sexy love scenes. We constantly try to give them everything.

MW: Bond is supposed to be about mystery and intrigue along with the action. So, we want to keep it that way. That's why Bond is unique, original, and has been around for 40 years.

In the earlier days of Bond, you frequently stuck with the same director, John Glen. Now there is a different director on every one of your films. What do you look for when searching for a Bond director?

BB: We look for someone who is a true filmmaker, whose body of work reflects diversity and style. We look for a director who has enough experience to be able to handle the complexities of multiple-unit shooting. We also need someone who, when we meet them and talk about James Bond, understands the essence of Bond. The director has to be up for the challenge of making a film with a character that is so well-established and has to be willing to push the envelope a little bit. We've been extremely lucky with our choices so far. We have picked some very interesting directors who have gone on to all kinds of films after James Bond. Lee Tamahori, who directed *Die Another Day,* is a special director and we thought his film, *Once We Were Warriors*, was a phenomenal piece of filmmaking. After we saw the film and met him, we sensed his genuine enthusiasm for Bond. It was simply great chemistry. Lee was the right guy and we were very, very lucky to get him.

MW: We actually wait until after we are done writing the script to attach a director. Then, it is a search to find the director that is right for the story. There are plenty of great directors out there, so we are always keeping our eyes open. We've discovered that it's good to get a director who is on the way up. The director has to bring a lot of enthusiasm to the set. This is key.

You have used two writers, Neil Purvis and Robert Wade, on back-to-back Bond films. What attracted you to them?

BB: We had hired them based on a script that they had written for a film called *Plunkett and Maclean,* which is a terrific sort of adventure film. It was dark, witty, sexy and inventive. Michael and I thought they were extremely inventive writers. I think, again, it comes down to chemistry. We liked their work. They came in. We sat down with them. Before they were hired, we spent weeks and weeks having discussions with them to see if they had the right attitude. They were big Bond fans and pitched great ideas. It takes a long period of time to get people used to working the way we do on these films. We are a true film series, so a lot of people come in with pre-conceived ideas. When you talk to them, you realize how often writers get stuck, mired in the past. When you were asking earlier, "What's the first film you remember seeing?"—I think for a lot of the general public, it was Bond. They can actually go back to where they were when they saw their first Bond film. Maybe they were sort of pubescent. So, you essentially find a frame of reference yourself, but it's actually like talking to an eight-year-old. You don't want someone like that writing or directing your new Bond film. I think it is about finding out whether or not we are all on the same page about the essence of Bond. It is a fine line between a Bond film and an *Austin Powers* film. We don't want to go off in the wrong direction.

MW: Because of the way we work, a lot of writers don't want to work with us. A typical writing process is six months, which includes meeting two or three times a week for hours and hours. After we assign the director, the final three months are spent refining the script and meeting daily. You have to really get along with people. It is that kind of intense brainstorming session that gets the job done.

How do you feel about the title of "producer" in film today?

BB: It is so hard to describe what a producer does. Often, you look at those credits with a list of seven executive producers on a film and there is usually a sound business reason for each one of those huge lists. In Hollywood, the development process for a film can go on for years and years. So producers can come and go, but the name still stays on the film. There are different types of producers, such as line producers and creative producers. It is really hard to define a producer in these times.

MW: Many times, they are associated with an actor as a business manager. Some people are promoters. They get their name attached to a script and, under contract, their name cannot be removed.

BB: It is very hard to get a film made. We are very lucky to be a part of a successful film series. However, since it is so difficult, there are many negotiations that go on behind the scenes. So, whether it is rightfully or wrongfully so, more and more people are getting their names on the production credits. Usually everyone who has their name attached has something to do with the film. True, sometimes they are removed from the process and all they get is their name in the credits. Such is the nature of the business.

The definition of the title of producer has become one of the big mysteries in Hollywood. Can you define what you do as producers?

BB: Michael and I are a true team and I think a good balance for each other. Michael's background is quite different and he understands the technical side. He is on target with all the CGI technology. We have slightly different interests, but we basically do the same thing and tend to compliment each other.

MW: I agree that primarily we do the same thing, but we use our strengths in different ways. As I said earlier, Barbara is very good at the scheduling and budgeting. She is also good at casting and dealing with wardrobe issues. I am probably not as involved in those areas. The point is that we both spend a lot of time putting the script together, attaching the right director, scouting locations and casting the picture. Then, we get into the execution part. It was an interesting situation dealing with our editor, Christian Wagner, who worked on *Die Another Day*. He told me that this was the easiest edit he ever had on a picture. I asked him why and he said, "You guys see every foot of rushes and then, when the director and I put it together, you come in with your comments and do it all in such an organized and smooth manner." Being a producer who is truly involved in the production helps every position and employee on the movie. We feel the basic challenge is to make sure that from the time we sit down to do the script to the time we are shooting the picture, we all are doing the same picture. So, when we all sit down for post-production and editing, the process is very smooth.

BB: As very involved producers, we know the script intimately. We know what was shot intimately. So, we know all aspects of the film.

MW: We remember alternative takes that we had seen in rushes. It is that kind of involvement in the process that makes you a successful producer. You have to totally live with the picture. We do look at all of the footage. Sometimes our directors can't sit and watch all the second unit stuff and model work because it gets too overwhelming. We are there to help out, to add another dimension of creative support.

Could you ever see yourselves directing an upcoming Bond installment?

BB: No, not me. It is too much hard work. I could see Michael doing it, though.

MW: No, I'm too old now.

BB: You have to have a specific type of brain to be able to handle the intricacies of directing. I don't have that type of brain.

MW: Barbara and I both like to be on the set and close by. When we are not on the set, we receive phone calls daily from the director, asking us what we think about this or that. We all toss around ideas and keep an open dialogue. So, our being there is comforting for the director. We also deal with the back and forth involving the studio. They bother us instead of bothering the director.

You have the longest-running series in film history. To what do you attribute to its enormous success?

BB: The success of the James Bond films is due to what Ian Fleming originally created. The Bond character is so interesting and exciting and offers so many possibilities.

MW: Yes, it is certainly flexible enough. Different unique actors like Sean, Roger and Pierce can play the 007 role, and each brings new excitement to it and a new interpretation to the same character. We managed to survive five changes in casting of our main character. It is really quite amazing.

BB: We have a very dedicated team of people who make these films with us. When our crew, cast and director steps on a James Bond set, they give it their all. They all want to do better than the previous installment. So, there is a constant sense of pride and achievement in the making of these films that goes up and down the ranks.

How do you feel about "take-offs" of Bond like *Austin Powers*?

BB: *Austin Powers* is an outright comedy and ours is an action adventure with a bit of tongue-in-cheek. Both films are very far apart. We have to be careful to not fall into "*Austin Powers* land" when we are writing a scene. I don't think they have the same problems we do. I don't think they sit around and say they are getting too serious. The frame of reference is so different. Our company's film, *Dr. No,* created this whole genre. So, many films and TV shows were born from our film series. As we said earlier, if there are good movies out there and they succeed, it just helps business. So, since *Austin Powers* is such a great spoof of the old Bond films, I think it just helps people enjoy going to the movies and seeing this sort of genre. It's all a win–win situation.

MW: If you're popular enough to be spoofed, then you are very lucky. If filmmakers take the time to invest time and money into a film that will spoof you, then it means you have had a great impact on them and the film industry as a whole.

What did you both learn as producers from watching your father Albert "Cubby" Broccoli?

BB: As far as I'm concerned, everything!

MW: I was with him daily from 1974 onward. We used to share the same office and worked right across from each other. You can't get any more of a mentor than that. It was special. That's for sure!

BB: His whole attitude towards making a film was very interesting. He made pictures for the public. It sounds pretty straightforward, but Bond is made for the audiences. Cubby loved standing at the back of a movie theater and hearing the audiences responding to a picture. When making these films, I think you have to make sure they're not too complicated, but always interesting and enjoyable. So, we keep that philosophy in mind. The Bond films never have been self-indulgent or say or do anything except entertain people.

MW: Sometimes people make films to impress other people in Hollywood. That's not what James Bond is all about.

Do you feel producers do not receive the credit they deserve? That the general public is way too focused on the director as being the filmmaker and not the producer?

BB: That can often be the case. There are fantastic producers out there. Take someone we really admire like Paul Vance. The man has gone to great lengths to get certain pictures made. Throughout the history of Hollywood, there have been producers who have put everything on the line to produce a picture and get it made. Samuel Goldwyn, because he believed in the film *The Best Years of Our Lives,* put up his house as security. I think if you have passion and determination, you can be a successful producer. I think it is important to know when to compromise and to know when not to compromise. Producers can get pretty deluded by the studio system. I think it is very easy for that to happen. It's a very difficult to get films made. Often producers are faced with all kinds of dilemmas about casting. A studio could say, "If you have this person and that person, we will make this film." If the producer knows that's the wrong choice, do you still make the picture with the studio or do you fight to try to raise funds on your own to make the film the way your experience tells you to make it?

MW: When I started getting involved, United Artists was the company that distributed Bond. Their philosophies were to get filmmakers into the mainstream — producers and directors. They supported them. Now that philosophy has died off. Today, there is a lot of development in-house and producers are primarily just hired. They can be fired easily.

Albert R. "Cubby" Broccoli, Roger Moore and Barbara Bach in publicity photo shoot for *The Spy Who Loved Me*. *The Spy Who Loved Me* © 1977 Danjaq LLC and United Artists Corporation.

BB: Most producers do not earn a living unless the film gets made. Some have a development deal. However, it can take years to get a film made. It is a very complex route to make it happen.

Do you think there is too much packaging going on in Hollywood today?

MW: A lot of talent packaging has come into play. There wasn't as much packaging back in the '60s and '70s. Now a lot of the agencies have gotten involved in packaging deals. They represent writers, actors, directors and they put together a whole package. The studios are going along with that. So, the producer's job of putting all the pieces together becomes less important.

How important is it to constantly communicate with your directors during production?

BB: Most directors need someone to talk to during production. I think a lot of times today, a producer will package a deal and then, once shooting starts, they tend to disappear. Then, the poor director is essentially stuck in the middle of a desert with a script that doesn't work and a bunch of actors who are miserable. The studio says, "We don't really care, just get the film finished and don't annoy the star."

MW: Then, they might even say, "Don't worry, we'll send down an executive." Usually, he or she stops by the set once in a while.

BB: Film is a collaborative medium. So, the director needs to collaborate with his or her cameraman and editor. Having a producer on set that the director gets along with is vital. The producer must stand up against people who are screwing up the film. "Cubby" used to say all the time, "The most important thing a producer can do is stop people from screwing up the picture." Again, it sounds terribly simple, but there are all kinds of people with good intentions who can, in fact, screw up a film.

MW: In the studio system, there are corporate power plays among various people. They want to make themselves seem effective and sometimes egos come into play. More and more directors I have talked to say, "We make the best films when we have good, strong producers."

BB: True, in this way, the director does not waste a lot of energy and valuable time in back-and-forth discussions with the studio. Instead, the director can get on with the business at hand. Directing a picture requires an enormous amount of energy, as well as mental and physical agility.

What about the old saying, "Too many chefs can spoil the broth?" Does that apply during the production of your films?

MW: I can't tell you how many days you get a call from someone at the studio level with a brilliant idea, completely out of left field. Then, you have to take the time to explain why the brilliant idea doesn't work.

BB: Or, that the idea can't possibly work because we shot the sequence three months ago in a faraway location.

MW: Or, that a person's brilliant idea on page 30 will totally destroy the picture from page 70 onward. You need patience and intense focus to be able to explain all of that. The director doesn't have the time to deal with it. So, it's better that we protect the director and we handle situations of that nature.

Since your Bond films are so anticipated, they are reviewed by critics with a fine tooth comb. Do you both think that you are thick-skinned when it comes to criticism?

MW: When I read a bad review, I burst into tears immediately (laughing).

BB: Yes, we always cry (laughing).

MW: Seriously speaking, Barbara and I take the good with the bad. Some people see the films and they love them and some hate them. However, through it all, Barbara and I never lose our focus. One of the pictures that I was involved in as a writer and producer generated this reviewer comment: "The producer, the director and the writer of this picture should be shot." So, I smiled and said, "I guess I get two bullets then." Criticism is simply the nature of this business.

Could you see yourselves doing anything else for a living?
BB: I feel that Michael and I could own a café. That would be fun.

MW: We hosted a birthday barbecue party this summer and I was doing the cooking. I got a little behind schedule, so Barbara came over and helped by cooking the fries and putting the food on plates. So, we began to feel we could open up a café (*laughing*).

BB: Yes, and a roadside café, at that. Michael and I could be short order cooks. So, if Bond goes under, we plan on becoming short order cooks (*laughing*).

What does the future hold for Michael G. Wilson and Barbara Broccoli?
BB: We truly enjoy what we do. We love making pictures. So, hopefully we will get to make some more. There are numerous projects on the rise. We are just moving right along.

MW: We produced the theatrical version of *Chitty Chitty Bang Bang* and we're hoping to take that to New York. There may be another totally different kind of picture we're working on and that has possibilities. Of course, the next Bond film is also in the works. Whenever we travel around the world, we're amazed to see how many people are so excited and anxious in every country, asking, "Oh, when is the next James Bond film coming out?" When you see that, it makes you happy and encourages Barbara and me to produce more Bond films and keep the tradition alive!

Barbara Broccoli Filmography

Die Another Day (Pierce Brosnan, Halle Berry) 2002 — producer; *The World Is Not Enough* (Pierce Brosnan, Sophie Marceau) 1999 — producer; *Tomorrow Never Dies* (Pierce Brosnan, Michelle Yeoh) 1997 — producer; *Crime of the Century* (Stephen Rea, Isabella Rossellini) 1996, TV — executive producer; *GoldenEye* (Pierce Brosnan, Izabella Scorupco) 1995 — producer; *License to Kill* (Timothy Dalton, Carey Lowell) 1989 — associate producer; *The Living Daylights* (Timothy Dalton, Maryam d'Abo) 1987 — associate producer

Michael G. Wilson Filmography

Die Another Day (Pierce Brosnan, Halle Berry) 2002 — producer; *The World Is Not Enough* (Pierce Brosnan, Sophie Marceau) 1999 — producer; *Tomorrow Never Dies* (Pierce Brosnan, Michelle Yeoh) 1997 — producer; *GoldenEye* (Pierce Brosnan, Izabella Scorupco) 1995 — producer; *License to Kill* (Timothy Dalton, Carey Lowell) 1989 — producer; *The Living Daylights* (Timothy Dalton, Maryam d'Abo) 1987 — producer; *A View to a Kill* (Roger Moore, Christopher Walken, Grace Jones) 1985 — producer; *Octopussy* (Roger Moore, Maud Adams) 1983 — executive producer; *For Your Eyes Only* (Roger Moore, Carole Bouquet) 1981 — executive producer; *Moonraker* (Roger Moore, Lois Chiles, Richard Kiel) 1979 — executive producer

Martin Richards

Martin Richards grew up in the Bronx with dreams of making it big. He was in his first Broadway show at nine years old and went on to become a singer playing famous venues like the Copacabana and the Latin Quarter in New York City, eventually traveling to Las Vegas to play the Sands. When his singing career didn't take off big time, Richards decided to start a career behind the scenes, first as a casting director for movies like On the Waterfront *and* Love Story, *and then as a Broadway producer when he raised $60,000 for actress Rue McClanahan and her revival of* Dylan. *After that, Richards became "Mr. Broadway," producing hit after hit:* Sweeney Todd, Crimes of the Heart, Grand Hotel *and, of course,* Chicago. *Shows produced by Richards and his company, The Producer Circle, have received an incredible 36 Tony Awards, the Pulitzer Prize, seven Outer Circle Awards and 17 Drama Desk Awards.*

Richards segued into movies, producing The Boys from Brazil *starring legendary actors Gregory Peck and Laurence Olivier,* The Shining *starring Jack Nicholson and* Fort Apache, The Bronx *starring Paul Newman. However, his ongoing labor of love was and is* Chicago, *which took him 27 years to get from stage to screen, bringing him his first Academy Award for Best Picture in 2002. Martin Richards resides in New York City and has numerous film projects on the slate.*

Having studied voice from the age of seven and since I was on Broadway by the age of nine, every movie I ever cut class for was a musical. Everything that Fred Astaire and Gene Kelly have ever done in their lives, I saw. But, my favorite movies are: *Mrs. Miniver, Now, Voyager, Wuthering Heights* and *Mr. Skeffington.* I also saw every Joan Crawford movie that she ever made. My heroes growing up were Spencer Tracy and Edward G. Robinson, who were in some amazing gangster pictures. Like every other male from my generation, I wanted to look like Tyrone Power and Tony Curtis. Ironically, I ended up being Tony Curtis' stand-in on three pictures. I have a very varied taste when it comes to films that I like. Growing up, I was a big dreamer and I went to the movies to dream.

Why did you segue from acting into producing theater and major motion pictures?

I started my career in entertainment as a singer. I was in my first Broadway show when I was nine years old. The very first production I was in was *Mexican Hayride* starring Bobby Clark, Rita Moreno and June Havoc. I played the newsboy in it. Then, as

I got older, I did acting and I kept getting parts on television shows. I was always being cast as a hood, which was so against type for me. But, I loved to sing and I sang everywhere for years when I was 14, 15 and 16. My mother kept saying to me, "With all of this acting and singing, you are going to eat out of a garbage can. What are you going to do with your life?" I actually listened to my mother for a brief period of time and I decided to go to college to study architecture. The reason I chose architecture was because my grandfather, who died of cancer at 55, was a great architect and actually built Radio City Music Hall. I lasted two years studying architecture. I truly hated it, so I went back to what I truly loved — singing. I sang everywhere: The Copacabana, the Sands, the Latin Quarter. The owner of the Latin Quarter was dynamic showman Lou Walters. In

Martin Richards. Photograph courtesy of The Producer Circle.

fact, I am still friendly with his daughter, Barbara Walters. I remember Barbara walking around with pigtails and braces. About that time, I recorded an album for a label owned by United Artists. I sold 250,000 copies of a song I did called "What Makes One Fall in Love." I also did musical commercials for Tootsie Rolls with Diahann Carroll. I then became the opening act at Basin Street for Herb Alpert and the Tijuana Brass. They wrote a song for me called "For Once in My Life" and they asked me to perform it. I performed it but refused to record it, because, at that time rock 'n' roll was on the rise. I had one more record on my contract and I wanted to do something more "cutting edge." Then, Bobby McFerrin wound up recording the song and it was a failure and I said, "I told you so." However, six months later Tony Bennett came out with the same song, sang it the same way I was doing it, and it became a mammoth, mammoth hit. Stevie Wonder eventually did it and it became another hit.

I really wanted to get booked in Las Vegas. I finally got Shelly Schultz, who was Johnny Carson's manager, to sign me. He booked me into the lounge at the Sands. I made $4,000 a week, which was the most I ever made. However, it was costing me personally $5,000 a week to make the show because I needed new arrangements, a new piano player, a bass guitarist and the back-up quartet. By the time I paid for everything, I was broke. My singing career never took off big-time. It was a shame, because after getting standing ovations at Basin Street, I, unfortunately, never made the jump from the middle to the top level of success.

I then started to put my life in perspective. I called my then agent Shelly and said, "My first agent, Tom Ward, who I used to help out occasionally at his office, asked me to come work for him. So, I am going to take a year off to do that." So over that year

I cast all the bit parts and extras for *The Seven Year Itch*, *Somebody Up There Likes Me*, *On the Waterfront*, *Butterfield 8*, *Love Story*, *The Out-of-Towners* and a million other pictures. I then got a call to work at Fox to cast with Alex Gordon. How I got into producing was that Rue McClanahan came up to my office and auditioned for me. She asked me to see a scene she was doing at Actor's Studio. She is a brilliant actress and could have done anything Geraldine Page did. I thought she was phenomenal in *Dylan* from the life of Dylan Thomas. It had been done before and I told her that she should really revive it. She said, "I don't know how to revive it." I found out and I raised $60,000 with all my friends and family. So I produced *Dylan* and it won the Obie Award and Rue won an Obie as well. Then, The Mercer Arts Theatre burned down. The man who was going to give us the $250,000 to move the show uptown ended up going across the street to a show that had a closing notice on it. The name of the show was *Grease* and he brought it uptown, instead, where it became the longest running show in history. So, if anyone ever tells you that there are any really set rules to success, it is not true. You can never guess anything. Bob Fryer came to me and said, "You cast *The Boston Strangler* for me, among other pictures, and you also raised the money for a few theater productions. My money man from Paris does not want to raise money any more. Will you come in and raise money for me?" I agreed to work with Bob and I raised what was, back then, the highest amount of money ever raised for any Broadway musical — $800,000. The show was *Chicago* and I did whatever it took to sell it — I danced it, I sang it, I acted it! I did whatever it took to make a sale! However, it makes it so much easier when you are dealing with a Bob Fosse, a Chita Rivera and a Jerry Orbach. It was incredible. That is how it all started.

Would you say, with the majority of the films you've produced, that you raised the money yourself or even invested your own money?

In the majority of the films that I've produced, the only investment I have personally made was to buy the book rights. I bought *The Shining* after Stephen King wrote *Carrie*. So, at that time, I probably gave him the most money for a book that he ever got, $500,000. I took a major gamble on it because we didn't know what was going to happen with it. I bought the Ira Levin book, *The Boys from Brazil*, for somewhere between $500,000 and $550,000. So, those were my major film investments. After we bought the rights to *The Boys from Brazil*, we worked on the script and then attached the director. We then got the studio interested on the basis of the director. I went out to LA and my agent set me up to meet a director, Robert Mulligan. Ironically, I was his casting director years before. I met with Mulligan and we had a great meeting. The next day, I got a call from Mulligan and he said, "I would love to change this book and make the two older guys into young guys." I said, "Bob, the book *The Boys from Brazil* has sold millions of copies and I love it the way it is." He said, "I am sorry, but I won't do it that way." I then replied, "Well, I guess you won't be doing it." My agent heard about it and said, "Marty you are not going to last in this town ten minutes." Anyway, Franklin J. Schaffner, who won the Academy Award for *Patton* starring George C. Scott, came in to direct and the film turned out to be a great success.

The Boys from Brazil (1978, Twentieth Century–Fox). Dr. Josef Mengele (Gregory Peck), the infamous Nazi geneticist, addresses his followers in his Brazilian sanctuary.

You had phenomenal casting in *The Boys from Brazil* with two legendary lead actors, Gregory Peck and Laurence Olivier.

Yes, we did. To work with Gregory Peck and Laurence Olivier was amazing. They were at the top of their game and deserved to be called "legends." They shared a true gift for acting but reflected very individualized styles and a perfect balance for this story. Peck was cast "against type" as the evil Nazi Dr. Josef Mengele and Olivier was equally brilliant as the old Nazi hunter tracking him down for Israel and for humanity. The first time I met Laurence Olivier, I didn't know how to address him. I said, "Do I call you Lord Olivier or do I call you Sir Laurence?" He politely replied, "You call me Larry." What a great honor to have been involved with both of them on this wonderful movie.

What made the casting even more interesting was that Olivier was fresh off of *Marathon Man* where he played the completely opposite character — a murderous Nazi fugitive.

Yes, I felt we cleverly switched it. Olivier got an Oscar nomination for our movie that year and, unfortunately, I feel he lost it because he was receiving the Lifetime Achievement Award. He got up and said admirably, "I would have rather won it for the picture." However, *The Boys from Brazil* was a wonderful experience for me.

Would you tell me how *The Shining* came about for you?

If you ever have the chance to read *The Shining* by Stephen King, you will see that it is the most frightening book you will ever read. Mary Lea and I were reading it in

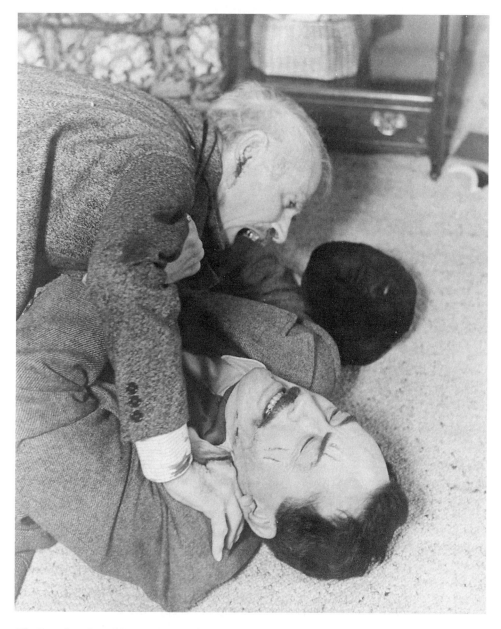

The Boys from Brazil (1978, Twentieth Century–Fox). Nazi hunter Simon Wiesenthal (Laurence Olivier) attacks the infamous Nazi Dr. Josef Mengele (Gregory Peck) in this exciting closing scene from the thriller based on Ira Levin's novel.

galley form in our house in Southampton. At the time, they were building our big house and we were reading it in the guesthouse where we lived for two years. Mary Lea used to joke and say, "Let's go look at the monument." (*Laughing*) Anyway, there was a bidding war for the book even in galley form, so we had to answer within 48 hours. Mary Lea and I were reading it simultaneously, passing the pages to each other. *The Shining*

was truly frightening and, to add to the drama, it was winter and so windy that the branches of the trees kept blowing against the window, making this eerie scratching noise, and it scared the hell out of us! The book was so terrifying that we were literally hanging onto one another. Mary Lea and I decided to buy the rights to *The Shining*. We steadfastly went after Stanley Kubrick to direct the film. Kubrick kept saying that he didn't want producers or bankers or even the chairman of the board of the studio on the set. Mary Lea, who never usually said anything because I am the big mouth, spoke up and said, "I am not a banker. I do not need the money. I want to produce and if Kubrick doesn't want us there on set, then screw him. We don't have to do the movie." Finally, Kubrick let Mary Lea and me on the set.

The Shining (1980, Warner Brothers). In this adaptation of the Stephen King horror novel, Jack Torrance's (Jack Nicholson) dementia takes a violent turn.

From being such a big fan of the book, did you like how the film version ultimately came out?

In the end, I am extremely proud of the picture. However, a couple of conversations with a few other objective people during the filming would have helped. Not that it would have made the film bigger or better. I just had some ideas to make the beginning of the film closer to Stephen King's original book. The movie was a big success and Stanley Kubrick is a brilliant director to have on my resumé. After the movie was finished, Kubrick called me from Scotland and said, "Tell me how are you going to see the movie. Are you going to see it with the suits or are you going to go out and see it in the movie theater?" I replied, "I am going to see it with Jack Nicholson in a theater near 42nd Street that they just built." Kubrick replied, "Finally, a producer that has brains." Kubrick even wrote me a letter on yellow paper that reads, "I finally met a producer who thinks like a producer should think. Looking forward to meeting with you again." I have cherished and kept this letter. But, my first call to Kubrick is even more interesting. I was a music major in Taft High School in the Bronx. When I graduated, one of the big idols of my high school at the time was Stanley Kubrick, because he graduated from Taft High School two years before me. I called him up in Scotland when we finally signed the deal. When I called, I didn't say my name or anything. I just started the conversation by singing to him on the phone our school anthem, "Hail Taft High! Hail Taft High!" Kubrick then yelled into the phone, very pissed off, "Who the fuck is this?" I sheepishly hung up and never called back. I never told Kubrick about it and I never even told him I went to Taft High School. (*Laughing*)

The Shining (1980, Warner Brothers). Young Danny Torrence (Danny Lloyd) tells his father Jack Torrence (Jack Nicholson) of a scary dream that will ultimately come true in the film.

Was Stephen King involved at all during the production?

No, and he was not happy with the opening of the movie. King went back and re-directed it for television and it turned out to be a big bomb. He had never done that before. Despite how good the script was and how tremendous the movie wound up being, it is not as terrifying as the book. When you are in the business for awhile, you know when you read good material, and that book was, and still is, amazing.

Did *Fort Apache, The Bronx* represent a major change of pace for you as a movie producer?

Definitely. Not only was it an extremely gritty police drama set in the beleaguered South Bronx of New York City, but it presented Paul Newman in a very different kind of role. He was absolutely riveting as a decent policeman who is pitted against every type of crazy criminal in the South Bronx, nicknamed Fort Apache. On top of it, he takes on his superiors, too, in what was a virtual Paul Newman tour de force.

Was there ever a film project that you really wanted to produce, but it unfortunately got away?

A book that I did not get the rights to and that I will never forget is *Kramer vs. Kramer* by Sam Cohn. I fell madly in love with the book. I lived the existence that it speaks of in Ocean Beach and Fire Island in general. I bid up to $35,000 and Cohn's agent called me up and said, "He doesn't want to sell it." Then, a few months later they announced that Stanley Jaffe and Sherry Lansing bought it. I then said to myself, "If he

Fort Apache, The Bronx (1981, Twentieth Century–Fox). New York City police officer Murphy (Paul Newman), a decent cop, consoles a nurse (Rachel Ticotin).

decides to produce it, he has to cast one of two people. He has to cast either Richard Dreyfuss or Dustin Hoffman." They hired Dustin Hoffman. Hoffman then hired the writer and everyone walked away with an Oscar. That film made many people's careers, including Sherry Lansing. But, everyone has stories about the ones that have gotten away.

It was over 20 years from when you produced *The Shining* to when you produced your Academy Award–winning picture, *Chicago*. Were you involved in theater at this time in your career?

Yes, I got heavily involved in Broadway. Mary Lea became ill and I came back to New York to be with her. I truly loved my wife. She was my whole life. When I came back, Mary Lea said to me, "I love musical comedy. We started our careers together producing musical comedy. Why don't we do that now at this stage of our lives?" In the interim, I produced *On the 20th Century,* for which we won seven Tonys. Then, I did *Grand Hotel,* which won the Tony, *Norman Conquests, March of the Falsetto, Crimes of the Heart* and many others. I produced about 30 Broadway shows and had about 15 hits. I really loved producing theater at that point in my life. But, turning *Chicago* into a major motion picture was my dream. After making it and winning the Oscar, I never imagined how exhilarated it would make me feel. All I want to do now is another movie.

Would you tell me about the many trials and tribulations of getting *Chicago* from stage to screen?

It took me 27 years from the time I bought the rights to *Chicago* to the time it finally appeared on the big screen. I spent nine of those years dealing with Miramax. Harvey Weinstein always wanted to do *Chicago* from when he first saw the production as a kid. He kept calling me about doing it. I wanted to produce it into a film, but after Bob Fosse died, I just threw the whole project into the drawer. I thought I would never be able to do this picture. Bob Fosse was my idol and my close friend. In fact, when I saw the first rough cut of our film version of *Chicago*, I started crying and I prayed and said, "Please, Bobby like it, because we do." It was always my dream that we would end up doing this film together. Anyway, Harvey kept calling me about doing *Chicago*. He was relentless. I knew the key to getting it on the screen was to attach the right director.

Take me through the process of attaching a director, and why you ultimately decided on Rob Marshall.

When I had seen *Strictly Ballroom,* I flipped over the work of director Baz Luhrmann. He made it a great success. I said to Miramax, "Get me an appointment with Baz Luhrmann and I will sign on tomorrow to do *Chicago* with you." They got me the meeting and Madonna was the witness to my signing the contract, because she was originally thought of to play Velma. Anyway, when I met with Baz Luhrmann he said, "I wouldn't dare touch the work of Bob Fosse. He is a genius and I just wouldn't dare." When I first met Baz, he was really still a kid. I told him, "This picture is an epic. Sit down in that chair and listen to me. I am older than you and smarter about this whole thing. This is your next big picture!" Baz still did not want to touch it. So, after *that* we went through considering many possible directors. After I saw *Cabaret* on-stage, I said to Harvey, "I just saw *Cabaret* and I loved it. Would you like to use Sam Mendes and Rob Marshall?" Harvey replied, "Who the hell is Sam Mendes and Rob Marshall?" So I said, "Go see the show." Well, nobody went to see it during that time. All of a sudden, after Sam Mendes won the Oscar for *American Beauty,* they decided to go see it. They sent Harvey's president at Miramax, Meryl Poster, who is a very bright young lady, and Julie Goldstein, who is equally as bright and a woman who is in charge of the musical division there. So, all of a sudden they have Rob Marshall up in the Miramax offices and they offer him *Rent.* He said, "No, Marty has been talking with me about doing *Chicago.* Not that I wouldn't direct *Rent.* I really want to do a feature." Rob had just won the Emmy for *Annie* on television and he did this gorgeous stage version of *Cabaret.* Well, in the end, Rob wound up directing *Chicago* and was nominated for an Academy Award for Best Director. When the movie became a big success, everyone was taking bows saying, "I discovered Rob Marshall." Rob Marshall is everyone's discovery except when Rob Marshall says it like it really was: "We know how it all happened, Marty." I reply, "Yeah, I know, but a little egotistically it bothers me every time I hear them say they discovered you." (*Laughing*)

Many of the actors and actresses in *Chicago* cleaned house at the award shows, many being nominated and many taking home Golden Globes and Academy Awards. Could you tell me about the superb casting of *Chicago*?

As far as the casting, the first person I attached and lucked out with was the wonderful Catherine Zeta-Jones. Michael Douglas is my wife's first cousin. So, we have

Chicago (2002, Miramax). Velma Kelly (Catherine Zeta-Jones) in one of the great musical scenes of this Academy Award–winning film.

always been very close. In fact, Michael was actually born in my father-in-law's mansion in New Brunswick. I first got to know him was when I was doing a play I discussed earlier called *Dylan*. Downstairs from us, they were performing *One Flew Over the Cuckoo's Nest*. I wanted to buy the rights to *Cuckoo's Nest* and I found out that Kirk Douglas had given the rights to his son, Michael Douglas. So, I called Michael and said, "I would love to produce *Cuckoo's Nest* with you." He replied, "If you have any money, I will definitely take it, but I am not letting anyone produce the film with me." Well, that was the end of that deal. However, we did end up speaking from time to time after that. When Michael fell in love with Catherine Zeta-Jones after his divorce, he invited me to their birthday party, because they were both born on September the 23rd. So, at the birthday party, Catherine got up and sang and she was amazing. I told her that I had the rights to *Chicago* and I said, "You would be an amazing Velma." Catherine eagerly replied, "I would kill to play Velma!" Then, when I saw her again on Christmas Eve, where we all sang around the piano, I was floored again by Catherine's voice. I said to her, "I can't believe how amazing your voice is. You could really play Velma and I am not kidding." Catherine said, "I actually come from the musical theater. I performed in *42nd Street* in London and was nominated for an Olivier Award." I then called Harvey Weinstein and told him that Catherine was interested in playing Velma. Harvey said, "You get me Catherine Zeta-Jones and director Rob Marshall attached and I will green light this production." I called Catherine and she got all excited about it.

Then, we had to cast the part of Roxie. I always wanted Goldie Hawn. I love Goldie so much both as a person and as a performer. I always felt this part would be perfect for her. Miramax said they wanted a young Goldie Hawn. We went down a list of names and Renee Zellweger was on everyone's list. I then said, "Can she sing and play skinny?" Miramax replied, "We heard that Catherine Zeta-Jones and Renee Zellweger both auditioned for the key part in *Moulin Rouge* and Renee came in second, Catherine third and Nicole Kidman was first." We had Renee come in and she was a size two and looking phenomenal. Renee then went into a private room with Rob Marshall and asked for all of us to stay out. Rob came out a few minutes later and, "She is wonderful!" I said to Rob, "What did Renee do?" He replied, "I showed her a few dance steps and she did those dance steps wonderfully. She also told me she was a gymnast and a majorette in high school." I then wondered if her singing voice would be good enough. We all went to lunch at the Four Seasons Restaurant and a fearless Renee got up in front of everyone at the restaurant and sang a knockout "Somewhere, Over the Rainbow." Rob then started to sing "Nowadays" and asked her to try it. She performed that wonderfully too. Rob said to Renee, "I swear on everything that is holy that you will be so brilliant in this movie that you won't believe it yourself!" So, that is how we cast Renee Zellweger.

Now for the part of Billy Flynn, my first choice always was Kevin Kline. I begged Kevin to do it and his agent begged him to do it. I then met with him and discussed it. Kevin said, "I don't want to play any more negative characters." Then, I wanted Kevin Spacey. He said, "The only musical I'll do is the one I bought the rights to about Bobby Darin's life." Harvey pushed for Travolta and he turned it down right away. I then heard Travolta say on television, "The biggest mistake of my career was turning down *Chicago*."

Then, we all made a list of possible actors and Richard Gere was on the list. I knew Richard did musicals in London, including *Grease*, and I was intrigued. But, casting Richard Gere as Billy Flynn was really by chance. One day, I went to a rehearsal and I heard a great voice from behind a closed door singing the song "All I Care About Is Love." I opened the door and saw it was Richard Gere and his voice teacher. I said, "Okay, I heard you sing the song. Now let me hear Richard sing it." The voice teacher said, "That *was* Richard!" I then said to myself, "Wow. We really lucked out."

As far as Queen Latifah was concerned, both Rob and I originally wanted Kathy Bates to play the part, Matron "Mama" Morton. Kathy auditioned and was brilliant. Queen Latifah auditioned three times and she sang incredibly. So, it was a very tough decision. Harvey really wanted Queen Latifah and we finally decided on her and she was nominated for an Oscar for Best Supporting Actress. Ironically, she was up against Kathy Bates. So, it all worked out in the end and Latifah's career is soaring.

As far as John C. Reilly, everyone wanted him to play the part of Amos Hart. I wondered if he could sing and John sent us three tapes of three auditions and we could not believe what we heard. He was signed immediately. Christine Baranski, who played Mary Sunshine, was also amazing and we never thought of anyone else. Lucy Liu did an amazing job playing Kitty Baxter. As far as the dancers are concerned, there was not one dancer in that picture that couldn't be a star on Broadway. They really proved it in the cell block tango scene. As far as *Chicago* is concerned, it was one of those casting situations where all the stars literally aligned in our favor. This movie was truly blessed all the way through.

Did you think Richard Gere was robbed by not being nominated for an Oscar for Best Actor for his portrayal of Billy Flynn?

I personally felt he was robbed, but Richard, who is such a gentleman, didn't even complain about it. If he would have allowed himself to be in the Best Supporting Actor category instead of the Best Actor category, not only would he been nominated, he would have won. How do you win a Golden Globe for Best Actor and not even get nominated for an Academy Award? It makes no sense to me.

When you won your Oscar for Best Picture, you were so genuinely happy and so sincere. I was so happy for you. How did it feel?

As I was walking into the Awards, everyone kept saying, "The Oscar is yours." I said, "Don't say that. I am very superstitious." I was very nervous and perspiring as I waited for the announcement for Best Picture. When they announced Roman Polanski for Best Director for *The Pianist* and Rob Marshall didn't win, I thought it was over. When Kirk and Michael Douglas announced my name, I was in total shock. When I walked up there, I was out of my mind. I stood up there and I was looking at a standing ovation of every actor and actress that has been acting for the last 30 years. It was completely mind-boggling. During my speech, I was trying not to forget anyone's name. When I won, all I had in my mind was my mother, my father, Mary Lea, my partner Bobby Fryer, Bob Fosse and all of the people who believed in me from the beginning. After I won it, I went backstage, turned the color ash and they asked if I wanted to sit down and have a glass of water and a tranquilizer. (*Laughing*) I said, "No,

I am walking right in and talking to the foreign press." I never understood why Rob never won the Oscar. I had said in every interview, "Thank you. I am overwhelmed by winning, but how can I win Best Picture without Rob Marshall winning Best Director." We won Best Set Design, Best Choreography, Best Music, Best Editing, Best Costume, Best Supporting Actress and then Roman Polanski won the Best Director Oscar for *The Pianist*. It just does not make any sense to me. Anyway, about an hour later, I was getting out of the limo and going to the *Vanity Fair* party. Behind the barricades there were six to ten rows of thousands of people. I got one foot out of the car and all the people started cheering, "Marty! Marty!" I then saw Kate Hudson and she looked so beautiful. I kissed her and grabbed her arm and I asked her to hold me and stay with me because I was totally overwhelmed. When the press came to speak with me, Kate said, "This is my Uncle Marty and he gave me my first turtle when I was eight years old." I then said, "Yes, and she gave it away because the turtle became too big." (*Laughing*) The whole experience of making *Chicago* was a major, major trip with the most exciting ending imaginable. What winning the Oscar does is that it makes you feel like Dracula. You feel like you got the taste of blood and you want it again and again. It was just a Cinderella night that I will never forget.

Do you think the success of *Moulin Rouge* helped propel Miramax to make *Chicago*?

Moulin Rouge was beautifully filmed, but it was not as commercially successful as *Chicago*. It certainly opened the doors for us and we were in a good position then because of it. Harvey Weinstein and Miramax have essentially made the first great commercial musical success on a movie screen in many, many years. But, the critics and public are eagerly anticipating what musical he will do next. It has to be at least equally as good or it has to be better. If it isn't equally as good or better, then it's got to be really inventive — something very daring and new. That was why I wanted to do *Sweeney Todd*. I wanted to do the first grand horror story as a musical and I wanted it done really, really bloody. But, they don't listen to producer's ideas as intently as a director's ideas. As a movie producer, when you come up with a good idea at a meeting, they look genuinely surprised as they say, "That is a great idea, Marty." It is almost as if they are surprised you had a great idea. I don't mean it to be nasty, but I think the industry and the world think that the "producer" title is synonymous with the word "money." They don't think of us as creative people, when we certainly are. I often sit back and say, "Why are they so surprised that I came up with a good creative idea? I have done some very successful projects. How many times do I have to prove myself?"

Do you feel that the title of "producer" holds any genuine credence today?

Being a producer is a very strange thing lately. When I first started in theater in the early years of my life, in my twenties, Cole Porter was writing songs like "Hey, Mr. Producer," and you were really a big deal as a producer. When I was growing up, we knew the name of every Hollywood producer that ever lived. I was a performer, so I knew it even better than most people did. On Broadway, it was powerful producers like David Merrick and Bobby Fryer. In movies, it was top producers like Selznick, Cecil B. DeMille, Louis B. Mayer, Darryl Zanuck and others. Even though they were studio heads, they were producers. What has happened today, in my opinion, is that movie producers are the most unsung heroes in Hollywood. They have become the entity that has done much of the crucial work and they get the least amount of credit. They put it all together and then after all of the decision-making and risk-taking, the producers are put on a back burner. Because of my Oscar, which was an incredible thing, all of a sudden I became the "flavor of the week." I was speaking to a great producer and a great man, Marty Bregman, who is one of the classiest gentlemen I have ever met. He's a person who I have a tremendous amount of respect for. We both agreed that the producer is the guy who puts the whole movie production together and then all of a sudden is considered invisible as soon as the director steps in. Producers don't have unions, so that is a major problem. Directors on movies today

Chicago (2002, Miramax). Lawyer Billy Flynn (Richard Gere) consoles his new client Roxie Hart (Renee Zellweger) in this 1920s jazz age era film.

become producers to a certain extent. Since the studio system stopped, there is less praise for the producer. But on the other hand, I understand why they got rid of the studio system, mainly because they were getting robbed blind. The studios these days have their own in-house producers who are called line producers, who they give an executive producer title to. The line producers come in and make phone calls after you have done all the work. Then they expect to stand next to you at the Oscars and take bows. If that sounds like sour grapes, it *is* sour grapes. I don't know how to emphasize this, but in my case you take 27 years to get a project made like I have on *Chicago*. Then spend nine of those years alone after working with Bob Fosse, who died. Then you work with Miramax for nine years. The thing that was wonderful about working with Harvey Weinstein was that he has the passion and always had the passion about this project. Interestingly, after the movie is made and it has become Oscar time, you are very limited in discussing the business side of your own picture. Frankly, you are happy enough that they are putting up the bread. The only people today who can say, "Fine, I'll finance it myself," are Ted Turner and Bill Gates.

Do you find it easier to get your projects moving faster after winning the Oscar?

The big difference for me now is that when I make a phone call, I get directly through to the president of the studio instead of speaking to the head story editor. Before that, I was speaking to the fifteenth story editor. This business is all about how hot you are at the moment. But, I have paid my dues and I have worked my way up. So, because of winning the Oscar, I am in a better position to make deals. I just made a deal with New Line Cinema. They love the writing and my ideas on casting, but they are not sold on the director. The director is a new talent who has made many music videos and has done one film. Now, this is a typical situation for a producer. After selling the project, the producer has to now go in to try to sell the director, which is what happened with Rob Marshall at the beginning of our deal with *Chicago*. But, people act like I just jumped on the scene out of nowhere. As I mentioned earlier, I produced *The Shining,* which was on the 15 all-time Best Pictures list. I produced *The Boys from Brazil,* which was extremely successful. I also produced *Fort Apache, the Bronx,* which was a huge success as well. In all of those pictures, I worked with some great stars like Paul Newman, Gregory Peck, Jack Nicholson, Laurence Olivier and so on. But everyone remembers the stars. They don't remember who the producer was. Now with *Chicago,* I think people will remember that it was definitely a producer-driven project, especially because of me winning the Oscar. That it is well documented, in articles and books like this one.

What projects will you be producing in the near future?

I just got offered to do a picture with Sony and another group of people about drag racing. I thought to myself, "What the hell do I know about drag racing?" Then, when we sat down and worked on the script, I got excited to put it together. It is a contemporary movie and it takes me as a producer to another level. I associate with people of all ages. I don't want to get older. So, this is a younger genre movie and that sounds like it will be fun. I am also begging Stephen Sondheim to allow me to do *Sweeney Todd,* which I have already done on Broadway, as a film. On the flip side, I am trying to bring *Bullets Over Broadway* to the theater. I am also writing a book. It is called *There Are No Rules, Just Surprises.* It is about my whole life and my marriage to Mary Lea and a bunch of lunacy and all the hard work that we all did leading up to the Oscar victory. Writing this book has been uplifting, but also a little bit painful for me. It's about a wonderful love affair with my wife, Mary Lea, and the marvelous life that went with it. My wife was my co-producer for a lot of my theater productions and my true love. She and Bob Fryer, who brought me into the original *Chicago,* lived to make this movie and she, unfortunately, died of Parkinson's a year before we started. Those are the two people who I really thanked when I got up there to accept the Oscar. You go numb up there. For someone who never stops talking, I was frozen. However, it has been an interesting life and I just want to go on working at what I love.

What advice can you give to someone who wants to start a career in producing theater and major motion pictures?

First of all, I believe that if someone really has a dream, a real dream, only that person can make that dream come true. People will often ask me, "What do you owe your success to?" I usually reply, "Which success? I have had many successes, but I have also had many failures." I feel you have to have tenacity, a belief in yourself, luck and good timing. I will say this to a performer, writer or director and I mean it: "If you want something bad enough and you have this little bit of talent and you stick with it long enough, you may not become a Stephen Sondheim and you may not become a Marlon Brando or Steven Spielberg, but you are going to work in the business that you love and there is no greater gift." Also, never take "no" for an answer. Parents will kill me when I say this, but parents usually never believe that it will happen for their children. They tell everyone else that it will happen for *their* children, but they never believe it for their own. That is my point of view. You have to be willing to sacrifice. It is not all fun and you get kicked around. No matter how good-looking you are, there is someone better-looking. No matter how talented you are, there are others who are more talented. But, if you believe in yourself, it will all fall into place. I'm living proof of that.

Martin Richards Filmography

Chicago (Renee Zellweger, Catherine Zeta-Jones, Richard Gere) 2002 — producer; *Fort Apache the Bronx* (Paul Newman, Edward Asner) 1981— producer; *The Shining* (Jack Nicholson, Shelley Duvall) 1980— producer; *The Boys from Brazil* (Gregory Peck, Laurence Olivier) 1978 — producer; *Some of My Best Friends Are* (Fannie Flagg, Rue McClanahan) 1971— producer

Paula Wagner

Paula Wagner started her career with dreams of becoming an actress. She appeared in theater productions and on screen, but when her acting career wasn't going where she wanted it to, she asked her agent for advice. Her agent told her to become an agent, herself. Initially opposed to it, Wagner then realized she could still be creative as an agent. She moved ahead full steam and worked hard to become one of the top agents in Hollywood, representing Demi Moore, Oliver Stone, Sean Penn, Liam Neeson and others. She bonded very deeply with one particular client, Tom Cruise, with whom she has been working with for over 20 years. Wagner ended her career as an agent to join forces with Cruise, becoming his producing partner and starting their own production company, Cruise/Wagner Productions. They have produced such major hits as Mission: Impossible, The Others, Vanilla Sky, Narc *and* The Last Samurai. *Paula Wagner resides in California and has many film projects in the works at Cruise/Wagner Productions.*

There were many films that affected me during my youth. The first film I remember seeing was *Gone With the Wind*. I think what affected me the most was the sweeping nature of the film — the melodrama, the emotion and the battle sequences. It was a beautiful movie that transported you into a very special world, a world that had some heritage for me because my family actually fought in the Civil War on both sides. Other films I loved during my youth were *How Green Was My Valley* and *A Tree Grows in Brooklyn*. Then my tastes changed and I got into the '40s *noir* films that portrayed these strong women who found the strength and courage to master their environment and conquer the world in their own way, all the while still being women. I loved all the Alfred Hitchcock films. As a child, I just loved going to the movies and being transported to distant places.

You went on to study at the theater school of Carnegie Mellon. Did the combined creative atmosphere of theater and love of film affect you and play a major role in getting you interested in acting?

I started going to the theater in my youth and I started acting in the local theater when I was 13. The first play I acted in was called *The Cave Dwellers* by William Saroyan. Then I played Adriana in Shakespeare's *The Comedy of Errors*. So, yes, a combination of film and theater made me want to be an actress. It was the concept of transformation. Starting with a character and then becoming that character was what was fascinating to me. My mother was such a strong mentor and influence for me. She said, "If you are going to go into acting, then do it the best you can and really study it." I then researched schools, but I knew Carnegie Mellon was considered the most renowned theater school since the turn of the century. You had to audition and they only chose a small, select number of students. I worked with an acting coach on scenes from *Joan of Arc*. Then, I auditioned for Carnegie Mellon and I got in on early admissions.

Did you study acting anywhere else?

Yes. I also studied at the great Hume Cronyn and Jessica Tandy's alma mater, the Neighborhood Playhouse, with Sanford Meisner, and later studied at the Yale Drama School while working at the Yale Repertory Theater. After Carnegie Mellon, I began to act on Broadway. My first role was in the original production of *Lenny*, the story of the comedian Lenny Bruce. I played 26 incidental roles, going on and off stage to change costumes, which was a real challenge. I then went on to perform in regional theater. I co-wrote a play in the mid–70s called *Out of Our Father's House,* which was based on the book *Growing Up Female in America* by feminist author Eve Merriam. It recounted the true stories that were written in diaries, letters and journals of American women. I acted in it as well. It was a piece that was done all over the world and is even performed today, a very timeless play. Rosalynn Carter brought it to the White House. In a sense, that was the beginning of my producing career because I put the project together from the ground up. I bought the book and I found a casting director. He directed and co-wrote it with me and it was performed Off–Broadway. Another milestone in my acting career happened when a member of the Yale Repertory Company called me in to replace a star who she said was so extraordinary that she was being brought to New York. She was that talented. Anyway, this actress was leaving a production of *A Mid-summer Night's Dream* because she was gifted and was being given a big chance in New York. I was brought in to replace her and the actress was Meryl Streep. I can honestly say I acted in her shoes. She was such an extraordinary actress then and is now. She was so powerful in the role and I truly admire her courage, dedication, energy and inventiveness as an actress.

Why did you leave acting to become a Hollywood agent?

I know this will sound simplistic, but one day I was a Shakespearian actress at Yale and the next day I was a Hollywood agent. I don't think there is anyone else in this business who has taken that kind of leap. (*Laughing*) I loved performing and I was a trained, devoted and committed actress. I first lived in Greenwich Village in New York City and I was kind of a bohemian actress. I then came out to Los Angeles and I had an agent at the time named Susan Smith, who was very talented. I told Susan, "I need to do something creative with my life. I need to move my career along quicker. Do you think I will ever act in a role of consequence in Hollywood?" Susan looked at me and said, "No. Well, at least not as an actress. However, I do think you would make a phenomenal agent." I said, "Are you kidding me? That is the last thing in the world I want to do. I am an actress. I am a creative person." I honestly had tears in my eyes when Susan told me what she felt. After my emotions settled, I thought about her advice. I began to realize that I have to make a living to survive. I had acted for a long time and I realized that maybe I could try being an agent for a short time. Well, I became an agent and that "short time" became 15 years. I first worked with Susan and then on October 1, 1980, I started working at Creative Artists Agency.

Who were some of the key clients you represented at CAA?

Directors like Oliver Stone and Kathryn Bigelow. Writers like Robert Towne, who wrote *Mission: Impossible*, among other top films including *Chinatown* and *Shampoo*. Besides working with Tom from the beginning, I worked with Sean Penn, Matthew Broderick, Kevin Bacon, Aidan Quinn, Eric Stoltz, Emilio Estevez, Demi Moore and Liam Neeson, among others.

You have gone on to have a 20–plus year career with Tom Cruise. Can you tell me about the first time you met him?

First of all, I saw some really wonderful footage of him as an actor from a film called *Taps*. In that picture, Tom played the part of David Shawn so fully and he was so compelling that I had to meet him. It was his pure commitment to the role that I was drawn to. Then, I met Tom and there was a wonderful intensity and warmth about him. There were also different layers of a person there. Tom had then, and still has, a pure, charismatic presence and the true ability to translate those qualities on screen.

What do you think the keys are to being a successful agent?

To be a successful agent, you need to have tenacity, extremely strong communication skills and you need to be thick-skinned. You have to possess the ability to be "barracuda-like" and tough when it comes to making deals, but at the same time, you have to maintain extreme rapport with your clients. When you go into a meeting to make a deal, you essentially are that client. Being an actress gave me invaluable insights as an agent. I could get into the character as well as the minds of my clients. I had to continually think, "What do my clients want so I can represent them fairly?" However, at the same time, you need to fairly represent the buyers to the client. I think a good agent needs to be ethical. In my world as an agent, when I said, "You've got a deal," that statement was better than any signed piece of paper. When I said, "We are walking and we do not have a deal," I meant that too. Lastly, you need a keen eye for talent and an extensive understanding of the business.

Do you think that your keen eye for discovering talent came from your time spent as an actress?

Absolutely. I knew from having "walked in the shoes" as an actress when an actor's or actress' performance is authentic. You look at someone and you understand how charisma translates into performance. Some people just exude that quality which can be arresting and compelling, like Tom Cruise.

Did you find that you were creatively stifled as an agent?

No, because you can be creative in anything you do. For instance, a scientist can be extremely creative. Albert Einstein was an artist. As long as I could be an inventor and think of new ways of doing things, I was fine. I think being an agent is quite cre-

Taps (1981, Twentieth Century–Fox). David Shawn (Tom Cruise) in full uniform.

ative in the sense of the following challenges: What kind of characters are you going to find for your clients to play? What kind of movies are you going to find for those clients who direct? How can you advise your writer clients on script changes? During my time as an agent, I was rapidly moving into the world of becoming a producer.

Why did you choose *Mission: Impossible*, the big-budget movie version of the TV series, as your first producing venture?

Tom called me up and said, "I love the old show *Mission: Impossible*. Paramount has the rights to it and I would love to make the movie." I agreed with him. When Tom and I commit to an idea as producing partners, we really go for it! We proceeded to try to find every way possible in a positive manner to make the movie happen. I liken it to Shakespeare getting certain inspirations from *Plutarch's Lives*— there was no new story. How about the fact that the greatest hit on Broadway right now is *The Producers*, based on a movie by Mel Brooks? My philosophy is that wherever you get the idea, go for it. Movies are based on books, songs, true stories, newspaper articles and, the most popular new source, old television shows. *Mission: Impossible* not only had a world-famous theme song, it had a great concept in that this group spearheaded by Ethan Hunt [the leader, played by Tom Cruise] get together and take on these impossible situations and conquer them successfully without being detected. They were to utilize any method possible to get the job done. Tom and I felt it was a great idea and Tom wanted to play the lead role. We launched the development process, attached a great director in Brian De Palma and wonderful screenwriters, Robert Towne and David

Mission: Impossible (1996, Paramount). **Ethan Hunt (Tom Cruise) is concerned as he confronts Clair (Emmanuelle Beart) in this highly successful movie.**

Koepp, and a super cast. Then, we eventually launched *Mission: Impossible II*. What is great about the two installments is that they are both "stand-alone" films. Each time a TV series is re-invented, the choice of director is key to the success of the film. Brian De Palma's *Mission: Impossible* is his vision and John Woo's *Mission: Impossible II* is his unique take on the series.

Do you give your directors a lot of freedom to make their own choices?

As a producer, I think your job is to commit yourself and to get involved with directors whom you respect and whose vision you understand, connect with and commit to. Then, you set out to help the director to complete his or her vision by protecting them from the studio, the budget problems, the physical production problems and sometimes from himself or herself. It is important for a producer to hold in his or her mind all of these aspects during a production because great movie making is also paying attention to details. So, as a producer, you have to be in touch with the details and "the big picture" at all times. I have a producing partner because the job of a producer is so vast and there is such a diverse arena of responsibilities at all times. I have a fantastic producing partnership with Tom. He gets very involved in developing the script with the director. Each motion picture and each new situation that you become involved in has its own rhythm and dynamic. You have to find the key elements of that particular production and that will determine how you function as a producer. It's probably the only job in Hollywood that means different things to different people. It's actually defined differently at different times according to what the range of needs are before, during and after production. Being a producer is a hard job. You have to be everything at all times to many different people. It's a complex job and if you ask five different producers what a producer does, I bet they will give you five different definitions. To be a good producer, you have to understand every job on the set. You have to know what the job of the boom operator is, what the job of craft service is, what the job of the cameraman is and how do the cameras work. You have to know everything. Earlier you referred to producers as the unsung heroes of Hollywood, but everyone on the set qualifies as an "unsung hero." Everybody works so very hard.

I read that you were extremely instrumental in bringing *Vanilla Sky* to the big screen. What first attracted you to producing this film?

I'd say certainly a wonderful story and a great character for Tom, but Cameron Crowe's interest really defined it for us because, ultimately, the filmmaker defines the film. We also had tremendous respect for Alejandro Amenabar, who directed the original version called, *Abre Los Ojos*. Alejandro eventually directed *The Others*, which Tom and I also executive produced. *Vanilla Sky* was ahead of its time, it dealt with extremely personal and infinitely relevant topics reflected in pop culture. The tag line was, "Love, Hate, Dreams, Life, Work, Play, Friendship, Sex." There was something very human about the movie. It was an unusual story of a man trying to find himself and his lost love and he would ultimately do anything for the love of his life. In one extreme moment, he made a mistake, and that one moment changed his entire life. Yet, he was still willing to sacrifice everything for hope in the future. Tom took incredible risks as an actor and Cameron also did extraordinarily daring things as a director. They had a tremendous trust between them. I thought it was a great story and working with Cameron was a bonus because he is an incredible storyteller who truly chronicles the souls of his characters in a very special and intimate way on screen. We are working with him on his latest picture, which Tom and I are producing with him. I hope this is the continuation of a long relationship with Cameron Crowe.

At Cruise/Wagner Productions, you have produced a few films without Tom Cruise in the lead role. One was the gritty *Narc* starring two fine actors, Ray Liotta and Jason Patric. How did you get involved with this picture?

After the filmmakers had finished *Narc*, Tom and I saw it and thought it was a fascinating movie from a new director with a fresh and exciting voice, Joe Carnahan. Tom and I have known Ray Liotta and Jason Patric for years and Ray was one of the producers on the film. Tom and I had a meeting with Joe and there was a very strong rapport and meeting of minds. The filmmakers asked if we would like to come on board as executive producers to help strategize the release of the film, which would ultimately bring a wider awareness of the picture. We agreed to help because we loved the movie and we loved the risks that it took. It was made for a couple of million dollars and the story of the making of the film was a movie in and of itself. The commitment by Joe, Jason and Ray to make this film was impressive and simply breathtaking. Our production company is here at Paramount Pictures, so we brought it to them and got Paramount on board. Then, we helped them finish the film in certain areas. Tom was incredibly supportive and lent his presence to *Narc* and its creators. When you believe in a filmmaker, as a producer, you absolutely have to support that filmmaker. So, we supported the writer-director Joe Carnahan to make this film what it ultimately should be.

Many people would say producing for Tom Cruise is easier than producing for any other actor because he has such a huge audience base already in place. I personally feel that you have even more pressure on you to make it right. Do you agree?

First of all, Tom and I produce together on our films. He is a wonderfully talented producer as well as an actor. Of course, involving his name and presence with a picture certainly launches a film. But I think that we as a production company are very diligent and extremely selective of what projects we get involved in. We've worked hard to build the name and reputation of C/W Productions and the challenge lies in upholding that image and taking it to the next level. So, each time it becomes more and more challenging. You are always striving for more and there in lies the biggest challenge for us. In Hollywood moviemaking, you are constantly under scrutiny and there are huge risk factors when you are operating at this level. But remember, real creators take risks. It boils down to coming up with a story that hasn't been told or a point of view that is new and fresh. That includes exploring different characters or going to a genre that perhaps has been done, but requires some reinventing. I think what we do when we make "Tom Cruise–starring films," or any other films for that matter, is to work toward doing something that hasn't quite been done before. That is the most difficult part for us. But, that represents an exciting element too!

Mission: Impossible II (2000, Paramount). Ethan Hunt (Tom Cruise), *sans* helmet, confidently rides his motorcycle.

How do you feel about your latest production, *The Last Samurai,* starring Tom Cruise?

Tom and I produced this with Ed Zwick and Marshall Herskovitz, who had been involved in the project for a long time. I think it was impeccably made and Tom gives an extraordinary performance. This was a different film for me but, in the final analysis, every film I do is different. Each time you go to the floor, you take your experience from other films with you. There are some professions in

Vanilla Sky (2001, Paramount). David Aames (Tom Cruise) and Sofia Serrano (Penelope Cruz) are about to share a passionate kiss.

which too much experience is not always considered good, but not film producing. In producing, the more experience you have, the better it is because you know how to steer the ship in the right direction. I may have extensive background and experience in producing movies, but I still learned a lot from *The Last Samurai* and I will continue to learn on each new picture.

You said earlier that everyone is an "unsung hero" on a film shoot. But just singling out producers for the moment, do you feel they are, in fact, "the unsung heroes of Hollywood"?

I think that maybe the general public does not understand the infinite involvement of a producer. However, anyone involved with moviemaking at any level understands that a true producer is the fuel that keeps the engine running. The producer is the crisis manager, the problem solver, the negotiator, the artist, the agent, the go-between, and the list goes on and on. You fill in the gaps and you encourage everyone on a picture to do their job to the best of their abilities. If a producer is doing his or her job right and can run a movie properly, then the actors and director can move forward to do their job creatively and in an uninhibited way. When producers do not do their jobs right, movies become much more difficult and complicated to make.

How hard is it today for women to make it in Hollywood?

The age-old question! (*Laughing*) My husband Rick Nicita, who is an agent and one of the partners at Creative Artists Agency, often jokes with me, "You are actually going

Vanilla Sky (2001, Paramount). David Aames (Tom Cruise) does it again as he is about to share another passionate kiss, this time with Julie Gianni (Cameron Diaz).

to another 'Women in Film' event? When are they going to have a 'Men in Film' event?" I say, "Maybe we will get to the point of having the 'People in Film' event where the genders are all one big happy family." (*Laughing*) The bottom line is that it's hard for anyone, male or female, to succeed in Hollywood. Work, focus and determination are basically what will get you there. I think you have to have really good, strong people around you. I do think we need more female writers and directors in this business. At the executive level, there are female role models like Sherry Lansing. Today, almost every studio has women in high-level positions and, like Sherry, some are even in charge of the studio. I think, as a producer today, women are accepted just as much as men. But, it is hard for anyone to become a producer. You need depth of experience because you also need a level of respect from everyone you are working with. Are there issues with men? Yes. Are there issues with women? Yes. But, it never stopped me and it will never stop me!

Well, you are a mentor in a lot of ways yourself. You are a mentor to actors and actresses, because not many actresses can say they replaced Meryl Streep in a role. You became one of the most successful agents in history. Now, you are an extremely successful producer.

I love mentoring. I really do. I like to help young women or men who are just starting out. I think helping youth is one of the reasons I am where I am today.

What do you think is your main strength as a producer?

I think my main strength is the ability I have to successfully bridge the two key worlds of filmmaking together. The two worlds I am talking about are the creative side and the business side. I look at filmmaking as renaissance art. Michelangelo and many great artists had to have financial backing behind them. I think that is what filmmaking essentially is. You can't make it without money and the business is the art. I have lived in both worlds, I am a strong communicator, and also, I think, I am a solid negotiator. I have a good sense of script and casting. I am involved from the conception of the film to the last DVD that hits the shelves. I am a total producer in the concept's purest form.

What does the future hold for you and Cruise/Wagner Productions?

Our goal is to keep making strong films about interesting people in exciting situations. I love the variety of projects that we are involved in. I am thankful for the chance to make a film like *Mission: Impossible*, or the chance to be involved with a cutting edge film like *Narc*, or to recreate a real-life drama such as *Shattered Glass*. I truly love diversity when it comes to films and filmmakers. I want to keep growing as a producer and to build an extensive library of films that have something special that we represent, and it involves a word that there isn't a lot of today, *quality*. Tom and I want to continue to produce films that take risks and dare to be different. I want to keep finding new stories and stay true to our highest goals and to the filmgoing audience.

Paula Wagner Filmography

The Last Samurai (Tom Cruise, Billy Connolly, Tony Goldwyn) 2003– producer; **Shattered Glass** (Hayden Christensen, Peter Sarsgaard, Chloe Sevigny) 2003 — executive producer; **Narc** (Jason Patric, Ray Liotta) 2002 — executive producer; **Vanilla Sky** (Tom Cruise, Penelope Cruz, Cameron Diaz) 2001— producer; **The Others** (Nicole Kidman) 2001— executive producer; **Mission: Impossible II** (Tom Cruise, Dougray Scott, Ving Rhames) 2000— producer; **Without Limits** (Billy Crudrup, Donald Sutherland, Monica Potter) 1998 — producer; **Mission: Impossible** (Tom Cruise, Jon Voight, Emmanuelle Beart) 1996 — producer

Dino De Laurentiis

Dino De Laurentiis was born on August 8, 1919, and has been making movies since he was 19 years old. After World War II, De Laurentiis became one of the most influential and powerful producers in Italy. He joined forces and worked closely with world-renowned directors Federico Fellini and Roberto Rosellini. In the 1970s, De Laurentiis set his sights on the United States and produced his first American film, Serpico, *starring Al Pacino. He has gone to produce hits like* Dune, Conan the Barbarian, Death Wish *and more. Dino De Laurentiis is an Irving Thalberg Award winner and has won Academy Awards for films such as* War and Peace *and* La Strada. *He is the quintessential independent producer, proving it again when he put up $10 million of his own money for the rights to* Hannibal, *which starred Anthony Hopkins and Julianne Moore. De Laurentiis resides in Los Angeles and Italy and has many projects in development, including another exciting movie based on Hannibal Lector, the movie going public's favorite serial killer.*

I grew up in Italy in a town called Torre Annunziata, which is not far from Naples. It is a very small town. At night, there was nothing to do but to go to the movies with my friends. The cinema could take me to a faraway place and I had always been infatuated with it from a very young age. Growing up, I collected photos of Italian and American movie stars. I would rip them out of magazines and paste them in my scrapbook. As a child, when I thought of cinema, I only thought of the actors and actresses. I had no clue how a movie was made or what went on behind the scenes or behind the camera. From an early age, I was always fascinated by the idea of being a part of the moviemaking business.

Could you tell me about your childhood and what it was like growing up during that era?

I was born right after World War 1. I am one of a family of seven children and we were all very close. My father owned a company that manufactured pasta and that was a major part of my childhood. When my father started the company, he was unable to afford the capital investment, so he first acquired the pasta via a third party, packaged it and then labeled it with "De Laurentiis." He then began distributing it throughout the entire province of Naples. People really loved the product. Eventually, my father made enough money to open a factory of his own. My father was a true entrepreneur. I learned what it took first hand to create your own business and that had a great influence on me during my youth.

You left home at the young age of 17 to attend the Rome film school "Centro Serimenatale Di Cinematografia." How important was this maneuver in your career?

I never liked school. I dropped out at 15 years old and went to work at my father's pasta company. I was a salesman and I traveled around Italy. My father was surprised at how well I could sell. Traveling at such a young age, I experienced many things and matured quickly. However, I began to get bored working for my father. I wanted to make my own mark on the world. I, too, had that entrepreneurial spirit. One day,

Dino De Laurentiis

during my travels, I found the answer in a poster ad for the school "Centro Serimenatale Di Cinematografia." I never liked school, until now. It was a school specifically designed for actors, directors and other technical positions in film. I applied to the school as an actor and got accepted. The only problem I had was to convince my father that I wanted to become an actor. I told him and he thought it was a ridiculous idea. After some begging from me, I think he saw the passion in my eyes and agreed to support me for my first year there. I thanked him and I was off to Rome!

Tell me about your time spent at the school.

I felt very free there to express my creative feelings. It was a great place to learn. I always thought I was good-looking enough to be an actor. However, after some time at the school, I realized I didn't have what it took. I did not contain the physical attributes that makes one a successful force in front of the camera. I then thought about studying to become a director, but that did not feel right either. I then began to read many, many books. I began to acquire a taste for good writing. I also knew I was very good at selling from my days working for my father. I realized that I should become a producer. I recognized all my strengths and weaknesses, and when someone can honestly do that with themselves, they can find their true calling in life. Mine was to become a movie producer.

What motivated you to produce your first movie at only 19 years old?

What pushed me was the genuine ambition and vision to become a producer. When you are young, you do not have the experience to produce movies. When I produced it, I did not have the experience of knowing if the script was good. At the time I thought I did, but I actually didn't. It was originally a German film so I decided to play it safe and do a remake, because when I saw the movie, I knew that with an Italian director and Italian actors, I could make a better movie.

How did you start working with the great director Federico Fellini?

After the War, there were a group of young movie-mad Italians with true vision.

The visionaries I am speaking of are Roberto Rosellini and Federico Fellini. At that time, it was almost impossible to make movies. We had no technological capabilities and there was no money to produce a film, but we decided to do it anyway. I met Federico Fellini when he was a humorist doing humor columns in newspapers. Fellini was also busy collaborating on various screenplays and stories. We decided to develop his writing projects. This was the true beginning of our movie life together. It was a sincere pleasure to have the opportunity to work with Federico Fellini, who was a creative and gifted director, in the truest sense of the words.

After the war, *Bitter Rice* [1949] was acclaimed as a major combination of the neo-realism of Italian post–World War II cinema and earthy sensuality. Did that set the pace for all the movies you did in Italy?

When the project came to me, I never thought it would have the universal appeal it did. I knew it was a simple story of life, love and death. But, when you make a movie that taps so uniquely into the audience's emotions, then you have a hit. I think this did set a pace for the movies I went on to do for the next few years, mainly because we got international recognition for *Bitter Rice*.

In 1954 *La Strada* won an Oscar for Best Foreign Film, and in 1956 *Nights of Cabiria* won another. Tell me about your transition from this type of Italian film of its day to the international movie *War and Peace*. Was this transition difficult?

The transition was not too difficult. With the success of my movie *Ulysses,* I had a good relationship with Paramount. Due to the size of this picture, *War and Peace*, Paramount was fairly particular about what director I could use. I originally wanted William Wyler, but in the end his visions for the film would have doubled the budget. I eventually settled on King Vidor, who told me he always wanted to direct *War and Peace.* You could write a whole book on my experiences with *War and Peace.* The casting of Audrey Hepburn was inspired and was key to the international success of the film. Don't forget, we also had other international movie "names" of the era like Henry Fonda, Mel Ferrer, Anita Ekberg, John Mills and others. That helped the international box office appeal tremendously.

You just mentioned your successful hit film *Ulysses,* starring Kirk Douglas. He was one of the first American actors you worked with in your career. What was it like to cast and work with American acting legend Kirk Douglas on *Ulysses?*

Kirk Douglas is a great actor. I came to America to find a star for *Ulysses* and in my opinion it had to be Kirk Douglas to play the role. I tried to make an agreement with his agents and I convinced Kirk to do the movie. Kirk came to Rome to shoot the film. We had a very good relationship. After the movie, Kirk was very happy how it turned out. I also introduced him to a woman who was the head of my publicity office, Anne Buydens, and I told her, "Take care of Kirk and see to anything he needs while he is in Rome." In the end, they wound up getting married.

War and Peace (1956, Paramount Pictures). Based on Leo Tolstoy's classic novel about three families caught up in Russia's Napoleonic Wars (1805–1812), the film featured Mel Ferrer with Milly Vitale (left) and Anna Maria Ferrera (right).

You remade so many films during your career. Why did you decide to remake *King Kong*?

Well, *King Kong* is a classic film that many, many people enjoy. It is a love story between a colossal ape and a beautiful woman and the story was always fascinating to me. If remakes are done correctly, they can be quite profitable. In the case of *King Kong*, I was definitely right to remake the film, because it wound up becoming a big box office success.

You also remade your own movie *Manhunter* into *Red Dragon*.

There are different reasons why I remade *Manhunter*. Director Michael Mann made a good movie, but represented on the screen only a part of the phenomenal book *Red Dragon* by Tom Harris. Mann brought to the screen only the part of the book that involved the investigation of the FBI officer. In all of the books by Tom Harris, he wrote about Hannibal Lector much wider. The part about *Red Dragon* in Michael Mann's movie totally disappeared. After the success of *Hannibal,* I thought that we could have another success by going back and representing the entire book, *Red Dragon*. We didn't actually re-do the movie, *Manhunter.* What we did was make the book *Red Dragon* in its entirety.

Ulysses (1955, Paramount Pictures). Returning to his homeland after the Trojan War, Ulysses (Kirk Douglas) is met by the ever-faithful Penelope (Silvana Mangano).

Speaking of Hannibal Lecter, you put up $10 million of your own money for the rights to the book, *Hannibal* by Tom Harris. Is your definition of a producer to put your money where your mouth is?

Yes, because the definition of what I feel is the true producer is one that does not go through a studio to buy a book. To me, a real producer finds the book and then buys it himself or herself. That is what I do and I have always done it during my career. By buying the rights to the book myself, I stay independent and I am in complete control of my product. Paying the initial $10 million was risky, but look how it paid off. It is the old story of risk vs. reward. This risk paid off with a great reward and then we ultimately did *Red Dragon*, and that was a huge hit, too.

Why did you go with Ridley Scott to direct *Hannibal*?

Originally, Jonathan Demme was going to direct the film. In the end, he changed his mind mainly because he felt he could not make a movie as great as the original, *The Silence of the Lambs*. When he rejected the project, I quickly hopped on a plane and visited Ridley Scott on the set of *Gladiator*. I suggested that Ridley read the novel that I bought the rights to. He read it, called me immediately and said, "Let's hire a screenwriter because I am in!" We then hired David Mamet to pen the script.

Could you tell me about the casting dilemmas, especially the role of Clarice Starling, originally played amazingly by Jodie Foster?

First and foremost, I knew we had no movie without Anthony Hopkins. When

Hannibal (2001, Universal). Clarice Starling (Julianne Moore) feels the intense stare of the deadly Hannibal Lecter (Sir Anthony Hopkins), who is standing right behind her.

he agreed to be in, I let out a very deep breath. As far as the role of Clarice Starling, Jodie Foster was not interested in reprising her role. I think Jodie did not connect with Clarice anymore. Universal was upset with her decision. Then we began to think of other actresses to play the part. I considered a wide array of important actresses to take the role of Clarice. Then, we decided on Julianne Moore, who is a truly gifted actress. She not only played the role, her presence was strongly instrumental in the reprising of the series.

How is it that Hannibal Lecter, who is a serial killer, has become loved by the public so much?

You see, Hannibal Lecter is the only serial killer in movie history that has a big cultural background that is extremely funny. Also, Lecter doesn't kill only to kill, he kills people that the public probably would love to kill themselves. (*Laughing*) So, even if he is killing, Lecter keeps his intensely human image with the public and for that they love him.

How did you assemble such a phenomenal cast for *Red Dragon?*

Ted Tally wrote a wonderful, wonderful script and that is how I assembled the cast. The talented actors in this film: Ed Norton, Emily Watson, Ralph Fiennes, Harvey Keitel, Phillip Seymour Hoffman, Mary Louise Parker and, of course, the magnificent Anthony Hopkins are attracted to great writing. I sent all of them the script and they all wanted in immediately. Writer Ted Tally's talent assembled this cast.

Red Dragon (2002, Universal). Hannibal Lecter (Sir Anthony Hopkins), a vicious killer prone to dining on his victims, is being escorted to his cell under major supervision.

Can you tell me about what many people predict will be your greatest movie ever,
    Alexander the Great?

You see, with *Alexander the Great* we are not in any race to compete with Oliver Stone. Oliver Stone has a particular vision of *Alexander the Great.* My vision is totally different. We are expecting a fabulous script from Baz Luhrmann and David Hare because Baz's vision of the movie is extraordinary. At that moment, we will decide when we are going to shoot it.

How many films have you made throughout your 60–plus year career?

God, there have been so many. I have made about 600 films. Now, these are films that I have help financed, acquired or distributed in the United States and abroad. I was a major distributor in Italy for many, many years. Remember that is where I started my career at the very young age of 20. Now, I am 84 years old. So, it is a long career.

You've worked with some of the greatest directors in the world — Fellini, Rosellini,
    Sydney Pollack, Sidney Lumet, Ridley Scott, Michael Mann and many more.
    Is there one director that stands out in an extra-special way?

Well, Fellini was one of the most talented directors I have ever worked with. I was involved with him earlier in my career and I was spoiled because he was so creative behind the camera. I have worked with so many great talents over the years that it is hard to single out just one because they all have their own unique ability to tell a story. From Rossellini to Sam Raimi to Milos Forman to Ridley Scott, I have been so lucky to collaborate with many of the greatest contemporary motion picture minds in the world.

What is the most exciting aspect of being a producer?

The most exciting part for me is the creative side of producing. The producer, in reality, is the soul of the movie. The producer is the one who chooses the script. He chooses the screenwriter. He chooses the director. Then, with the director and the producer in a collaborative effort, together, chooses the cast. The producer follows all of the steps of the movie until the final cut, including the promotion of the movie. That means that if the movie is a big success, the producer shares the merit with everybody else. I also believe that if the movie is a flop, the responsibility of it being a flop is on the producer, because it means he made some kind of a mistake. Maybe the producer made a mistake choosing the story or the screenplay. Or maybe the producer made a mistake choosing the director. Basically, something went wrong for the movie to fail and I believe that the fault is on the producer's shoulders. Also, in my experience of producing film, the real star of a movie is the script—not the actor or the director. Because, with a good script and a mediocre director you can make a very good movie, but with a bad script and a great director you still make a bad movie. The real star of any movie is the script!

Do you feel that producing a movie is like the birth of a child? Are the films ultimately your children?

I do think of my films as my children. I am so close to my films that you can't feel any other way about them. Early Academy Award–winning movies of mine like *War and Peace* and *La Strada*, and more recent movies like *Hannibal* and *Red Dragon*, all mean so much to me. You see a producer stays with a project from the conception of an idea to the promotion of the picture, to the DVD release. So, in a sense, it is like seeing your child born, teaching it to walk, watching it go through puberty and then sending the child off to college. So, yes, all my movies are like my children. They are my extended family.

After numerous box office successes, does raising funds for film ever get easier or is it always a constant battle with each new production?

When you have a great script, the money will come. I have a track record of producing film for over 60 years. Sure that helps when convincing an investor to put up millions. However, when you are in any business for that stretch of time, you have failures as well as successes. One hopes you have more successes, but business of any kind is risky and investing in film is highly risky. However, the returns can be very grand. A really good script will attract all kinds of ingredients for a movie, including the money.

Over the years, you have produced sci-fi, mob movies, Westerns, psychological thrillers — everything. Is one of the keys to your success *variety*?

Variety is the spice of life. I am always up for trying something I have not done before. The main thing I am attracted to is still, basically, a great story. I don't care what the genre is as long as it is a story with emotion, heart and excitement. I want my audiences to leave the theater satisfied.

There are many producers who have disappeared in this business. In your opinion, what is your method to staying strong, powerful and focused in your career?

I will answer you with another story. Very often I speak to students in colleges. A few years ago at Columbia University, I was having fun talking to the film students there. One of the students asked me, "Can you tell me how I can become a movie producer like you?" I replied to him with two answers. The first, was essentially that anybody can be taught how to produce a movie. However, secondly, I pointed out that there is something that I cannot possibly teach you and nobody can teach you. When Picasso was young, his teachers were teaching him how to paint and draw. Picasso became famous because he started using colors such as yellow, blue and red in a very original way. For this reason, Picasso became a "one-of-a-kind" and famous all over the world. That means he had something very special inside himself, something artistic that brought him to use the colors in that way. This is the same premise for a producer. There is a type of producer who knows only the mechanics of how to make a movie. Then there is also a producer who has inside himself the intuition that I call, in Italian, "Pallino" [to be obsessed]. The "Pallino" gives the drive to create the movie in a certain way. I can tell you that even though I am 84 years old, in the movies you never get old because the creative aspect is extraordinary in this business. The movie industry is not an industry of prototypes. In every movie, we have different challenges creatively and artistic problems. They have to be solved in very different ways. If I do *Hannibal,* I'll have certain problems to solve. If I do a movie like *U–571* about the Second World War, I will have a different range of production problems. This variety of problems that a producer must take care of always keeps you on the edge and at the top of your game. Once you have that gift, you will have it forever. There are truly no age limits as far as producing movies. I believe my career is testimony to the fact.

What are your most interesting or unusual experiences producing in Italy and in Hollywood?

The most interesting experience in Italy ranges from *La Strada* to *Nights of Cabiria* to *War and Peace.* When I was producing *War and Peace,* I was also able to produce *La Strada.* With an artistic movie like *La Strada,* no Italian distributor wanted to touch it or co-produce. I was only able to do it through Paramount because they wanted *War and Peace.* I told them that I would agree to give them *War and Peace* if they would make *La Strada,* too. This I will never forget. In America, problems are different. When I told myself, "I will go to America to become a producer there," I came to New York. However, it was a different world, a different culture and a different public. It is a whole different way to make movies. I said to myself, "Maybe I was wrong. I don't think I will ever become an American movie producer." The only thing I could do was to try to make an American movie. If, through this movie, I can show to myself, not just to the public, but to myself, that I can produce a very successful movie here in the United States, only then I will stay in America. Then I started to look for my first project. I looked right and left. One day I called writer Peter Maas who I knew very well. I did *The Valachi Papers* with Mass. I asked him, "Are you writing something new?" He replied, "I am writing *Serpico*." I said, "What is *Serpico*?" He explained to me the real-life story of heroic New York police officer Frank Serpico. I thought it was extremely interesting. I then asked him, "Can I read it?" He said, "I only have the first chapter done—the first 20 pages." To make a long story short, I convinced Maas to let me read his first 20 pages. He gave me the pages and I read them. In the first 20 pages of the book, Peter Maas explained only the character of Serpico. I quickly became fascinated by Frank Serpico. I said to myself, "What a movie needs to be successful is a compelling personality and a strong character." If you can create a story around that character, the book doesn't have to be exceptional. I knew that I could make a story around that strong personality of Frank Serpico. In fact, one can achieve that with any strong character. So, I decided to buy it. I met with Peter Maas and said, "I will buy the rights." He looked at me shocked and said, "The book isn't finished. You are actually buying this whole thing in the dark?" I said, "I don't care. I am buying this on the spot." At that time, I paid an amount close to $500,000, the equivalent in those days of $5 million. I had the right intuition because *Serpico*, starring Al Pacino, was a big hit. I made a successful movie with the public and the critics alike. Most importantly, I showed to myself that I was able to make major movies in America.

It appears that the new generation of producer has somehow lost the prestige of the title of "producer." What is your reaction to this?

I wouldn't say it that way. There are two categories of producers. On one level, there's a producer like me, who is absolutely independent from the studios and who works for himself or herself. When we have a project ready, we go to the studio to make a distribution agreement. These kinds of producers today are few and far between. There are almost none. There is a second category: Those producers, who if they want to buy a script or a book, have to go to a studio. They have to wait while the studio reads the book, then the studio "powers-that-be" may agree or not agree to cut a deal. Finally, if they decide to buy it, at that point the producer basically works for the studio because the studio is in command. They have the project in their hands. The studio decides on the director, actors, everything. My type of producer follows his or her own path. When I get to the point where I make an agreement with the studio, I bring the script completely ready. I have done this with my own money, work and credibility. I do not know how many of these style producers are left. Very, very few, I can tell you that.

How does it feel to have another producer in the family, your daughter, Raffaella?

It feels great. She is an independent producer but right now we are actually thinking about doing a project together. I helped her to make her first movie in Bora Bora. She is a wonderful producer and a wonderful daughter.

Serpico (1973, Paramount Pictures). Based on Peter Maas' book (the true-life exploits of undercover New York City cop Frank Serpico), the film contributed significantly toward making Al Pacino a major movie star.

What are your plans for the upcoming year?

My future plans are wrapped up in the films that I am waiting to make. Soon, Tom Harris will give me the script about a young Hannibal Lector. Through this new *Hannibal* movie, I want to explain to the public the motivations of why he became a killer and a cannibal. It will be an extremely interesting and original movie that will bring us back in time. I am also continuing to develop *Alexander the Great*. Those are my plans for now.

Since you and your family all started in the pasta business, what pasta do you eat now in your home in the United States?

The best Italian pasta in America, DeCecco.

Besides making movies, what do you truly love?

My family!

Dino De Laurentiis Filmography

Alexander the Great project (Leonardo DiCaprio, Nicole Kidman) 2005 — producer; *Red Dragon* (Anthony Hopkins, Edward Norton, Ralph Fiennes) 2002 — producer; *Hannibal*

(Anthony Hopkins, Julianne Moore) 2001— producer; *U-571* (Matthew McConaughey, Bill Paxton, Harvey Keitel) 2000— producer; *Breakdown* (Kurt Russell, J.T. Walsh, Kathleen Quinlan) 1997— producer; *Unforgettable* (Ray Liotta, Linda Fiorentino, Peter Coyote) 1996— producer; *Slave of Dreams* (Edward James Olmos, Sherilyn Fenn) 1995 TV— producer; *Assassins* (Sylvester Stallone, Antonio Banderas, Julianne Moore) 1995— executive producer; *Solomon & Sheba* (Halle Berry, Miquel Brown, Norman Buckley) 1995 TV— producer; *Army of Darkness* (Bruce Campbell, Embeth Davidtz) 1993— executive producer; *Body of Evidence* (Madonna, Michael Forest, Joe Mantegna) 1993— producer; *Once Upon a Crime...* (John Candy, James Belushi, Cybill Shepherd) 1992— producer; *Sometimes They Come Back* (Tim Matheson, Brooke Adams) 1991 TV— executive producer; *Desperate Hours* (Mickey Rourke, Anthony Hopkins, Mimi Rogers) 1990— producer; *King Kong Lives* (Linda Hamilton, Brian Kerwin, Peter Elliott) 1986— executive producer; *Manhunter* (William L. Peterson, Kim Greist, Joan Allen) 1986— producer; *Maximum Overdrive* (Emilio Estevez, Pat Hingle, Laura Harrington) 1986— executive producer; *Silver Bullet* (Gary Busey, Everett McGill, Corey Haim) 1985— producer; *Year of the Dragon* (Mickey Rourke, John Lone, Ariane) 1985— producer; *Cat's Eye* (Drew Barrymore, James Woods, Alan King) 1985— producer; *Dune* (Francesca Annis, Jose Ferrer, Leonardo Cimino) 1984— executive producer; *Conan the Destroyer* (Arnold Schwarzenegger, Grace Jones) 1984— executive producer; *The Bounty* (Mel Gibson, Anthony Hopkins, Laurence Olivier) 1984— executive producer; *The Dead Zone* (Christopher Walken, Brooke Adams, Tom Skerritt) 1983— executive producer; *Amityville II: The Possession* (James Olson, Burt Young) 1982— producer; *Conan the Barbarian* (Arnold Schwarzenegger, James Earl Jones) 1982— executive producer; *Ragtime* (James Cagney, Brad Dourif, Elizabeth McGovern) 1981— producer; *Flash Gordon* (Sam J. Jones, Melody Anderson, Max von Sydow) 1980— producer; *Hurricane* (Timothy Bottoms, Mia Farrow, Jason Robards) 1979— producer; *The Brink's Job* (Peter Falk, Peter Boyle, Gena Rowlands) 1979— executive producer; *King of the Gypsies* (Sterling Hayden, Susan Sarandon, Brooke Shields) 1978— executive producer; *The Serpent's Egg* (Isolde Barth, Heinz Bennent) 1977— producer; *The White Buffalo* (Charles Bronson, Jack Warden) 1977— executive producer; *Orca* (Richard Harris, Bo Derek, Charlotte Rampling) 1977— executive producer; *Drum* (Warren Oates, Isela Vega, Pam Grier) 1976— producer; *King Kong* (Jeff Bridges, Charles Grodin, Jessica Lange) 1976— producer; *Three Days of the Condor* (Robert Redford, Faye Dunaway) 1975— executive producer; *Mandingo* (James Mason, Susan George, Perry King) 1975— producer; *Porgi l'altra guancia* (Bud Spencer, Terence Hill) 1974— producer; *Death Wish* (Charles Bronson, Hope Lange, Vincent Gardenia) 1974— producer; *Uomini duri* (Lino Ventura, Isaac Hayes) 1974— producer; *Crazy Joe* (Peter Boyle, Paula Prentiss, Rip Torn) 1974— producer; *Neveroyatnye priklyucheniya italyantsev v Rossii* (Andrei Mironov, Ninetto, Davoli) 1973— producer; *Serpico* (Al Pacino, John Randolph, Jack Kehoe) 1973— executive producer; *Lo Scopone scientifico* (Alberto Sordi, Silvana Mangano) 1972— producer; *Causa di divorzio* (Enrico Montesano, Senta Berger, Catherine Spaak) 1972— producer; *The Valachi Papers* (Charles Bronson, Lino Ventura, Jill Ireland) 1972— producer; *Io non vedo, tu non parli, lui non sente* (Alighiero Noschese, Enrico Montesano) 1971— producer; *La Spina dorsale del diavolo* (Bekim Fehmui, Richard Crenna) 1971— producer; *A Man Called Sledge* (James Garner, Dennis Weaver, Claude Akins) 1970— producer; *Waterloo* (Rod Steiger, Christopher Plummer, Virginia McKenna) 1970— producer; *Una Breve stagione* (Christopher Jones, Pia Degermark) 1969— producer; *Io non scappo... fuggo* (Enrico Montesano, Alighiero Noschese) 1969— producer; *Napravleniye glavnogo udara* (Yevgeni Burenkov, Vladlen Davydov) 1969— producer; *Barbagia* (Terence Hill, Don Backy, Frank Wolff) 1969— producer; *Fräulein Doktor* (Suzy Kendall, Kenneth More) 1969— producer; *L' Amante di Gramigna* (Gian Maria Volonte, Stefania Sandrelli) 1969— producer; *Nerosubianco* (Terry Carter, Umberto Di Grazia, Anita Sanders) 1968— producer; *Roma come Chicago* (John Cassavetes, Gabriele Ferzetti) 1968— producer; *Barbarella* (Jane Fonda, John Phillip Law) 1968— producer; *Anzio* (Robert Mitchum, Peter Falk, Robert Ryan) 1968— producer; *Banditi a Milano* (Gian Maria Volonte, Don Backy) 1968— producer; *Capriccio all'italiana* (Andriana Asti, Laura Betti) 1968— producer; *L' Odissea* (Bekim Fehmui, Irene Papas) 1968— TV producer; *Diabolik* (John Phillip Law, Marisa Mell) 1968 — producer; *Lo Straniero* (Marcello Mastroianni, Anna Karina) 1967 — producer; *Le Streghe* (Silvana Mangano, Annie Girardot) 1967 — producer; *Matchless* (Patrick O'Neal, Ira von Furstenberg) 1966 — producer; *Se tutte le donne del mondo* (Mike Connors, Dorothy Provine) 1966 — executive producer; *La Bibbia* (Michael Parks, Ulla Bergryd) 1966 — producer; *Menage all'italiana* (Ugo Tognazzi, Anna Moffo) 1965 — producer; *Thrilling* (Luigi Battaglia, Federico Boido) 1965 — producer; *I Tre volti* (Goffredo Alessandrini, Nando Angelini) 1965 — producer; *Cadavere per signora* (Sylva Koscina, Sergio Fantoni) 1964 — producer; *Il Disco volante* (Alberto Sordi, Silvana Mangano) 1964 — producer; *La Mia signora* (Lamberto Antinori, Maria Canocchia Alfredo) 1964 — producer; *Il Giovedi* (Walter Chiari, Michele Mercier) 1963 — producer; *Il Maestro di Vigevano* (Alberto Sordi, Claire Bloom) 1963 — producer; *Le Ore dell'amore* (Ugo Tognazzi, Emmanuelle Riva) 1963 — producer; *Il Boom* (Alberto Sordi, Gianna Maria Canale) 1963 — producer; *Il Diavolo* (Alberto Sordi, Ulla Andersson) 1963 — producer; *Il Processo di Verona* (Silvana Mangano, Frank Wolff) 1963 — producer; *Il Commissario* (Carlo Bango, Pasquale Campagnola) 1962 — executive producer; *Mafioso* (Albert Sordi, Norma Bengell) 1962 — executive producer; *Barabbas* (Anthony Quinn, Silvana Mangano) 1962 — producer; *The Best of Enemies* (David Niven, Michael Wilding) 1962 — executive producer; *Il Federale* (Ugo Tognazzi, Georges Wilson) 1961 — executive producer; *Maciste contro il vampiro* (Gordon Scott, Leorna Ruffo) 1961 — executive producer; *Una Vita difficile* (Alberto Sordi, Lea Massari) 1961 — producer; *Il Giudizio universale* (Mario Abussi, Anouk Aimee) 1961 — producer; *Crimen* (Lamberto Antinori, Bernard Blier) 1960 — producer); *Il Gobbo* (Gerard Blain, Anna-Maria Ferrero) 1960 — producer; *Io amo, tu ami* (Giuliano Gemma, Peter Marshall) 1960 — executive producer; *Le Pillole di Ercole* (Piera Arico, Nedo Azzini) 1960 — producer; *Tutti a casa* (Alberto Sordi, Eduardo De Filippo) 1960 — producer; *Sotto dieci bandiere* (Van Heflin, Charles Laughton) 1960 — producer; *5 Branded Women* (Silvana Mangano, Jeanne Moreau, Vera Miles) 1960 — producer); *La Grande guerra* (Alberto Sordi, Vittorio Gassman) 1959 — producer; *Ladro e cameriera guardia* (Mario Carotenuto, Fausto Cigliano) 1958 — producer; *La Tempesta* (Silvana Mangano, Van Heflin) 1958 — producer; *This Angry Age* (Silvana Mangano, Anthony Perkins, Richard Conte) 1958 — producer; *Fortunella* (Piera Arico, Nando Bruno, Guido Celano) 1957 — producer; *Malafemmina* (Maria Fiore, Nunzio Gallo, Aldo Bufi Landi) 1957 — producer; *Le Notti di Cabiria* (Guilietta Masina, Francois Perier) 1957 — producer; *Guendalina* (Jacqueline Sassard, Raffaele Mattioli) 1956 — executive producer; *War and Peace* (Audrey Hepburn, Henry Fonda, Mel Ferrer) 1956 — producer; *La Bella mugnaia* (Vittorio De Sica, Sophia Loren, Marcello Mastroianni) 1955 — producer; *Le Diciottenni* (Marisa Allasio, Margherita Bagni) 1955 — producer; *La Donna del fiume* (Sophia Loren, Gerard Oury, Lise Bourdin) 1955 — co-producer; *Ragazze d'oggi* (Marisa Allasio, Eduardo Bergamo) 1955 — producer; *Mambo* (Silvana Mangano, Michael Rennie) 1955 — producer; *Ulysses* (Kirk Douglas, Silvana Mangano, Anthony Quinn) 1955 — producer; *Attila* (Anthony Quinn, Sophia Loren, Henri Vidal) 1954 — producer; *Un Giorno in pretura* (Peppino De Filippo, Silvana Pampanni) 1954 — producer; *Miseria e nobiltà* (Toto, Liana Billi, Leo Brandi) 1954 — producer; *Siluri umani* (Paolo Bergamaschi, Nerio Bernardi) 1954 — producer; *L' Oro di Napoli* (Toto, Lianella Carell, Pasquale Cennamo) 1954 — producer; *La Strada* (Anthony Quinn, Giulietta Masina) 1954 — producer; *Anni facili* (Nino Taranto, Armenia Balducci) 1953 — producer; *Il paese dei campanelli* (Ricardo Billi, Carlo Dapporto) 1953 — producer; *La tratta delle bianche* (Silvana Pampanini, Vittorio Gassman) 1953 — producer; *Fratelli d'Italia* (Ettore Manni, Paul Muller) 1952 — producer; *Jolanda la figlia del corsaro nero* (Silvio Bagolini, Ignazio Balzamo) 1952 — producer; *I sette dell'orsa maggiore* (Carlo Bellini, Tino Carraro) 1952 — producer; *Totò a colori* (Toto, Mario Castellani, Virgilio Riento) 1952 — producer; *Gli undici moschettieri* (Pina Gallini) 1952 — producer; *Anna* (Silvana Mangano, Gaby Morlay, Raf Vallone) 1951 — producer; *Europa '51* (Ingrid Bergman, Alexander Knox) 1951 — producer; *Guardie e ladri* (Ernesto Almirante, Pietro Carloni) 1951 — producer; *Totò terzo uomo* (Toto, Ughetto Bertucci, Liana Billi) 1951 — producer; *L' Ultimo incontro* (Jean-Pierre Aumont, Laura Carli, Giovanna Gallletti) 1951 — producer; *Accidenti alle tasse!!* (Riccardo Billi, Mario Riva) 1951 — producer; *Il Brigante Musolino* (Amedeo Nazzari, Silvana

Mangano) 1950— producer; ***Napoli milionaria*** (Toto, Eduardo De Fillipo) 1950— co-producer; ***Il Lupo della Sila*** (Silvana Mangano, Amedeo Nazzari) 1949 — producer; ***I Pompieri di Viggiù*** (Nino Taranto, Toto, Vanda Osiris) 1949 — producer; ***Riso amaro*** (Silvana Mangano, Maria Capuzzo) 1949 — producer; ***Adamo ed Eva*** (Erminio Macario, Isa Barzizza, Gianni Agus) 1949 — producer; ***Molti sogni per le strade*** (Checco Durante, Massimo Girotta) 1948 — producer; ***Il Cavaliere misterioso*** (Vittorio Gassman, Maria Mercader) 1948 — producer; ***La Figlia del capitano*** (Irasema Dilian, Amedeo Nazzari) 1947 — producer; ***Il Bandito*** (Anna Magnani, Amedeo Nazzari) 1946 — producer; ***Malombra*** (Isa Miranda, Andrea Checci) 1942 — producer; ***L'Amore canta*** (Vera Carmi, Maria Denis) 1941— producer

Robert Chartoff

After a summer job as an assistant to a talent manager in the Catskill Mountains, Robert Chartoff knew his life's work would be devoted to the entertainment industry. He became a personal manager of talent for many years and then made the transition, through his connections with studio executives, to being a producer of major motion pictures with his partner Irwin Winkler. Early in his career, he and Winkler produced Point Blank *starring Lee Marvin and* The Gambler *starring James Caan. An associate of Chartoff's suggested that he and Winkler take a look at a film called* The Lords of Flatbush *and to take an even closer look at one of its fine new actors, Sylvester Stallone. After watching it, Chartoff was convinced that Stallone had the potential to become a young Marlon Brando. Chartoff called Stallone into his office for a meeting. Well, that meeting resulted in* Rocky, *which ultimately turned out to be Robert Chartoff's Academy Award–winning picture. Chartoff and Winkler have gone on to produce five* Rocky *installments and turned that very series into an American tradition. He has produced classic pictures like* Raging Bull, New York, New York *and* The Right Stuff. *Robert Chartoff, an avid world traveler, resides in California.*

Like every kid, I loved movies. I just loved the whole idea of going on a Saturday afternoon to the theater. It was a great escape for me because movies were sexy, scary, fun and adventurous. They were just filled with emotions. However, I never dreamed during that point in my life that I would go into this field. It was far from any thought in my mind when I lived in the Bronx as a kid growing up on Gunhill Road. It was only later it looked like it would become a reality. I can't say that it was anything that inspired me. I wasn't a kid that was inspired by movies so that's why I got into the movie industry. When the opportunity happened to get into this field, I really wanted to do it. I would say my preparation for this business was more my education than being a fan of film.

What was it about your education that prepared you for your career in film?

I have a liberal arts education and after college I attended Columbia Law School. However, it was through my English composition courses that I learned what character is all about. I also learned about character from life in general. Character is so important in telling a story. I learned the value of character and I learned the strength of character and, in turn, it strengthened me as a person and a producer.

74

Describe your first introduction to show business.

During college and before I attended law school, I worked for an uncle who was an agent in the Catskill Mountains. He booked talent for Catskill hotels and I worked for him during the summer for three years straight. That was my first introduction to show business of any kind. I knew when I finished law school that I wanted to be in this field in some capacity. So, when I graduated, I chose personal management and proceeded to do that for about half a dozen years. I managed talent, first comedians, then actors and later singers. Through that I got to meet studio people and started to make some serious connections. Also, through my managing, I found a great script entitled *Point Blank*. I showed it to executives at MGM and they decided they wanted to make the film. That was in the late 1960s and it starred Lee Marvin, Angie Dickinson and Carroll O'Connor. I produced it with my partner Irwin Winkler and that's how it all began.

Robert Chartoff

Did you use your extensive knowledge from managing talent towardm your transition to becoming a film producer?

We actually ended up doing another production prior to *Point Blank* for MGM. That was our very first picture deal. It was an Elvis Presley movie. It couldn't have been a better entry because Elvis films were very formula-driven at that time. So, everyone else knew exactly what they were doing and we were essentially there with the opportunity of learning around others. It turned out to be kind of a producing apprenticeship, a very unique opportunity to learn.

Has the anti-hero always attracted you to a story when committing to produce it? For instance, two successful films you produced early in your career, *They Shoot Horses, Don't They?* and *The Gambler,* both focus on lead characters down on their luck.

What attracts me to a script is a good story. In both cases, you are right. They are anti- heroes and in both cases they were not saved by the story. I can't say I am necessarily attracted to anti-hero stories. I feel I'm attracted to characters with vulnerabilities. I have no partiality in regards to that. In both films I had great directors who knew the main characters extremely well. Sydney Pollack, who directed *They Shoot Horses, Don't They?,* delivered such a wonderful film and is always such a great guy. We were lucky to get him for this movie. It was challenging to sign him. It was hit-or-miss whether we would or not. Sydney is a man who came out of television, essentially.

Maybe he had only one or two feature films prior to ours. But he is so smart and so well put together. Sydney truly understood what the picture and characters were all about. It was a last-minute decision. We had someone else in mind but, ultimately, went with Sydney. As far as the film *The Gambler*, James Toback wrote a great script, and our director Karel Reisz really knew the characters well. When the script came to our attention, I read it and loved it. I personally always loved gambling, not excessively but for fun. It was a truly great opportunity to produce that film. Karel Reisz is such a smart, sensitive director and he had done such great films in England like *Saturday Night and Sunday Morning* with Albert Finney. James Caan was perfect in the lead role of *The Gambler*. We were lucky to have such a great director as well as a lead actor who was so talented and working with us during his prime.

You and Irwin Winkler made the *Rocky* series into an American tradition. How did *Rocky* start for you?

Irwin Winkler and I had an associate by the name of Gene Kirkwood and he was friendly with Sylvester Stallone's agent. I never heard of Stallone and was not really excited to meet him. Gene then told me to see the *The Lords of Flatbush* with Stallone. I watched the movie and I was very impressed with him. I thought Sylvester Stallone had the potential to become a young Marlon Brando. A meeting was then arranged for me to meet him. He came to my office and, again, I was very impressed by him. He was so smart and so funny, clearly nothing like the character he played in *The Lords of Flatbush*. I enjoyed the meeting and wasn't sure where we would go with it, but I was pleased to have it. I told him so. Literally, as Sylvester was leaving my office, he stopped to tell me he was doing a little writing. He asked, "If I send you a script, will you read it?" I said, "Sure, send it over." He then sent over *Paradise Alley*. I read the script and I felt it had lots of problems. However, it did have some serious potential, the potential to become something quite wonderful. I called his agent and told him we would be prepared to option this script and develop it, if Sylvester wanted to do so. The agent, who was so eager for the meeting in the first place, all of a sudden backed off and said, "Maybe Sylvester should call you directly on this one." So, he arranged another meeting and Sylvester came into the office and somehow, apologetically, said, "Look, I've had this script for years. No one ever liked it and, just a month ago, I optioned this script to someone for $500 so I could pay my rent. So, I don't really have control of the script and I shouldn't have given it to you in the first place." From my point of view, I didn't really care because it was an "okay" script, but I just had a feeling about it. The texture was very attractive. Then he said, "Look, I have another idea for a screenplay about a boxer. Would you read it if I write it?" I said, "Sure, send it over." Six weeks later he brought in what was the first draft of *Rocky*. There was so much in this script that I liked, but what I liked most was the ending. In the end, Rocky Balboa lost the fight to Apollo Creed. However, something more important happened. He won by achieving his personal goal. That was very rare in American cinema. My partner Irwin Winkler read the script, and also liked it. Our associate, Gene Kirkwood, who brought Sylvester to us in the first place, also liked it. So, we were all in agreement. For the next six months, we worked on the script with Stallone before we sent it to anyone. When it was finally done, we showed it to United Artists, the company

Rocky (1976, United Artists). Rocky (Sylvester Stallone) listens to Paulie's (Burt Young) plea to assist him in training for the championship fight in this Academy Award–winning picture.

we were working for on an exclusive basis at that time. Mike Medavoy, who was an executive in the LA office, loved it. Since United Artists' principal offices in those days were in New York, Medavoy had to convince them, which was not easy.

What was the budget to produce *Rocky*?

It was $950,000. That was in 1976. The reason it was so low was because Stallone would not sell the script unless he played the lead role. The studio did not feel comfortable about financially backing a more or less unknown. No one knew at that moment he would go on to superstardom. At that time, Stallone didn't have a penny to his name. The studio made many offers to buy the script, but he turned them all down. Stallone never wanted to direct it, but we were totally committed to him acting in the picture. He knew this was his big opportunity, an opportunity that may never happen in his life again.

Many of the key, well-cast supporting actors went on to be nominated for Academy Awards for the film. Could you take me through the casting process of *Rocky*?

Before we cast anyone, we signed on John Avildsen to direct. He was heavily involved in the casting as well. As far as the casting process went, Burt Young was easy for us to cast for the role of Paulie. We knew right off that we wanted Burt for the part. He is a multi-talented actor and had been in two or three movies of ours prior to *Rocky*.

Rocky II (1979, United Artists). **A weeping Adrian (Talia Shire) responds to the torment of her brother, Paulie (Burt Young).**

For the part of Mickey, we had given the script to Lee Strasberg, who had just done *The Godfather Part II* and was just kind of hot. Strasberg wanted to do the picture, but he also wanted too much money. So, I called Burgess Meredith, who frankly, I wanted all along. We both lived in Malibu, so one evening I dropped off the script to him. Burgess read the script that night and loved it. Ironically, the same night he got a call from Lee Strasberg and they spoke on the phone for awhile. Burgess literally had the script in his lap as he asked Strasberg what film he was doing next? Lee said, "I'm doing a script called *Rocky*." Burgess did not let on we had given it to him. Well, you all know how that story ends. Burgess Meredith played a brilliant Mickey. For the part of Adrian, we had a lot of fine actresses read. Carrie Snodgrass was going to do the part but she wanted $75,000 and that was too much money. So, we auditioned Talia Shire for the role. Talia had done *The Godfather* as Connie Corleone, but no one really knew of her. She auditioned and we just loved her. Talia came in and completely won us over. Sylvester and Talia did some scenes together that were directed by John Avildsen during the audition. They were absolutely perfect together. We immediately cast her and were extremely lucky to have her for the part.

Carl Weathers is an interesting story. We originally had another actor for the role of Apollo Creed, but I wasn't too keen on him. We were only a few weeks away from shooting and, at about seven at night, we were all talking about the part. I felt there had to be someone else. So, I picked up the phone and called an agent I knew. Back then, there were agents who principally dealt with African-American talent. Now, that talent is spread out everywhere, as it should be. I called this woman agent and said we were desperately looking for this character, a boxer, who can act and play this part. She said, "There is someone in the office right now who I feel could do it." She then yelled out, "Hey, Carl, do you ever box?" Then, a deep voice came over and said, "Sure, I can box, why?" She then told me there is somebody here right now who boxes and is an ex–Oakland Raider. I said, "Gee, it sounds good. I'd love to meet him." She begged off and said, "Sorry, but he's leaving tonight on a flight for Oakland." I said, "Culver City is on the way to the airport, so tell him to stop by my office on the way and we'll meet him." I called Sylvester and John, they agreed to come in and we waited. Carl came in an hour later, at 8:30. We gave him two pages to read. He went outside for a few minutes and came back in with his shirt off. Sylvester took his shirt off. They did the scene together and it worked out perfectly. Carl had the perfect voice, the perfect body. He was Apollo Creed. Then, after the scene, Carl said with a straight face, referring to Stallone, "If you get a real actor, I can do a lot better." There was dead silence. Then someone said, "This is Rocky. He is playing the lead role." Stallone actually found it very amusing and really wanted Carl for the role, as we did as well. In that movie, we had a series of great breaks and great miracles. We were very lucky

The basic theme of *Rocky* is a million-to-one shot for an unknown fighter to win. Did you think your possibility of winning an Academy Award for Best Picture with *Rocky* was a million-to-one shot?

All I can tell you is that on the last day of filming, I bought a leatherbound pad and a pen for Sylvester. I walked up to him and said, "Now, go write the sequel." So, I kind of believed we had something special. I never believed we would capture the world's imagination the way we did. I knew in my heart that we had something unique and it was a great movie, the personification of the American Dream.

Many fans of the *Rocky* series say Clubber Lang was his best opponent. Personally, I believe it was because his dialogue was written so well. Did Stallone write the part of Clubber Lang with Mr. T already in mind?

That's a very interesting question. I don't think Sylvester wrote the part for Mr. T. However, when we got Mr. T, he was perfect for the part.

With all the fame and adulation, not to mention the financial success, did Sylvester Stallone change much as a person from the first *Rocky* to *Rocky V*?

By the time he did *Rocky V* he was 15 years older. He changed in that respect. However, he always found the truth in the character and himself. I don't think he took a different approach to the role. He was a bona fide star making three movies a year for top dollar. The truth is that Sylvester will always be Sylvester. I don't think fame changed his relationship with me. He's always respected the fact that I gave him his first big break in movies. It is important to remember where you came from.

Many people say *Rocky* is the best installment, while others cite *Rocky III*. Which was your most enjoyable one to produce?

How could it not be the first *Rocky*? It won the Academy Award, was a smash hit and came out of nowhere. It was one of the greatest experiences of my life. For any producer to have that gift once in a lifetime, it is pretty thrilling. The budget was $950,000 and it has gone on to make over $200 million. So, it's an easy answer to that question.

As a producer, are you trying to recreate that success? Are you waiting for that *Rocky* script to walk through your office door again from another unknown actor with a dream?

No, I never look at it that way. I just look at what scripts I can relate to and what scripts I would like to make. That's essentially why I make films. I make films that interest me. Things I'd like to see. I don't worry about what the audience is going to like because I have no idea what they will like. I make a movie to the best to my abilities, put it out there and hope that people respond.

When it came to the marketing of the *Rocky* movies, did you get involved with the promoting aspects, such as trailers, posters, toys, etc.?

As far as making the picture, the release of the film, the trailers promoting it and the movie posters — oh yes, I'm heavily involved. Every true producer who wants to succeed in this business gets involved with that. These are the key elements to the success or failure of a movie.

Rocky III (1982, United Artists). Rocky Balboa (Sylvester Stallone), wearing his championship belt, poses confidently.

You produced *New York, New York* with director Martin Scorsese. During the production of that film, did Scorsese pitch you the idea of producing *Raging Bull*?

It was either during that production or immediately after. I am not sure if he optioned the rights to the book, we optioned it, or Bobby De Niro optioned it. What *is* important is that it's such an unusual take on the American Dream.

What was the difference between Sylvester Stallone's preparation for his role in *Rocky* and Robert De Niro's preparation for his role in *Raging Bull*?

So different physically in the sense that Bobby had to lose all the weight initially to play the part of the young, lean Jake LaMotta. Then, actually stopped production for three or four months, so Bobby could put on weight for the second half of the movie. I think their approaches to acting are very different. Sly wrote the character and knew

Rocky IV **(1982, United Artists). Paulie (Burt Young) attempts to restraint Rocky (Sylvester Stallone), who travels to Russia to fight the Soviet champ who killed his friend during a previous bout.**

the character intimately. So, right off the bat, that's an extreme difference. Both are very different guys. I wouldn't begin to tell you what their qualities are as actors, but Sylvester is more over-the-top and less classically trained. He takes the character on like that. One thing is for sure, Bobby and Sly are both brilliant actors. Everybody acknowledges De Niro to be so great, but Sly is underrated because of the films he has

Raging Bull (1980, United Artists). Jake La Motta (Robert De Niro) is ordered to his corner by the referee (Martin Denkin) after knocking out Tony Janiro (Kevin Mahon).

chosen to be in. Action movies. Or maybe they have chosen him. I thought Sly was absolutely brilliant in *F.I.S.T.*

What was the budget for the movie *Raging Bull*?
    The budget was $13 million.

Was the real Jake LaMotta actively involved during the production?
    Jake LaMotta was certainly present. He was a very powerful resource and advisor to the picture and always valuable to have on-set.

Raging Bull (1980, United Artists). Joey (Joe Pesci), brother and manager of boxer Jake La Motta (Robert De Niro), whispers to him conspiratorially.

Many people say that *Rocky* is the greatest boxing movie of all time, while others single out *Raging Bull*. How does it feel to be the producer of both?

Personally, I don't even like boxing. I like movies and I like solid drama and I feel both movies are filled with that. I love the fact that people still think about these films all these years later. That kind of lasting impact is truly rewarding to me.

Not many producers were successful in making factual outer space movies. What made you want to take a chance on the non-fiction book *The Right Stuff* by Tom Wolfe?

It's simply a great story. There were great real-life characters in it. Chuck Yeager, who broke the sound barrier, was extraordinary. It was about the real pioneers, the other heroes of our generation, the astronauts. It was Tom Wolfe's imaginative story that made it possible for me to produce it. That was the inspiration for the movie. It was obvious to me, from reading the book, that there was a good movie in it. I never thought otherwise. Actually, the book was given to me as a house gift. John Gorman, who was staying with me, bought the book and gave it to me to read. We had worked on a Tom Wolfe project together, so we knew a lot about Tom's story telling abilities. The book had just come out and he thought I might be interested in reading it. I thought it was great. I gave it to Irwin. He felt the same way and we proceeded to produce it.

The Right Stuff (1983, Warner Brothers). Capt. Leroy Gordon (Dennis Quaid) gets prepared for flight in the adaptation of Tom Wolfe's non-fiction book about the beginnings of the U.S. space program.

Any obstacles in the production process, particularly the challenge of making the film seem real?

There were always obstacles, especially in the early 1980s when you are dealing with computer generated images. It was a tremendous chore to get these effects done. It was extremely challenging and we didn't really know if we could get the stuff to work and look real.

As the title of producer is being bandied about throughout the film industry, how do you define your job as a producer?

The first challenge is to get good material and you are ultimately no better than the material that you get. Putting my producing job in the broadest terms, once you get a script you like, your next step is to develop it. You need to develop it thoroughly, which is a year process or more. Then you get the best possible director. You get the best actors for the parts and then you have to stay with the project intimately while it's being shot. Then you go through the editing process. All of these elements are vitally important in making a successful movie. I feel this is what a producer should do. From the beginning to the end, you have to be fully involved, totally immersed in the production.

On your productions, do you carry over the same crew from picture to picture?

Well, we do hire the same crew whenever possible. If you have good people, you want to keep them. As a producer, you always try hard to find the best crew possible. Like everything else, quality is so important. The best people make the best movies.

You discovered Sylvester Stallone, among other great talents. What do you look for when auditioning an actor or actress?

The first criteria is if they can act and that is not easy to find. There may be someone who looks good for the part, but can't act. It is a very demanding profession. It's not easy. What you begin to discover, as a producer, is that there are lots of people who are acting, but there are very few who are truly gifted. That's why there are very few stars around. It's not a fluke. If you find someone that is really good, you want to embrace them and utilize them toward the best level they can possibly attain.

The entertainment industry changes as quick as the fickle tastes of the public. What is your take on that?

In reality, it has changed for me because I have changed. I have been in and out of this business for the last 35 years. There are new influences now: CGI, television, reality shows and the list goes on. They market films for a much younger audience now. The people who run the studios are different. Now they are conglomerates that are more accountable for their films than they used to be. There was a time "back in the day" when a studio head would say, "I like this film. Let's make it." Now they want a marketing report first and numerous other things. So, I have changed and the business has changed too.

With a proven track record in producing movies, does financing for your projects come easy?

I am about to start a picture now and it was very tough to find the financing. It was really, really hard. I think if you want to do a picture that is not in the studio mold, and you have to find independent sources of money, it is an extremely difficult challenge. I think it is more difficult now than ever. The economy right now is a big part of it. Increasingly, money has to come from Europe. When you are getting money outside the United States, getting access to money is harder. I was essentially brought up in the studio system, where you pitch it to a studio and if somebody says yes, then you make the movie. Now, the financing is coming from insurance companies, banks, from people who are not necessarily from the film industry. So, it makes my job a lot harder. As a producer, you have to convince the money man, whoever it is, that he is going to make money on the picture. Whether it is an insurance man, banker or a studio, they want to know that you believe it will make money. First you have to believe it and then it is your job to present it with that same intense passion to the potential investors. It is much harder when you are dealing with bankers. They usually don't share your dream. They just look at the bottom line, and that is difficult. The money aspect in my mind is the least enjoyable part of the producing process.

At this point in your life, what is important to you?

My family is really important to me. I spend as much time as I can with them. I really love to travel. I also have been busy working on a charity that I have been running for 14 years in India. So, that is what I have been doing and it is a big part of my life.

I think the whole world wants to know the answer to my next question. Will there be a *Rocky 6*?

No comment, but there might be news about it shortly.

Robert Chartoff Filmography

Country of My Skull (Samuel L. Jackson, Juliette Binoche) 2003 — producer; *Straight Talk* (Dolly Parton, James Woods) 1992 — producer; *Rocky V* (Sylvester Stallone, Talia Shire, Burt Young, Tommy Morrison) 1990 — producer; *Rocky IV* (Sylvester Stallone, Talia Shire, Burt Young, Dolph Lundgren) 1985 — producer; *Beer* (Loretta Swit, David Alan Grier) 1985 — producer; *The Right Stuff* (Sam Shepard, Scott Glenn, Ed Harris) 1983 — producer; *Rocky III* (Sylvester Stallone, Burt Young, Talia Shire, Mr. T) 1982 — producer; *Raging Bull* (Robert De Niro, Joe Pesci) 1980 — producer; *Rocky II* (Sylvester Stallone, Burt Young Talia Shire, Carl Weathers) 1979 — producer; *Uncle Joe Shannon* (Burt Young) 1978 — producer; *Comes a Horseman* (James Caan, Jane Fonda) 1978 — executive producer; *Valentino* (John Ratzenberger) 1977 — producer; *New York, New York* (Robert De Niro, Liza Minnelli) 1977 — producer; *Nickelodeon* (Burt Reynolds, Ryan O'Neal) 1976 — producer; *Rocky* (Sylvester Stallone, Talia Shire, Burt Young) 1976 — producer; *Peeper* (Michael Caine, Natalie Wood) 1975 — producer; *Breakout* (Charles Bronson, Robert Duvall) 1975 — producer; *The Gambler* (James Caan) 1974 — producer; *Busting* (Elliott Gould, Robert Blake) 1974 — producer; *Thumb Tripping* (Bruce Dern) 1972 — producer; *Up the Sandbox* (Barbra Streisand) 1972 — producer; *The Mechanic* (Charles Bronson) 1972 — producer; *The New Centurions* (George C. Scott) 1972 producer; *Believe in Me* (Jacqueline Bisset) 1971 — producer; *The Gang That Couldn't Shoot Straight* (Jerry Orbach, Robert De Niro) 1971 — producer; *The Strawberry Statement* (Bruce Davison, Kim Darby) 1970 — producer; *Leo the Last* (Marcello Mastroianni) 1970 — producer; *They Shoot Horses, Don't They?* (Jane Fonda) 1969 — producer; *The Split* (Gene Hackman, Donald Sutherland) 1968 — producer; *Point Blank* (Lee Marvin, Angie Dickinson) 1967 — producer

Lauren Shuler Donner

Born and raised in Ohio in 1945, Lauren Shuler Donner knew at a very young age that she wanted to work in the film industry. After graduating Boston University with a degree in film studies, she moved to Los Angeles to work in entertainment. After struggling for a year, she got a job at the NBC Studios and performed many different jobs, including pulling cable and wire on The Tonight Show. *After she learned how to operate a camera, she went on to become a camera operator on local news and television shows.*

After awhile, Lauren got the urge to tell other people what to shoot. The first feature film that she produced was the smash hit comedy Mr. Mom, *one of the ten top grossing films of that year. Shuler Donner was responsible for two of the most popular "Brat Pack" movies of the '80s,* St. Elmo's Fire *and* Pretty in Pink. *In her long and successful career, she went on to produce the hit movies* Free Willy, Bulworth, Any Given Sunday *and* You've Got Mail *with Tom Hanks and Meg Ryan. One of her latest productions,* X-Men, *which opened to a staggering $57.5 million, was the largest non-sequel opening in film history. Combined, her films have grossed well over $1 billion worldwide. Recently, Girls, Inc., an organization dedicated to inspiring all girls to be strong, smart and bold, honored Shuler Donner for the example she has set for girls and young women. Lauren Shuler Donner resides in Los Angeles with her husband, director Richard Donner.*

The first movie I ever saw was Walt Disney's animated film *The Song of the South.* I loved it so much and ended up loving animation from that point on. Even today, I love it. I am looking toward producing an animated film soon. While I was growing up, my first cousin and I used to go to the movies a lot. I remember seeing several Marilyn Monroe films and being absolutely in love with her. I also loved Abbott and Costello movies. As I got older, I went through a big Francois Truffaut and Federico Fellini period. Also, *The Graduate* with Dustin Hoffman and *Midnight Cowboy* with Jon Voight and, again, Dustin, made huge impressions on me. *The Deer Hunter* with Robert De Niro was phenomenal. That's when I said to myself, "Wow! I would love to make a movie like that." I lived far away from Hollywood. I grew up in Columbus, Ohio. I had a Midwestern suburban childhood. It was sort of uneventful. Unfortunately, I was sick a lot. I had kidney problems from years 9 'til 12. The doctors had told me I would be on medication for the rest of my life. I think those early obstacles in my life had a lot to do with my drive to succeed. Looking back, I had a great childhood. I had a terrific gang of friends growing up. My friends and I would put on shows. We'd sing songs and make up plays and stand in front of the fireplace and put on performances for each other. Those were my first signs of a real interest in show business.

Did you have any family members working in the movie industry?

No, not at all. I had no uncles or cousins in Hollywood. I'm from Ohio, as is most of my family. My father was a businessman, a wholesale distributor. My mother was a housewife. My father did encourage photography. He loved his camera. He gave me a camera as a gift and I quickly grew to love mine as well. I was always writing, drawing and taking photographs as a child. I was, and still am, a terrible artist. However, I do think getting comfortable with a camera at a young age contributed to my moviemaking.

Where did you attend film school?

I went to Boston University and majored in film. My career aspirations developed early on. When I figured out that for the rest of my life I wanted to make movies, I became obsessed with it. I was truly single-minded about it. I did not, however, enter immediately into the film business. That was mainly because I was in school in Boston and I had grown up in Ohio. Of course, while I was devoted to movies, in the beginning I didn't realize that I had to come out to LA in order to make them. Actually, there was a professor at Boston University that had been to Hollywood and he encouraged me to go out there. I had done a one-on-one study with him and he felt I had something special and he really pushed me to go out to Hollywood.

Do you feel your education at Boston University offered you enough practical knowledge of film and the process of making movies?

I found it enormously helpful. Boston University, mind you, is not USC, UCLA or AFI. When I moved to Los Angeles, I looked at all of those schools and I was floored at the extent of film equipment and resources they had available to their students. However, BU did have enough classes and resources to make me comfortable in real production situations. I was comfortable in the editing room because I had worked on a flat bed. I was comfortable filming because you had to make your own movies. So, this education gave me a great practical knowledge of how a production is done. I did take some acting classes at BU and realized very quickly that acting was not for me. The only area at the time that they did not have classes in was screenwriting. BU now has screenplay classes available to their

Lauren Shuler Donner

students. I picked up screenwriting when I moved to LA. In the end, my education at BU gave me a great all-around background and working knowledge of what goes on during a production. It really helped give me confidence on the set. Boston University was a good school to go to.

How did you pay the bills and support yourself when you got to Los Angeles?

When I first came out to LA, I talked my way into an assistant film editing job where I was cutting negative film from A+B roll. I knew what I was doing because I had done that in the little editing room at Boston University. The company I was working for made educational and medical films. I knew nobody in the business when I came to LA. I cut out ads in the yellow pages and knocked on doors. At one point, I got lost and ended up at NBC. I had no intention of getting into television, but I was right there, desperate to move ahead in entertainment, and I began complaining about my situation to the front desk woman. She finally let me see a woman in NBC's Human Resources Department. I was told they had nothing at the moment, but if a job opened up, they would give me a call. Later, while I was editing, I got a phone call from the woman at NBC. I couldn't believe she actually called me back. She told me that they had something called Vacation Relief. What that meant was that when one of their employees went away on vacation, you could "temp" in their place. They brought me on board and I was excited to be there. What I did at NBC was videotape editing, pulled cable and wire on soap operas and I did sound on *The Tonight Show*. I was involved in many jobs and in many capacities. After a while, I felt it was all kind of boring. So, I said to myself, "Lauren, what do you really want to be doing?" Well, I always loved the camera ever since my father introduced it to me as a kid. So, the guys on *The Tonight Show* taught me how to operate the camera. When I finally got the grasp of it, I asked NBC to be transferred into local news because I knew I didn't have enough experience for them to let me shoot *The Tonight Show*. I got transferred and I shot all the local news and stayed there for quite a while. Then, I freelanced and was extremely busy shooting everything. I shot game shows, sitcoms, commercials, movies and so on. I basically was a "freak" because no women were doing it. After a couple of years of being behind the camera and proving to myself that I could do it, I decided I wanted to tell other people what to shoot.

How did you get the opportunity to produce and have the power to tell other people what to shoot?

I was able to transfer my experience from being involved in so many aspects of production into becoming a creative executive at Motown Productions. My friend told me about a story editor job at a production company called Motown. So, I went in for an interview. They gave me a script and said, "Take it home and read it and tell us what you think." I read it and gave them five pages of constructive criticism. That script was for a film called *Thank God It's Friday*. They really liked my criticism and hired me. Ultimately, I became the associate producer on *Thank God It's Friday* and that was my first feature. Then, Joel Schumacher wrote and was to direct a film for NBC. It was an NBC movie and Motown was the production company. The person who ran Motown was in New York City doing *The Wiz* so I was the only one left to produce the film and I got the job. However, Motown dissolved and therefore there was no requirement for them to be involved. I was 27 and I went to see Charlie Engels and begged him to let me still produce the movie: "Believe in me and I promise I will make you a great movie." He said to me, "When I was about your age I said the same thing to someone who ultimately hired me. So in order to pay him back I'm going to give you a chance." It was great. Five years ago I heard the name of that man who had given Charlie Engels a break in a restaurant. I turned around introduced myself to that man and said, "Thank you — you are responsible for my career." Joel was terrific and believed in me and allowed me produce. The film was very, very well received.

What was the transition like, from producing for the small screen to your first big screen producing effort, the big box office success *Mr. Mom* starring Michael Keaton?

During my time at Motown, I made a lot of relationships with writers. Since we were Motown, all we got were very one-dimensional scripts such as *Black Tarzan*. We never got any good material, so we had to come up with our own. Through this facet of my job at Motown, I got to meet many great writers. I figured out that since I knew enough writers and had enough good ideas, I could now set up a few projects on my own. So I left the company. During that time, I read *National Lampoon* and I read a great story by this writer named John Hughes. I called him up and told him he was really funny. We hit it off very well, probably because we were both Midwesterners. One day while we were talking, he told me his wife went to Arizona and he was left alone to watch after his two boys. John had no clue how to handle them on his own. He had never been to the grocery store; he had never operated a vacuum cleaner and so on. John was so ignorant that, in his ignorance, he was hilarious. He had no idea what to do with these kids and he said to me, "Do you think this would make a good movie?" I said, "It sure sounds funny to me." John then decided to write the script called *Mr. Mom*. When he was done, he sent it to me. I read the script and I thought it was hilarious. John flew out to Los Angeles and we did some rewrites. By the end of our collaboration, I felt we had a truly wonderful script. Producing *Mr. Mom* was a huge learning experience for me.

What did you learn from *Mr. Mom*?

Well, I was young and so was John Hughes. People said it to us that it was a TV movie and we thought it was for the big screen. We eventually agreed with them because we didn't know any better. John had a TV deal with Aaron Spelling, so we brought him on as an executive producer. Then the players involved were upset because John was writing out of Chicago instead of Los Angeles. They fired John and brought in a group of TV writers. In the end, John and I were muscled out. It was a good movie, but if you ever read John's original script for *Mr. Mom,* it's far better. Then they decided it was right for the big screen and not for television. So, what I learned as a producer on *Mr. Mom* is to trust your initial instincts and to fight for what you believe in.

You produced one of the biggest '80s cult movies, *St. Elmo's Fire*. Was it the ensemble cast of characters so brilliantly written that attracted you to the project?

Since I produced *Amateur Night at the Dixie Bar and Grill* for Joel Schumacher,

Mr. Mom (1983, Twentieth Century–Fox). Jack Butler (Michael Keaton), an auto executive, loses his job and stays home with his kids as his wife Caroline Butler (Teri Garr) becomes the breadwinner. Here they are at the wives' office picnic.

he approached me to producer *St. Elmo's Fire*. Joel Schumacher and Carl Kurlander wrote the script. I thought the script was excellent. They added so much texture to the characters. Every one of them was so well-defined. Anyway, the head of Columbia agreed that I could produce *St. Elmo's Fire* and we were off.

With the casting of *St. Elmo's Fire* you created the infamous "Brat Pack," with the then-unknown actors Emilio Estevez, Ally Sheedy, Judd Nelson, Andrew McCarthy, Rob Lowe and Demi Moore. Can you take me through the casting process of *St. Elmo's Fire*?

One of Joel Schumacher's major strengths is casting. From him, I believe that has become my strength too. I am a better casting producer because of Joel and I learned so much working for him. During my career I have put a lot of actors on the map and have made a lot of careers happen. I learned from him that if you want to cast people in your leads, you have to cast "sex." You want to cast the person that the audience wants to go to bed with. So, with that in mind, we began casting *St. Elmo's Fire*. John Hughes, who was still a friend of mine, had a helping hand in the casting process. John was shooting *The Breakfast Club*, a tiny little movie that nobody thought would go anywhere. John recommended a lot of his cast. He suggested Emilio Estevez, Ally Sheedy and Judd Nelson. Among all the people that we saw, and upon John's recommendations, they turned out to be the best choices and were really good actors. We felt each one of these people were, in fact, right for the roles. Our two lead characters were the hardest roles to cast. We looked for awhile and finally settled on Rob Lowe. He was definitely the right guy. Till this day, I think it was Rob's best role because Joel got such a great performance out of him. I have to say that Demi Moore was a walking talking "Jules." Demi came to our office on a motorcycle. She was obviously a "natural" in the truest definition of the word with a unique sense of style that can only be described as a genuine "original." Her hair was kind of a mess. She had this perfect raspy voice. She was the character. Once she walked in, we immediately hired her. We knew Demi Moore was the one to play Jules.

Throughout your career, you were an executive producer on films like *Volcano*, *Bulworth* and *Just Married*. Other films like *Dave*, *Radio Flyer* and *Pretty in Pink* had you credited with a producer title. Do your duties change when you are credited with a different title?

Absolutely. My definition of an executive producer is a person who's "once removed" from a project. In some of those films, I was not directly involved. For instance, in *Volcano* I was involved and in *Bulworth* I was not. It really varies, but my duties are definitely different when the title is different.

Any film that involves a portrayal of the President of the United States is very risky. What made you want produce *Dave*, a film with Kevin Kline as a presidential look-alike who's launched into the White House after the real president of the United States suffers a stroke in embarrassing circumstances and slips into a coma?

It was a pleasurable experience to produce that film. Getting it made was a tough battle.

St. Elmo's Fire (1995, Columbia Pictures). A promotional shot of the beautiful Jules Jacoby (Demi Moore) and handsome Billy Hicks (Rob Lowe).

Initially, I sent the script to a studio that I was under contract with and they felt nobody wanted to see the President being imitated by anybody else. At the time, Ronald Reagan was the President. The studio strongly thought the audience did not want to pay money to watch that. They then said, "Why don't you make him a president of a different country?" We said, "No way." I waited three years until my contract was over and I wasn't exclusive any more. Then I made the deal with Warner Brothers, who strongly believed in *Dave*.

How did it feel when *Dave* was ultimately nominated for an Academy Award for Best Original Screenplay?

It was a great feeling. This business is always about believing in your own instincts.

You've Got Mail (1998, Warner Brothers). Joe Fox (Tom Hanks) looks deep into Kathleen Kelly's (Meg Ryan) eyes when they finally unite as a loving couple at the end of the film.

How did the film *You've Got Mail*, starring Tom Hanks and Meg Ryan, come about for you?

At my company, The Donners' Company, we were in development and looking at the Turner film library. They had a lot of great old movies. I had an executive named Julie Durk who brought *The Shop Around The Corner* to my attention. She showed me this old movie with James Stewart and Margaret Sullavan. I remembered seeing it years ago and when I watched it again on her recommendation, I fell in love with it a second time. It is very sweet. The problem was that in the original movie they were pen pals and it was very dated. Julie said, "I like this movie." I said, "So do I." However, I wasn't sure what to do to update it. This was 1992 and I had just gotten on the Internet and began exploring chat rooms and all that fun stuff. I guess comparing the number of users today to back then, I was on the Internet very early. One day, while chatting on the Internet, I stopped and said to myself, "Oh my God, here is my answer to remaking *Shop Around the Corner.* The Internet." I called the head of Turner and told her and she felt that this was a wonderful idea. Then, she suggested Nora Ephron to direct, which was the best idea in the world. Nora and her sister Delia wrote the script. Nora directed the film and produced it with me as well.

How was it to work with acclaimed director Nora Ephron?

It was a truly wonderful experience. Ernst Lubitsch, who is one of the most famous romantic comedy directors ever, directed *Shop Around the Corner* in 1940. I wondered who could top him. Then, when Turner recommended Nora Ephron, I agreed right away because I feel Nora is the best writer and director of romantic comedy in the business today. She understands the specifics in this film genre and what is necessary for it to be successful. Nora had just come off of *Sleepless in Seattle* and I felt incredibly lucky to have been able to work with her on *You've Got Mail.* Nora is so smart and witty and uniquely Nora. Nora and Delia have such distinctive voices when it comes to their writing. They grew up in a family of writers. The parents, Henry and Phoebe Ephron, wrote famous movies like *Daddy Long Legs* for Fred Astaire, *Desk Set* for Katharine Hepburn and Spencer Tracy and many others. I knew that Nora would be perfect to direct *You've Got Mail.*

Were you worried about your lead actors being behind their computer terminals for a third of the movie and still coming off compelling while keeping the audience interested?

Yes, that was our biggest concern. We thought, "How are we going to make this thing come alive?" We talked about it a lot with many different solutions. For instance, having them read aloud, seeing what they are typing, voiceovers while they were walking around the city. As you can see in the movie, we came up with a lot of creative and effective solutions. Nora thought that, especially early on in the film, they should be on the computer as little as possible because we knew that later on in the movie there would be a point where we would have to listen to these letters and see them at their computers for long stretches of time. We did not want the audience to feel trapped early on so that they anticipated spending most of the time watching people at computers. An important part of the solution to this problem was Tom Hanks and Meg Ryan because they are two of the most talented performers in the business. I believe when you think romantic comedy, you think Tom Hanks and Meg Ryan. Everybody loves them, so whether they are at their computers or not, the audience still loves them. We also had a great supporting cast like Greg Kinnear, Parker Posey, Steve Zahn and the hilarious Dave Chappelle.

Why did you choose an expensive place like New York City to shoot the movie when you could have shot this story anywhere?

It did not turn out to be too expensive. The reason Nora based *You've Got Mail*

You've Got Mail (1998, Warner Brothers). Kathleen Kelly (Meg Ryan) speaks openly about relationships and love at an outdoor café in New York City.

in the Upper West Side of Manhattan was that she felt it was a small community in the way that the village in *Shop Around the Corner* was a small community. She felt the Upper West Side was a village. To establish this, Nora showed scenes at the beginning of the film of bread being dropped off outside these closed little stores to make the audience feel like they were in a village even though they were in a metropolis like New York. From the West 90s to the West 50s, from Central Park West to the Hudson River, Nora felt it was just like a small village. She felt one could travel around those streets and possibly bump into the same people all the time. Therefore, she felt it was the same sort of setting, but more contemporary. It is the kind of place where there could be a great big bookstore and still have someone own a little bookstore. It turned out to be the perfect place to shoot.

On the football film *Any Given Sunday* with Al Pacino and Cameron Diaz, how was it to produce for controversial director Oliver Stone?

He is a very fascinating director. The man is brilliant. He was lovely to produce for. Oliver was collaborative in the development of the script. He was very respectful of our opinions with regard to the casting. When we got into production, he was very much like a general who enters a war in battle. Rather than being as "hands-on" as I usually am on a picture, I was "hands-off" during the production period of *Any Given Sunday*. I did this because I don't think that my getting involved would have benefited Oliver Stone. I gave input, but not to the extent I usually do on one of my productions. In this case, I felt it had a better effect. As a producer, you want to do whatever is best for the movie. If it's best for the movie to let the director follow his vision, then go with it. I totally trust Oliver Stone's vision. You are hiring Oliver Stone because you want his take on the script and therefore you must listen to him.

To produce a film with so many cameras, numerous technical advisors, stadium shooting where you need many extras, as every producer knows, it is extremely difficult and costly. Did you run into budgetary problems with *Any Given Sunday*?

Yes, we did. We ran into money problems because initially we had it budgeted at a higher figure and then Warner Brothers asked us to take $10 million out of the budget in order for them to green light *Any Given Sunday*. Taking out the money was not a realistic way to make a movie, because $8 million of the $10 million ultimately crept back in. So, I was very busy trying to balance the budget on that film.

What attracted you to transporting the classic comic book *X-Men* to the big screen in film format?

What attracted me to the idea of producing *X-Men* were the characters. When I started reading the biographies of each character, I was very impressed. Each person is so psychologically complex. The first one I read about was Wolverine. He is such a tragic hero. Wolverine has no memories of the past. He is dealing with unrequited love. I got so fascinated with his background and I just kept reading further and couldn't wait to delve into the other *X-Men* characters. I thought if we treated the Marvel comic book realistically and not as a comic, then we could make the film successful. I felt that if it appealed to me, then it could appeal to anyone. It was a world I really wanted to get into and that I didn't know too much about. I did not grow up reading the comic books of *X-Men* like a lot of people did. However, even though I "came to the party" late, when I got there, I really liked what I saw.

What made you feel that Bryan Singer had the skills and talent to direct this?

I loved the film Bryan directed called *The Usual Suspects* with Kevin Spacey, Chazz Palminteri, Benicio Del Toro and Gabriel Byrne. *X-Men* is a multi-character piece and I saw from watching *The Usual Suspects* that Bryan could handle directing multi-characters. I also saw that he could get great performances out of his actors. I noticed he had a great stylistic eye and that was very important because *X-Men* has a lot of style. Once we met, Bryan agreed with me that he, too, wanted to make the big screen version of *X-Men* realistic. We had to approach it differently and in a way that I was ultimately opposed to, but it all worked out. With Bryan's intelligence, directing skills and point of view, I felt he was the right guy for the job.

Was the original creator of the *X-Men* comic book, Stan Lee, involved in the production of your film?

Yes, Stan Lee was involved and very helpful in the first installment of *X-Men*. However, he was not involved during the production of *X-Men 2*.

What was the budget for the first *X-Men*?

The budget was $75 million.

Any Given Sunday (1999, Warner Brothers). Tony D'Amato (Al Pacino) yells out the game plan to his players.

Did you feel that $75 million for an event type film like *X-Men* was a low budget?

Yes, I thought $75 million was low. On the other hand, ask a producer on any movie if they think the budget is low and they will always say, "yes."

For box office purposes, was it a major concern for you to have *X-Men* come across as interesting to not only children, but to adults as well?

Yes. First and foremost, we needed to make it interesting to the pre-existing fan base. Bryan and I wanted it to first be attractive to them. The comic book has been around for 38 years and is not only popular with kids, but with adults in their thirties and forties as well. So, because of the nature and evolution of the product, we had to appeal to both children and adults. Then, of course, if you want to make a hit movie, it is imperative to cross over.

The original release date for *X-Men* was Christmas 2000. Then, in the middle of production, the studio hit you with a new release date of July 2000. Did that six-month-earlier release date hinder your production in any way?

Summer release is the greatest possibility for success with a film. It offers the best availability for audiences to attend. That date in July was a good date for us. We were destined to do more with that date. Did it crunch us? Absolutely. We didn't even have a preview trial screening for *X-Men*. We didn't have our visual effects done until right before we had to turn over our on-screen credits. We were working 24 hours a day, seven days a week. I do believe that some things suffered because we didn't have the time or the money for the visual effects to make them precisely right. However, I still think we did a great job. Looking back, I wouldn't have traded that summer 2000 date for anything.

Did you run into any problems with CGI during *X-Men*?

All the CGI was difficult. Mystique was the most difficult character to deal with. We did a lot of research into how to make her skin blue without hurting actress Rebecca Romijn-Stamos. It took eight hours to do her make-up each time. Then, once we got the make up on, we had to learn through computer graphics how to morph. We didn't want just regular morphing. Bryan and I both felt that we had seen it in the Michael Jackson videos and we wanted to do the morphing differently. So, we came up with the idea to make her skin like scales and each one would pop out of her and down her body. Even Wolverine's claws were computer graphically enhanced and created so we had to make the metal look real. It is the reality of it all that makes it a good film.

What character in *X-Men* can you personally relate to the most?

I don't know if I can relate to anyone personally, but there are ones that I love. I love Wolverine. As I said earlier, he was the first character I read and fell in love with. I also love Storm for her mutant power ability of changing the weather like Mother Nature. However, I think I can relate to mutants on a whole because they are outsiders. In my life, particularly during my childhood, people were predominantly Christian in my suburb. Jews were expected to live on certain streets and couldn't join certain country clubs. Growing up, I couldn't go to certain schools. So, because I was Jewish as a child in my small town in Ohio, I felt like an outsider, a mutant in my own way. Through this, I can identify with being a mutant on a whole, but not a particular one.

Do you find it risky to produce a project of this nature with a huge fan base anticipating the movie?

Yes, it is very risky. The Internet scared us to death during production because of the concerned fans' constant e-mails about the film. They wanted to make sure we met their expectations for the uniforms, casting and locations. They were watching our every move. I tried to send back the message asking the fans to please give us some more freedom. We were not a comic book. We were now a movie and we needed some dramatic liberty. Years ago, when a producer-director like Billy Wilder directed a movie, nobody commented on the Internet or in chat rooms about whether he was doing the right thing. So, it can be stressful.

Did the budget go up substantially from *X-Men* to *X-Men 2*?

The budget did go up somewhat because the actors got more money than they did before. Also, you want to raise the level production-wise because you have to top yourself. In order to do that, you have to spend more money. So, the budget went up a bit.

X-Men (2000, Twentieth Century–Fox). Storm (Halle Berry), who has the ability to create hurricanes like Mother Nature, is, in fact, creating one in this shot.

However, it will not cost as much as most of the blockbuster movies that are coming out in summer 2003.

The definition of the title of producer has become one of the big mysteries in Hollywood. Can you define what you do as a producer?

My duties as a producer are as follows: I have to find material, whether it is from a book or script. I shepherd the script and make notes and get it in good-enough shape to attract a director and a studio to finance the project. I personally don't raise money as other producers do. I have studio backing. Then, after I get the studio, I get involved with the director. We discuss the film in-depth and make sure we have the same vision. I supervise the pre-production and, with the director, I get involved in the casting process. It is my favorite part of putting together the movie. With the director, we figure out where we are going to film and how we are going to shoot it, whether going on location or actually building the sets. We prepare a budget. With the budget in mind, I figure out if we are going to buy the clothes or are we going to make them. What visual effects do we need? What cinematographer is going to supervise the visual effects? Who is going to shoot the film? How long are we going to shoot the movie? So, my job as a producer is creative and also involves the production side of things. Since I produce multiple movies at a time, I hire a line producer to take care of the film as well. That's to make sure each department is doing their job and we're not overspending. My job is more in the area of making sure everything is moving forward — that the art department knows what they're doing, that the wardrobe looks right and so forth. Once we start filming, the movie is turned over to the director. As a producer, I have learned that you really can have only one captain on a ship. I am there to solve problems when there is a problem with an actor or actress, or if a location falls through. I watch the filming very closely. If I come up with an idea to make the film funnier or to go faster, I will suggest that to the director. At the end of the shoot, I get involved in the cutting room and with editing, music and video effects. Then, I get involved with the studio in marketing and distributing the movie. To be a successful producer, you have to wear many hats and make sure you wear each hat correctly.

You said that your favorite aspect of producing is the casting process. Are there any actors or actresses that you have personally discovered?

I discovered Michael Keaton. I cast him in *Mr. Mom*. Prior to my film, he had done *Night Shift*, but not too many people saw it. *Mr. Mom* made him a big star. As I said earlier, Joel Schumacher and I cast Demi Moore in her first role as Jewels in *St. Elmo's Fire*. In *X-Men*, I was the one who pushed for Hugh Jackman to play Wolverine. I believe that my push got him cast in the movie. In the film *Timeline* that my husband Richard Donner directed and I produced, we cast an actor named Gerald Butler who plays the role of Andre Marek. We put him in his first major role and I believe he will be another big male star. So, those are just a few.

Do you find there are more obstacles being a woman in the entertainment industry as opposed to being a man?

It is hard to say. It will always be a male-dominated business. I think with the success of myself and other women producers, it has gotten a lot easier. Today, women don't enter the film business with preconceived notions thinking that they can't produce a movie. Sure, men still all go on rafting trips together and deals are struck, but I think today a woman has as good a shot to succeed as a man.

Can you tell me about your production company, The Donners' Company, in which you are partnered with your husband, director Richard Donner?

I run the company because my husband, Richard, doesn't like the development process. The big secret is that we have only done three movies together. I think we work together every ten years. The employees at my company are always looking for good material. We do read unsolicited scripts, but only if they are given to us by an agent or lawyer. The writer also has to sign a legal release form that protects both parties. The writer has to sign it before we read the script. You are always looking for that big script to come in the mail, but through my own experience, it has never happened.

Is this business more of who you know instead of what you know?

I think it is 50-50, who you know and what you know. I really do. I am always encouraging younger people to make alliances with people their age in the business, because people grow up and move up the corporate ladder as I did with my career. Also, a big part of it is whom you know. I think a lot of life is luck and it's what you make out of it. There is timing, but everything is truly luck and hard work. I definitely believe in hard work more than I believe in luck.

Variety — is that the element that keeps you on top of your game with continuously successful movies?

It keeps me interested and it's more fun this way. I can't imagine being one of those producers who only does one kind of movie. It is just much more exciting to expand one's horizons. It opens up the possibilities of stories you can explore, a whole world of ideas.

This business, many say, is a Catch-22 for writers and directors. Basically, if you don't have an agent, you can't sell a script and if you haven't sold a script, you can't get an agent. What guidance can you offer to a screen writer?

I would tell writers to *write*. I think if you're a decent screenwriter and if you have a good script, it will ultimately get into the hands of an agent or a production company. If you are talented and persistent, you will get noticed. Also, writing a great script is the best way to get into the film business. Once you are successful as a screenwriter and have sold a couple of movies that have been made into hits, you have bargaining room. Basically, you can to say to a production company or studio, "Hey if you want to buy this script from me, I have to direct it." That's what happened to Steven Soderbergh, Barry Levinson and Nora Ephron. This is what many other writers who turned directors have done in their careers.

What steps should a director take to make it in this business?

For a director, it is a little harder. You need a reel. You have to have directed terrific television or you need to have done well at a film festival like Sundance. Your commercial reel can be really good and yet you have to display a talent for telling stories. You need to take certain steps before you will be considered to direct a feature film. One of the best ways is to raise your own money for an independent film.

Do you feel that producers are, in fact, "unsung heroes"?

Absolutely. I don't think that the movies would be as good as they are without the producers being a guiding force. All the producers that I know feel that way as well. We all have a saying: "If the producers went on strike tomorrow, no one would care." That's the irony.

To what do you attribute your continued success as a producer?

I believe it is because I have a good story sense. I also feel that since I am such a big fan of movies myself, I can possibly understand more accurately what the audience wants and can translate that to the end product up on the screen. Another key factor is that I'm capable of working well with directors.

What does the future hold for Lauren Shuler Donner?

I want to do animation. I have a project at Universal involving animation. My next movie is called *Constantine* starring Keanu Reeves at Warner Brothers and a movie called *Labor Day* starring Jet Li at Disney. I have just optioned a lovely book, *The Secret Life of Bees*, which a young director, David Gordon Green, is developing with me. So, those are the next steps in my career, with a lot of exciting projects on my plate.

Lauren Shuler Donner Filmography

Timeline (Paul Walker, Frances O'Connor) 2003 — producer; *X-Men 2* (Patrick Stewart, Hugh Jackman, Halle Berry) 2003 — producer; *Just Married* (Ashton Kutcher, Brittany Murphy) 2003 — executive producer; *Out Cold* (Jason London, Lee Majors) 2001— executive producer; *X-Men* (Patrick Stewart, Hugh Jackman, Halle Berry) 2000— producer; *Any Given Sunday* (Al Pacino, Cameron Diaz) 1999 — producer; *You've Got Mail* (Tom Hanks, Meg Ryan) 1998 — producer; *Babes in the Wood* (Karl Howman, Denise Van Outen) 1998 TV Series — producer; *Bulworth* (Warren Beatty, Halle Berry) 1998 — executive producer; *Free Willy 3: The Rescue* (Jason James Richter) 1997 — executive producer; *Volcano* (Tommy Lee Jones, Anne Heche) 1997 — executive producer; *Assassins* (Sylvester Stallone, Antonio Banderas, Julianne Moore) 1995 — executive producer; *Free Willy 2: The Adventure Home* (Jason James Richter, Michael Madsen) 1995 — producer; *The Favor* (Elizabeth McGovern, Brad Pitt) 1994 — producer; *Free Willy* (Lori Petty, Jason James Richter) 1993 — producer; *Dave* (Kevin Kline, Sigourney Weaver) 1993 — producer; *Radio Flyer* (Lorraine Bracco, Elijah Wood) 1992 — producer; *Three Fugitives* (Nick Nolte, Martin Short) 1989 — producer; *Pretty in Pink* (Molly Ringwald, Andrew McCarthy) 1986 — producer; *St. Elmo's Fire* (Rob Lowe, Demi Moore, Emilio Estevez, Ally Sheedy) 1985 — producer; *Ladyhawke* (Mathew Broderick, Michelle Pfeiffer) 1985 — producer; *Mr. Mom* (Michael Keaton) 1983 — producer; *Amateur Night at the Dixie Bar and Grill* (Don Johnson) 1979 TV — producer

Michael Phillips

Born in Brooklyn, New York, in 1943, Michael Phillips spent every Saturday after-noon of his childhood at the movie theater — never as a student of film, but as a pure movie goer. With no intentions of entering the film business, he graduated NYU Law School and decided to go right into a Wall Street broker's job, with plans to get rich quick. One day he got a phone call from an actor friend by the name of Tony Bill. Bill tried to convince Michael and his wife, Julia Phillips (who went on to write the controversial bestselling book You'll Never Eat Lunch in This Town Again*), to move out to LA to become movie producers. They agreed to go to the West Coast and their partnership ensued. Michael's second film,* The Sting, *won him an Academy Award at only 30 years old. He has gone on to produce* Taxi Driver, *directed by Martin Scorsese,* Close Encounters of the Third Kind, *directed by Steven Spielberg,* The Flamingo Kid, *directed by Garry Marshall, and many other hit films. Michael Phillips currently lives in Beverly Hills, California.*

When I was three years old, my aunt took me to see my first film, *Dumbo,* and it scared the hell out of me. I was born in 1943 and grew up in Brooklyn, New York. During my childhood, I could walk to the neighborhood theater and for 25 cents see two features and ten cartoons. I spent every Saturday, all day, in the movie theater. I was just a true moviegoer and I was not a student of film. I particularly remember having a love for science fiction films. So, this was my early experience. The sci-fi classic *The Day The Earth Stood Still,* directed by Robert Wise, changed my life. I stayed in the theater and watched it three times straight. The others films I enjoyed were B movies like *Mighty Joe Young* and *When Worlds Collide.* I liked to be transported beyond reality and most of the movies I enjoyed were ones where I was transported somewhere. I still like to go to another world.

Tell me about your childhood in Brooklyn.

Looking back, it seems almost ideal now. It was an apartment building and it was safe. Kids were let out of their houses to play in the streets. Actually, it was the perfect environment. I have a brother, Mark, who is five years younger, and he is the best brother in the world. I love him dearly. Both of my parents are alive and are 85 years old. I am lucky. Growing up, my father was a garment manufacturer. My mother was first a teacher and, then, a housewife. I never thought I would get into the family garment business. I grew to hate the dress business. My father thought I would have a love for it if I worked from the bottom up. So, he had me pushing racks of dresses around the streets of Manhattan and putting tags on bags and on garments. I quickly developed a genuine hatred for it!

Why did you choose the film industry for a career?

I worked in other fields before the film business. I first discovered the stock market in college. I went to Dartmouth initially and then to NYU law school. In law school, I knew I was not going to be a lawyer. I went right into a Wall Street job after graduation and I had plans to get rich quick. I entered at the peak of a Bull Market and soon discovered that when a Bear Market rolls around, you no longer feel like a genius. I was there for two years and, during that time, I was afflicted with a stiff dose of reality. My late ex-wife, Julia Phillips, had started in the movie business as a story editor in New York. Julia was not interested in her job any longer. An actor friend, Tony Bill, told us about opportunities for young producers to produce films in Hollywood. So, we shook hands with Tony and decided to form a company while we held onto our other jobs. Tony sent us scripts and one day he sent us an audiotape of a movie about con men that David Ward, a USC film student, spoke to him about. I listened and quickly felt this was something special and wanted to buy it! David Ward sent us a sample of his writing, which was a screenplay for *Steelyard Blues*. We pooled our money together to option the con man movie. Julia and I had $2,500 and Tony Bill had $1,000. So, we gave it to David for an option on the as-yet-unwritten *The Sting*. David also threw in a four-month option on his film school thesis, *Steelyard Blues*.

We got Mike Medavoy to be our agent. At the time, he was a junior agent and his only client of consequence was Donald Sutherland. He gave *Steelyard Blues* to Donald and, then, Donald gave it to his then girlfriend, Jane Fonda. They had just come off the success of *Klute* together. They were very politically active at the time and saw real political content in it. Two weeks after we acquired the script, we had two studios competing to finance it. It was amazing! Julia and I came out to LA and were rookies. but we engulfed ourselves in the project and the process. *Steelyard Blues* did not turn out to be a great movie. We were overwhelmed by inexperience. Here we were, first-time producers. We had a first-time writer, first-time cameraman, first-time art director and first-time director, who was chosen by Jane Fonda. We had a power-crazed production manager who was very successful at manipulating us with his expertise, so it turned out to be a mess.

Michael Phillips

However, in struggling with the editing for a year, we got an education. It had an important and happy ending for me. I learned what not to do.

How did *The Sting* come to your attention?

David Ward was writing *The Sting* at that time we were shooting *Steelyard Blues*, so we were already in business with Universal with *The Sting* before *Steelyard Blues* came out. The pain of its flopping was softened a great deal by the enthusiasm we had being the producers of something that was going to be a major and wonderful film.

How did you attach two of the hottest actors of that time, and now certainly two legends, Paul Newman and Robert Redford, to the project?

Tony Bill had shown the script to Robert Redford. He was not attached yet, but there was a definite flirtation there. We really sold the script on just the pure excellence of the writing. We had two studios competing heavily for it, and in the end, Universal just gave us everything we wanted. Then the head of business affairs of Universal showed the script to director George Roy Hill because he had an overall deal there. George loved it and we were excited because at that time he was one of the top directors in Hollywood. Hill in fact directed *Butch Cassidy and the Sundance Kid*. Hill came in first and, then, Redford committed to playing the role of Johnny Hooker in *The Sting*. George had been a very close friend of Paul Newman. Out of friendship, each would send the other the scripts they were working on. Newman read *The Sting* and immediately called Hill. He said, "I want to be in this." Hill replied, "No, because Redford is already playing the lead." He answered, "No, I want to play *Gondorff*." Well, the part of Gondorff was really written for Peter Boyle, who was to portray it as an over-the-hill slob of a guy. For a few days, we wrestled with the idea of casting Newman, because you have to believe he will screw Redford over in the end or it doesn't work. Ultimately, Hill gave the nod and said, "We can make this work with Newman." I thought that you can't kick a gift horse in the mouth. These guys were great together.

Newman worked six weeks and Redford worked 13. *The Sting* cost $4.5 million to make. Back then, Paul Newman and Robert Redford would get $500,000 a picture and George Roy Hill was the top director, getting $450,000 a film. The above-the-line today is $20 million to $30 million. That is where the big costs have gone up to. If a top actor gets $20 million today, that is 40 times what Paul Newman was making. During shooting, I was in awe of Paul Newman. I had a hard time talking to him because I had been such a fan. He is a very down-to-earth guy, and doesn't create distance, but I was a little awestruck. Essentially, Newman's character was secondary, but he loved the writing. In the final analysis, it was the script that was the magnet for the talent. It was not a sell job. *The Sting* is still the best script I have ever read.

Paul Newman's entrance, "Sorry I am late, I had to take a crap." What great dialogue!

Yes, and that is why he wanted to play the part—that real and great dialogue. It was the train scene that he said won him over to play the part.

The Sting (1973, Universal Pictures). The acting duo from *Butch Cassidy and the Sundance Kid* triumphs again as Johnny Hooker (Robert Redford) and Henry Gondorff (Paul Newman), con men, in this Academy Award–winning film.

The Sting was your sophomore project. With the casting of top talent on this film, were you quickly convinced that a great script will bring great talent?

If you sit and read 100 scripts, you will find that they are pretty much all interchangeable, on a Grade B level. When a good script comes along, it just screams out to you, "Grade A!" David Ward never told us the ending and we never saw it until we read the first draft. It is a joy to read a great script. The script for *The Sting* made me a believer in material. There can be a half a dozen directors who can do it, or a half a dozen actors or actresses. However, the script is the most important thing and your true starting point.

Did you feel from the get-go that *The Sting* had all the right ingredients to win an Oscar for Best Picture?

Believe it or not, I rehearsed my Oscar speech before we rolled our first shot. It was naïve, even though it worked out that I won. In a way, I wish it came later in my career, because I think I would have appreciated it more. I was only 30 years old at the time. I didn't appreciate how lucky I was. We were nominated for ten awards that year and so was *The Exorcist*. I thought because they had stronger reviews that *The Exorcist* was going to win. But, there started to be a lot of public squabbling and bad press among the filmmakers of *The Exorcist* prior to the Academy Awards. Everyone was getting so tired of hearing the controversy that I think it soured the voters. I think the filmmakers behind *The Exorcist* somehow short-changed themselves by having these internal battles covered by the press. I felt that if the Academy Awards were held in January, *The Exorcist* would have won. It was a phenomenon.

I remember the Academy Awards being very exciting. I didn't say in my speech what I had carefully prepared to say. When I got up there, I just babbled. It was a dream. It was amazing. One of my first major lessons as a producer, I learned from that experience. The producer does not get much credit for the film. After we won, our phones did not ring. The reality truly set in. We found it just as hard to get a script financed. If we walked into a studio and it was not the same type of film as *The Sting,* then nobody was really interested. The next film I produced was *Taxi Driver*. I spent three years spinning my wheels. Today, the movie business is driven by marketing and this is a big and fundamental shift. It is the nature of how to do business today. Films are so costly now that studios want to be sure that what they put out there, in the highly competitive world of opening weekends, gets noticed and is somewhat pre-sold. By the time it opens, hopefully the film is already familiar and you know the cast. You bet the farm on the opening weekend. Almost 80 percent of the advertising is spent on the two weeks before the opening weekend. There is no second chance. In the '70s, a big release was 200 theaters, one or two theaters per city, with most of the advertising money spent on print. It was more open to creative gut thinking than now.

Supporting characters like Robert Shaw and Charles Durning were extremely well-cast and I feel were key in the success of *The Sting*.

The casting of Robert Shaw was a last-minute accident. We had hired and made a deal with Richard Boone to play the part of Doyle Lonnegan. Somewhere along the way, he got cold feet. He was offered $125,000 and, then, he disappeared to Florida. Hill called Boone and he would not return his call. Finally, Lou Wasserman called him and he didn't return his call either. By the way he was behaving, we figured he dropped out. We had a start date and we went through a few names and finally cast Robert Shaw. He was great. Hill resisted him because Shaw wanted $150,000, but he got the part. When he was in LA prior to the beginning of shooting, he injured himself playing racquetball. So the limp Shaw has in the movie is real, but he cleverly turned it into a character trait and said it was an old war wound from the Chicago back alleys.

When you first read Paul Shrader's script for *Taxi Driver,* what was your initial reaction?

When I first read *Taxi Driver*, it knocked me out. Julia and I used to live on Nicholas Beach, north of Malibu. Next door to us lived Margot Kidder. Her boyfriend was Brian DePalma. DePalma and I were friends and we used to play chess together all the time. There was a magazine reporter by the name of Paul Shrader who was doing an article on him for a film magazine. Brian had told me that this guy Shrader had written an interesting script. It was not something DePalma was into, but he felt I might like it. I absolutely loved it. I was really impressed and had never seen anything like it. It is amazing to think Paul Shrader wrote *Taxi Driver* in eight days. It just must have burst out of him.

Could you identify with the struggles of main character Travis Bickle?

There was something so universal and profound going on in his main character, Travis Bickle. The loneliness was what I was captivated by. I could understand Bickle but could not identify with him. He reflected the need to prove to yourself so that you are alive. So we decided to option *Taxi Driver*. I began the process of discovering that nobody wanted it. Paul Shrader urged us to see a rough cut of *Mean Streets* and we were quickly impressed by the director Martin Scorsese's work. We also discovered actor Rober DeNiro in that movie. So, we would let Scorsese direct as long as he had DeNiro in the lead role. Then, we ran around town trying to get it made. Both Scorsese and DeNiro were respected, but not enough to get an investment in a film. I think the picture came to fruition because everyone hung in there and truly believed in it. I have a very close relationship to *Taxi Driver*. I felt that it was my baby. I bled for that film to get it made.

I am surprised you had to fight so hard to get your next picture made after winning an Academy Award for *The Sting*. Is that what this business is all about for producers?

The big directors get to push the studios around, so the studios, in turn, get to take it out on the lesser-known directors. We were going over-schedule and they did not have a lot of faith in *Taxi Driver*. David Begelman, the then head of Columbia, gave it a green light because he got the talent for such a bargain basement price. The budget was $1.5 million. The producers got $45,000, Marty got $65,000 and DeNiro got $35,000. The only one that cost money was Cybill Shepherd. She got $100,000. Cybill was popular and insurance for the studio. Begelman didn't like the script. Nobody liked it, even after it was made. It was just a strange and violent film. The ratings board wanted to give *Taxi Driver* an X rating. We played a game with them. We desaturated the color of some of the blood at the end and sent the film to them so many times that they became desensitized. We got congratulated on changes that we never made.

Top: The Sting (1973, Universal Pictures). Big time racketeer Doyle Lonnergan (Robert Shaw) casts a suspicious eye on con artists Henry Gondorff (Paul Newman) and Johnny Hooker (Robert Redford) in 1930s Chicago. *Bottom: Taxi Driver* (1975, Columbia Pictures). Cabbie Travis Bickle (Robert De Niro), in director Martin Scorsese's award-winning film, daydreams on the job.

Taxi Driver (1975, Columbia Pictures). Travis Bickle (Robert De Niro), a psychotic New York City cabbie, tries to save child prostitute Iris Steensma (Jodie Foster), with whom he becomes infatuated.

How did you deal with all of the Screen Actors Guild rules with a then 12-year-old Jodie Foster playing a prostitute?

An adult had to be with her at all times. Her mother and her sister came to the shoot and filled that need. We also brought a social worker and tutor with us from California. There were serious limitations on the hours that a child could work. As a producer, I worked around it. There was certain content where her character was supposed to put her hand between DeNiro's legs and, naturally, we had to use a double.

How was it to work with director Martin Scorsese on such a small budget?

It was great. Marty was so creative, even with such a small budget. What he was turning out every day was jaw-dropping. These swirling shots of New York City were so imaginative. We would send the dailies to the studio and I would excitedly call and say, "Aren't they great!" The studio would only mundanely comment, "You're two days behind schedule." Nobody there seemed to enjoy *Taxi Driver* or really understand that we were making an extraordinary film.

As a producer, how did you handle the studio when they were breathing down your neck about the schedule, for instance on an inspired film like *Taxi Driver*?

I would just tell the studio that we would definitely get back on schedule. You'd then have to lie to them by saying you'll drop this shot and drop that shot. Plain and simple, you just lied. You have to protect your film, because at the end of production, the studio will be happy with a terrific film and forget about the fact you went a little over-budget. A producer's job is to have a sense of what is important and what is not. The director thinks everything is important. Sometimes you have to make trade-offs and shoot it smaller and tighter, use less extras, and on this *other* scene do it bigger and better. It is an important role as a producer to set the priorities. Ultimately, it is the director's film. But during the process, if you think he is wrong you have to let him know.

Do you have any interesting anecdotes from the filming of *Taxi Driver* for all the film buffs out there?

The most famous line in the movie, "Are you talking to me?," is not in the script. It was purely an ad lib by Robert DeNiro. I was on the set every day, but that moment when they did that line, I was unfortunately not there. When I saw it in dailies, I thought it was amazing. I asked Marty, "What did you tell DeNiro? What kind of direction did you give to get him to ad lib that wonderful dialogue?" Scorsese said, "I just said, 'Do something.'"

What was the difference between directors Martin Scorsese and George Roy Hill?

George's approach was to plan everything out and making the movie was an execution of that plan. Marty treats a movie like a living, breathing thing. He tries to create something real on the set. Marty will depart from the script if it will make the movie better. Their styles are 180 degrees opposite. Just learning from both of them was wonderful and I was on the set every day. When the director first comes on board, you know more about the movie than he or she does. Then, there is a point in the movie when the director knows more than the producer does. I love the process of working with writers the most. The process of conceiving the film, then attaching a director and a cast—I really enjoy it. Bringing all these vital elements together to make the best movie a producer can is a special sense of accomplishment. During shooting, I am more of a trouble-shooter. I hang in there throughout the shooting because if I can find two little things wrong every day that I can point out to the director, that ultimately adds up to 120 things to help make the movie that much better. Most of the time, the producer is worrying, looking at his or her watch and thinking "How are you going to be able to get everything done?" But, *The Sting's* production ran like a clock. If I have any mentor in the film business, it is George Roy Hill. I learned so much from him.

With the studio giving you negative vibes, were you extremely nervous to show the first cut of *Taxi Driver*?

The studio hated the rough cut. We loved it as much as they hated it. Opening day in New York, at the matinee showing, there was a line around the block. The people just sniffed out a winner. It got great reviews and the head of distribution for Columbia Pictures admitted to me that they left a lot of money on the table by not spending more aggressively. He said Columbia could have spent more, but they did not feel confident in the project. In the afterlife, it has become a classic. Everybody had points on the project and enjoyed a good profit. But still, it was a labor of love, even at starvation wages.

How did *Close Encounters* and your collaboration with director Steven Spielberg come about?

While we were editing *The Sting*, Steven Spielberg was editing *Sugarland Express* on the same lot. We would have lunch all the time and talk about science fiction movies we both liked. One day, he called me and he said, "I want to come out to the beach and talk to you and Julia about a project I think you might like." So, Spielberg came to the house and said, "I want to make a movie about UFOs and Watergate." This was actually nothing like how *Close Encounters* turned out to be. We had been big fans of his from *Duel*, the television movie that Spielberg had directed early in his career. It is still, to this day, better than any TV movie I have ever seen. He was so strong with the camera and such a great storyteller. On the basis of that, we went ahead with this project. We set up a deal at Columbia, but we had trouble getting the story working to our satisfaction. Finally, Steven said, "I have this offer to do a movie about a shark at Universal. What should I do?" I said, "Go do it." So while he was directing *Jaws*, I would bring writers out to him at Martha's Vineyard. After several drafts, finally Steven announced that he, personally, wanted to write the screenplay. So, he did. As we started moving towards production, Julia and I were divorcing. I told Julia to take the lead on *Close Encounters*. I was burned out from *Taxi Driver* and said she should be the on-set producer. I was involved in the conceptual side of the movie and what it was all about. Julia went to Alabama and fought all the battles and I went to visit the set for a couple of days. Unfortunately, during post-production, Julia had some drug issues and had to be removed from the picture. So, I took over during editing. But, I want to emphasize that Julia deserves the credit for doing most of the work.

Since you had many problems with the script, in the end, did you like how the film *Close Encounters* ultimately turned out?

I was thrilled with how it turned out. When I saw Steven's cut, I remember using the word "cornucopia," because that is exactly how it struck me. The last 40 minutes of the film just came and came and came. Early on, we talked about the ending. We had big debates on whether the aliens were good guys or bad guys. Of course, as I mentioned, I was always a big fan of *The Day the Earth Stood Still*. It is one of my favorite movies of all time. So, if the aliens were good guys, then what could be the climax? I urged that just the meeting of the two species was a big enough event in itself. Spielberg kept saying, "I am not sure it is enough." That is why I think he gives us the ending he did. I think he was a little insecure that there wasn't a conventional dramatic climax so he just gave more and more and more. The last 40 minutes, I must have watched 100 times and I can still watch it again and again. I was very happy with the film. We were in a fish bowl at the time because Columbia Pictures was on the verge of bankruptcy and they bet everything on this one picture. When we had a preview in Dallas, a reporter by the name of William Flanagan who wrote for *New York* magazine sneaked in, and his headline of the story was, "*Close Encounters* Will Be a Colossal Flop."

He wrote a very negative, distorted and very biased attack to assassinate the film. The next morning the stock of Columbia Pictures dropped 20 percent. Everybody was on the phone, frantic. However, in the theater, you could see that the audience loved it. My eyes were telling me that we had a great film, but there were some extremely nervous moments.

Did Spielberg have a totally different style of directing from Scorsese and Hill?

He has a little of both. Spielberg really loves his actors. He would always say, "Get me good actors and a good cameraman and directing is not hard." He would never give himself credit. It is fun working with him because of his enthusiasm and lack of pretension. Steven always welcomed ideas from the cast and crew. We had six different times when we thought we wrapped the film and each time Steven would come up with another great idea to shoot. I think we had six wrap parties! (*Laughing*)

Do you think it is important to relate to your directors on a friendship level?

I think it is very important. It is a lonely experience for the director. If you are supportive and helpful as a producer, it can make the picture better. You always start a movie thinking that it is terrific and half the time it is not. My favorite memories are when I had a close relationship with the director.

When attaching a director to a project, do you have a certain formula you follow?

I like two types of directors. My favorite experiences have come from working with a second-time director because I feel I can give my advice and contribute a lot. You feel good about being involved. You feel much closer to the project. However, if you can get a "superstar" director to direct your film, you may not be as involved, but you have a chance of a really great film and first-class treatment all the way. So it depends on the material, principally, in the final analysis. However, I still always try to get the best director possible.

Do you have close relationships with studio executives?

I like any studio executive who likes my idea for a movie.

You have produced many classic films. What is your favorite movie that you have produced?

I can't choose. I love the three films we discussed. Also, *The Flamingo Kid* was a happy memory for me in a lot of ways. It grew out of my weekend basketball game at Garry Marshall's house. He had made one film at that time called *Young Doctors in Love*. Of course, he was a giant success in the television business with *Happy Days, Laverne & Shirley, The Odd Couple* and the rest. We were talking about what film he wanted to do and he mentioned a "coming of age" story. I had been involved with the script for *The Flamingo Kid* for many years. Garry liked it. So, we put it together and got the financing. The budget was $9 million. Working with Garry Marshall on a film is like something I have never seen. He keeps the crew happy. He keeps us laughing. He creates a happy little family bubble around the picture. But, yet, this was only his second film and he was just a little wobbly. He needed some help in a lot of his decisions. So,

I helped Garry. It was one of those pictures where Garry and I looked at each other and wondered if it was ever going to work at all. We could not tell from the dailies. We weren't sure if Matt Dillon's performance was going to work. Matt was sort of fighting Garry the whole way through. He had never done a comedy before.

If you had all these complications and doubts, why did you ultimately choose Matt Dillon for the lead role?

We needed a young man of leading stature and he was the right age. It was a gamble because we were not sure if he could do this sort of thing. There was a short list of actors to play this role. We could have had Tom Cruise. He came in for a reading, but we passed. We didn't know he was going to be a big star. This was before *Risky Business*. At that time, Matt's career was much bigger. The studio wanted a star. It was a tough role to cast. I was very relieved at Matt's performance. We honestly thought at first that we might have a disaster on our hands. It was a nice surprise when the picture actually worked and did well. Garry was a total joy to work with and he has been a great asset to the world. He just wants to make people laugh. It was a nice surprise when the picture actually worked and did well.

Do you view all your movies as "your children"?

The Flamingo Kid (1984, ABC Motion Pictures). Brooklyn teen Jeffrey Willis (Matt Dillon) gets a summer job at a fancy beach club on Long Island and tries to impress California college coed Carla Samson (Janet Jones).

Yes, if I am really close to them, I do. If I am close to the process of birthing the film, I especially do. The movie *Taxi Driver* would have never been made if it weren't for me. I slept with that script for three years. I wouldn't give up and I fought hard to keep the package together. Marty had to go off and do other things. I have had a different relationship with each film. When you get along with a director, there is no positioning. It is a true team. If the director knows you, he knows he is on your side and vice versa. The producer job during production is to do whatever it takes to help the director make the best film he's capable of. In retrospect, I think, overall it was *The Sting* that I felt closest to. Winning an Oscar at age 30 as a producer was not fully appreciated at the time. But, it also liberated me from the illusion that if I only had a hit film and won an Oscar, it would totally change my life. I know what it is and what is isn't. Michael Douglas and I were talking after he won the Oscar for producing *One Flew Over the Cuckoo's Nest* and he asked me, "After you won your Oscar, did the studio want to do more pictures with you?" I said, "No." Douglas then said, "I am having exactly the same experience." The director is considered to be the "filmmaker" and the fact that the producer initiated the project still does not give the studio the feeling that we can pick another winner. Hollywood is far too blinded by actors, directors and name talent.

What do you know about the history of the title of producer?
Producers traditionally come from the clothing business. Directors come from the theater. Producers were always carpetbaggers who came to Hollywood with entrepreneurial skills and not a lot of education in film. There are very few producers who went to film school and became producers. Notable exceptions are Joel Silver and Jack Rapke. Most people who go to film school want to be directors, writers and cinematographers. The kind of producer that I represent, and most of the people reflected this in the early part of my career, were essentially hustlers and people who did not have a background in film, just a love of film. With most producers, 99 percent of the time, it is operating with other people's money. In the business that I am in, it is the professional companies that finance film. True independent producers, who raise $400,000 here and $50,000 there, I really admire because it is really hard to stitch something together piece by piece. My network of relationships is not in the area of piecemeal buyers of film rights. It is in the mainstream of Hollywood agents, filmmakers, studios, execs, etc. I pretty much work for companies which finance films. I stay more on the creative side than the business and financing of the films.

How do you feel about the "producer" title and its undefined existence in Hollywood today?
I don't know what a producer is any more. I do know that getting a movie made is a miracle in itself. Getting it to be good is a double miracle. I was lucky to have worked in the '70s. Back then, a producer really had a job. He was the entrepreneur who initiated the project. He or she was expected by the studio to play the key role of gatekeeper between the creative and business sides of the production. The talent worked very differently then. The degree of studio involvement creatively is so much greater now. A meeting with a writer at a studio today often involves six people in a room taking notes and giving their points of view. The studio is actively in control and involved with creative decisions they would have never dared to get involved with before. All my friends who are producers are complaining that it's the toughest time in the industry that they have ever experienced. I think the job has largely been taken away. I think the directors have gone behind the producers' backs and shaken hands directly with the studios to do business. They are saying, "What do we need him for? Screw the producer." And they are doing fine—or so they think. On the other hand, it is ridiculous to have so many producers get credit. I think we should give credit where credit is due. I choose stories purely based on the kind of exciting movies they'll become. Generally, I am mostly struck by ideas that are original. The originality of an idea is the first consideration for me. Today, familiarity is a virtue that is prized. It is the opposite of originality. The more original a concept, the harder and harder it is to be a producer today.

I don't see many original producers on the horizon. There are exceptions like Scott Rudin, Jerry Bruckheimer, Brian Grazer and Joel Silver. They are unique because they have constantly turned out many films that are successful. They have earned the right and secured the confidence to make the films they like. Other producers are trying to sell things to studios that are getting increasingly conservative in what they want. Today, audience familiarity with the idea and something that is pre-sold is a guiding force in the decision-making process by a studio. Old TV shows, comic books, that is what they like right now. Today, if you define yourself successfully in a certain type of film genre, you have a position in the industry, but you have problems if you want to go another way. I am different. I like variety. After *The Sting,* I got a ton of con man scripts. After *Close Encounters,* I got tons of sci-fi scripts. That was not what I wanted. I wanted to do something very different. To me the ideal meal would be an endless variety of appetizers coming by on a conveyor belt. As far as movies, I would like them never to be the same.

What are your true strengths as a producer?

I am in touch with what I like. I have belief in my taste and I always get along with talent.

In turn, what are your weaknesses?

Playing the game the way it is supposed to be played today is a problem for me. I am still betting on my course of action, which is to focus on the material and to bring talent to the material. You keep adding to a package until it ignites. In the case of *The Sting,* the script was enough. On other movies, I have had to add more and more talent to achieve financing. Money is always a problem. Some producers are terrific socially. Some are terrific with material and some are great with financing. You find your own strengths and go from there.

Has your career as a movie producer been fulfilling to you?

Being a producer is a great job when you are allowed to do it and are actually making movies. Primarily, you are calling people, nagging them to read your scripts and following up. *That* part I don't particularly like. I wish I could make every movie I want to make. It is a privilege producing films and it is a career that can span your whole life. It is something I genuinely love. There is the success, but you have to define it for yourself. Whether it puts money in your pocket or not, there is the sense of personal triumph — the personal relations you establish and make. Only you can measure that.

Michael Phillips Filmography

Impostor (Gary Sinise, Madeleine Stowe) 2002 — executive producer; *Mimic* (Mira Sorvino) 1997 — executive producer; *Mom and Dad Save the World* (Teri Garr) 1992 — producer; *Eyes of an Angel* (John Travolta) 1991— producer; *Don't Tell Mom the Babysitter's Dead* (Christina Applegate) 1991— executive producer; *The Flamingo Kid* (Matt Dillon) 1984 — producer; *Can-*

nery Row (Nick Nolte) 1982 — producer; ***Heartbeeps*** (Andy Kauffman, Randy Quaid) 1981—producer; ***Close Encounters of the Third Kind*** (Richard Dreyfuss, Teri Garr) 1977 — producer; ***The Big Bus*** (Stockard Channing, Joseph Bologna) 1976 — executive producer; ***Taxi Driver*** (Robert De Niro, Cybill Shepherd, Jodie Foster) 1976 — producer; ***The Sting*** (Paul Newman, Robert Redford) 1973 — producer; ***Steelyard Blues*** (Donald Sutherland, Jane Fonda) 1973 — producer

Martin Bregman

Martin Bregman was born in New York City in 1931. After attending college at Indiana University and at New York University, he got his first job at the Kenneth Later Agency, a company representing top talent. After working his way up at the firm, he went on to become an agent and business manager for some of the biggest stars in entertainment (Barbra Streisand, Faye Dunaway, Candice Bergen, Alan Alda and other top talent). Bregman is credited for discovering, in an off–Broadway show, one of the greatest actors of our time, Al Pacino. After managing Pacino's career and negotiating to put him in the classic film, The Godfather, *he decided to become a movie producer.*

Bregman produced his first film, Serpico, *starring Pacino, in 1973. His second film, the controversial* Dog Day Afternoon, *brought him an Academy Award nomination for Best Picture. Since then, he has gone on to produce the hit films* Scarface, Betsy's Wedding, Carlito's Way *and* The Bone Collector. *In 1974, he founded the New York Council of Motion Pictures, devoted to encouraging film production in New York City. Martin Bregman, who lives in Manhattan, has several projects currently in development at his company, Bregman Productions.*

Nothing affected me in my youth to enter the film business. I had no ambition to become a film producer when I was young. I came from a middle-class background and didn't know anyone in the entertainment industry. I didn't have an uncle in the business. So, that ambition flowered much later on in my life. Like every other kid, I went to the movies, seeing Saturday matinees, double features, everything. However, there was no moment in my life when I looked up at a screen and said "Ah, ha! That is what I am going to do with the rest of my life."

Could you tell me a little bit about your education?

I attended two colleges, Indiana University and New York University. My studies had nothing to do with the entertainment industry. They were normal college courses like language, physics, English literature, but no preparation for the film business. The only preparation I ever had was during my senior year of high school when I wrote and directed the school play. It was an original concept. Also, I was a member and soloist of the All City Choir here in New York. Those are my only two theatrical background experiences and they had nothing to do with film.

How did you first get introduced to the field of talent management?

My first job out of college was working for a theatrical agent. Then, I became a junior agent for many years. At the time, I was mostly dealing with nightclubs in New York City. The agency was called the Kenneth Later Agency. That was my introduction to the entertainment business. I really enjoyed it there and was an agent and business manager for many years to follow.

During your management career, who were some of the stars you represented?

Some of my clients over the years were Candice Bergen, Faye Dunaway, Barbra Streisand, Alan Alda and Al Pacino.

Martin Bregman. Photograph by Ralph Nelson.

You are credited with discovering actor and icon Al Pacino. Can you tell me about the first time you saw Al Pacino perform?

A client of mine at the time, Faye Dunaway, suggested that I go see an off–Broadway play called *The Indian Wants the Bronx* and to take a close look at this brilliant young actor named Al Pacino. So, that's what I did. I went to the show and saw Pacino perform and I thought he was truly sensational. Afterwards, I went backstage to meet him, personally. I introduced myself and we talked for awhile. I gave him my business card and suggested that he come see me. Several weeks later, Al showed up at my office, not knowing what I did or how I could help him. I was very happy that he showed up. I told him what we could do together and how I could help start his career in film. I didn't give him his ability to act. His ability was and is there. We agreed on working together. I signed him as a client and our relationship ensued from there.

Could you tell me about your segue from managing to producing your first film, *Serpico*?

I represented Pacino then and I knew at that point in my life that I would like to get into filmmaking. I was looking for good material to develop. I was seeking a gangster film, or a cop film, basically a street film that I felt Pacino would identify with and something he would be wonderful in. At that time, I met with Sam Cohn, who represented Peter Mass. He had just written an extraordinary piece for *New York Magazine* about police officer Frank Serpico. And that's how it all started.

Did you read the magazine article and immediately identify with police officer Frank Serpico?

I related to the subject matter and found it very interesting. I found it exceptionally

Serpico (1973, Paramount Pictures). Frank Serpico (Al Pacino) goes undercover in disguise to expose corruption in the New York City police department.

real. It wasn't the kind of cop story that you normally read. It was very different and was about a very unusual sort of man, Frank Serpico.

Your next film, *Dog Day Afternoon*, is based on a true story about a homosexual who holds up a bank so he can buy his male lover a sex change operation. This was 1975 — how did the studio executives react to the concept of your film?

Not very well. It is interesting, because if I pitched that idea to a studio today, I can only imagine the reaction I would get. It would have never been made. There was a young executive at Warner Brothers then who was kind of tickled by the idea. Why he was, I have no idea. He never made it as a studio executive. That was probably due to his bizarre tastes. Thank God they were bizarre. He helped us glue this film into Warner Brothers' plans. It is obviously a very bizarre subject. How do you pitch this, especially today? A young man has given up his family to hold up a bank so he can buy his male lover a sex change operation! I don't think it would go past the first five minutes of the introduction. However, it went on to be nominated for an Academy Award for Best Picture.

What did you personally see in the script to go out on a limb and fight for it to be made?

I saw everything. It is a phenomenal story. There is humor, drama and fascinating characters. In my opinion, back then it was a perfect role for Pacino.

There are various similarities between *Dog Day Afternoon* and *Serpico*. They are both true stories. Both include law enforcement. Al Pacino stars in both. Sidney Lumet directs. Was your thought process, "Since it worked once with *Serpico*, let's try it again?"

Al Pacino is a great actor and I knew he would be perfect for the role of *Sonny*. I had a wonderful relationship with a fine director in Sidney Lumet, so I contacted him first. When you are a producer you always want the best and these two were the best director and actor for the production of *Dog Day Afternoon*.

You remade the film *Scarface* and the film became a phenomenon. How did the idea to remake this movie come about?

I was watching television late one night because I couldn't sleep. I began to watch the original *Scarface* with Paul Muni. I was fascinated by it. I felt if this film were updated, it would be a wonderful gangster film. I was looking for a role exactly like this for my client, Al Pacino. So, that is basically how I got introduced to it. The rise and fall of an American businessman and gangster was the subject that interested me.

Did you see anything pertinent in the original *Scarface* that you consciously wanted to put in your version?

No, nothing. It was just a concept. My film had nothing to do with the first film.

Why did you choose Oliver Stone to write the script?

He is a wonderful writer and I felt he could absolutely gel with this. I knew it was his kind of material. I have been a good friend with Oliver for a long time, so I contacted him and hired him as the screenwriter. No one else could have brought the texture that he did to these characters. I knew he could do a masterful job, which he did.

As a producer, whom did you call upon to help create the reality of the drug world when writing the script for *Scarface*?

Oliver and I did our own research. We went down to Miami, Florida and obtained a lot of useful information. We got a lot of help from the U.S. Attorney's Office there. They opened up their files and showed us their tapes. They were of major assistance. The head of the Organized Crime Bureau, Nick Navarro, who was Cuban, was vital in helping us with the picture. They all were great consultants to us because they, too, wanted to see this anti-drug film made.

You originally hired Sidney Lumet to direct *Scarface*. Why did you end up having Brian DePalma direct, instead?

Lumet didn't agree with me. We had creative differences. Sidney wanted to make it more of a political story than I felt it was. He was more interested in blaming the President's administration for the influx of cocaine that was here in this country. My experience and my knowledge were different than Sidney's. I felt you could blame the Reagan administration for many things, but you could not blame them for bringing cocaine into this country. They had nothing to do with it. We decided to split at that moment.

Top: Dog Day Afternoon (1975, Warner Brothers). Based on a true story, this thriller centers on bisexual Sonny (Al Pacino), who negotiates with police as he attempts to rob a bank to obtain money for his boyfriend's sex change. *Bottom: Scarface* (1983, Universal Pictures). Tony Montana (Al Pacino), a Cuban refugee, is powerful in the drug trade until this final stand-off.

In *Scarface,* you cast many lesser-known actors who were phenomenal in supporting roles. Could you tell me about the casting process of the then-unknown Michelle Pfeiffer?

We were looking for an actress for the role of Elvira for a long time. We were pretty much reading everyone in New York. I got a call from Michelle's then agent and he said that he had a wonderful young actress. The agent read the script and loved it. He asked me to fly Michelle from LA to New York. I said we could not do that. We were not about to pay for her transportation. I probably shouldn't be saying this, but I have always worked on the basis that if an actor or actress wants to pay for his or her own transportation and genuinely makes an effort to come and see me, I will pick up the tab. However, they have to do this first, before I agree. So, Michelle paid for her own transportation. She came in and was sensational in the reading. We auditioned at a small theater on the West Side of Manhattan and, again, a lot of women auditioned for this role. But, she was pure magic. More importantly, Pacino reacted to Pfeiffer more than he reacted to anybody. I knew right then and there that Michelle Pfeiffer would get the part of Elvira. Nobody ever heard of her. Nobody knew who she was at that point in her career. I knew when I watched Michelle and Al together, that she was it, the actress we were searching for.

Many feel that the controversial "chainsaw scene" in *Scarface* is in bad taste and is way too gruesome. Do you agree?

No, because you just heard the sound of the chainsaw. You never saw it physically cut anyone. It was very Hitchcock and that was because we had a very fine director in Brian DePalma. There was no violence in that scene. It was something you as a viewer imagined, much like the shower scene in *Psycho* that Hitchcock became famous for. Again, DePalma saw it that way, so it was done that way. It was conceived that way. *Scarface* was conceived like an opera, over-the-top and flashy — flashy colors, flashy people, flashy music. The women were sensational-looking. Everything about Miami had to look terrific. You couldn't do a film about that world after having spent some time down there, the way it was, because it was so ugly. I wasn't doing a documentary. My intention was to do a movie about that world in an over-the-top fashion. I thought that we had done that when Pacino's character, Tony Montana, leans over and inhales cocaine from a pile that must have been a foot and a half high. I figured the audience would get it. The audience got it, but the critics didn't. They thought it was stupid. Some of my contemporaries thought it was unbelievable, sick, bad storytelling, all the things that it wasn't. *Scarface* has gone on to be a classic film. It has become a benchmark.

How were the reviews from movie critics?

We didn't get good reviews. We got slaughtered, actually. However, we got one good review that was important from Vincent Canby of *The New York Times*. The other big reviewers panned us. Many of those reviewers, if not all of those reviewers today, point to it as a benchmark film. Well, so much for reviewers.

Tell me about your battles with the MPAA and getting a rating for *Scarface.*

The first rating we got was an X rating, which was stunning to me. There certainly was no nudity or sex in the film. The violence was also choreographed. The drug world is a violent world, but it certainly was not *Debbie Does Dallas*. The then head of the rating board was not smart and decided to take us on. We went to a hearing with 21 experts to overturn the rating. Among them, I brought two psychiatrists, the feature writer for *Time* magazine and the head of the organized crime bureau in Miami, who was a narcotics agent. I brought some very key people in to testify and we got the rating reduced. This experience was very much like a trial. The ruling was 18–2 and we won. We beat them because we presented an intelligent position — an intelligent and planned defense and offense. Unfortunately, the opposing side, the head of the MPAA, Mr. Hefner, at that point was, in my opinion, not qualified and was never qualified.

Why did you consider re-releasing *Scarface*?

I wanted to get *Scarface* re-released for quite awhile. It is a classic film. It has changed the business. It has become a huge film in the inner city, a huge film with young people. Al Pacino is best-known not for *The Godfather*, not for Michael Corleone, but he is best-known for Tony Montana and *Scarface*. He always will be. It is a film that has impacted the whole world and something that has gotten more and more popular in the after-life.

You have had a long relationship with another Al, Alan Alda. You have produced four of his films. Could you tell me about your overall experience collaborating with him?

I represented Alan Alda for many years. I represented him when we were making films together. He is a very gifted writer, a very gifted actor and a very gifted director. Alda is a multi-talented man. We made several good films together. Two really stand out for me. One was *The Four Seasons*, and the other is *The Seduction of Joe Tynan*, which I still think are wonderful.

In films such as *One Tough Cop, The Bone Collector, Nothing to Lose and Sea of Love*, law enforcement has played a major role in these and so many of your other movies. Do you have a personal fascination with it?

Well, I think everyone does. That's why I think that well-done films in this genre get great box office results, provided that you do not produce "shoot-'em-ups." I think the films that I have produced like *Sea of Love* are a kind of different facet of police work. You have to deal with the character in order to make something interesting. These were the films that I was interested in, or that interested me.

After producing hit films for so many years, does it ever get easier to find financing for your pictures?

No, it is not easy because the financing of a motion picture is a tough world. Films today have gotten very, very expensive. Most people who sit in the financing position are not filmmakers. So, it is a non-filmmaker being asked to commit 30, 40, 50, 60 or more million dollars of their company's money for a film that may or may not work. That is extremely hard. So, as a producer, you have to do some serious selling.

Top: Scarface (1983, Universal Pictures). Elvira Hancock (Michelle Pfeiffer) dances the night away with Tony Montana (Al Pacino), a Cuban refugee drug lord, in this classic American gangster film. *Bottom: The Four Seasons* (1981, Universal Pictures). Jack (Alan Alda) and Kate (Carol Burnett) find that marriage is like waves — it has its ups and downs.

Do you think studio heads just look at the immediate bottom line and not the dream and creative vision?

If you look at the films that are being made today, I think you can answer your own question. The movies are being made for 12-, 13- and 14-year-olds.

In 1974, you founded the New York Council of Motion Pictures. I read that you are currently a chairman. Can you tell me about this organization?

This organization, the Mayor's Advisory Council, started with only nine members. It was started by myself and a close friend of mine named Louis Rudin, who was in the real estate business. Louis Rudin has done a substantial amount for this city, this organization among his contributions. Lou came to me right after I made *Dog Day Afternoon* and *Serpico*. The producer of *The Taking of Pelham One Two Three* contacted Lou and was having difficulty in getting the then mayor of New York, Abe Beame, to cooperate with the film. Mayor Beame read the script, felt it was anti–New York and then turned him down. Lou called me and asked me to go down to City Hall with him, which I did, and we had some serious meetings down there. Ultimately, we met with Mayor Beame and told him that what he was doing was wrong, and told him he was creating a censorship board. Beame denied it and I said he was wrong. I opened my big mouth and said, "Mr. Mayor, when the media gets ahold of this story, you are not going to look too good." Then, some heated words led to another and he sent us to the deputy mayor. We finally got permission from the deputy mayor to produce the film. From that point on, Lou and I started the advisory council. The advisory council in those days were the heads of every union here. Teamsters, IA, those were the people we had on the council. Now, it is kind of an honorarium. At the time we started the council, I think the entire budget spent on film and television was $50 million. When I left, it was somewhere around $4 billion. So, we did a lot of great work there. They are carrying this on. New York is an element and a story in itself. If it wasn't, you wouldn't work here. It is not cheap. In fact, it is more expensive than other places.

Can you define what you do as a producer?

There are very few producers left. I am pretty much of a dinosaur in this business. What a producer should do, I believe, is to be involved every minute of the day. He should field any problem that comes up. He should start with the material and be part of the creation of the material. I never simply bought scripts. I developed almost everything I have done. The projects have come from ideas, books, newspaper articles, or from remakes. Once in a while, I see a script that I would like to do, but it usually belongs to someone else. Essentially, a producer should be the guy flying the airplane. So, I am a pilot, flying in the left seat. I'm the guy who is up there taking the risks, flying, and the guy who is literally doing it. That is what a producer does. Most producers don't do much. There are exceptions. There are a lot of producers who are managers. They manage an actor. There are a lot of producers who are husbands and boyfriends of an actor or actress. The title of "producer" means absolutely nothing today. People in the business know what I do. However, the audience doesn't care. Producers don't become famous.

Producers are the ones who actually discover talent and give many directors and actors their first breaks, correct?

Yes, that is correct. They have the ability to recognize talent. It does not make you richer and it does not make you smarter. It is an ability to find the material, recognize the potential and then to find that actor or actress who is perfect for that specific role. It does take talent and vision.

You said earlier that you consider yourself a "dinosaur" in this business. What aspects of this industry have changed?

The financial aspect of the business has changed. *Serpico* cost $3 million to make. If we tried to make it today, it would probably cost somewhere around $50 million. So, that part has changed and that is obviously one of the biggest considerations when you are producing a movie. However, the passion to make great art has been tarnished because of the studios' lack of risk-taking. They want only "sure bets" these days.

There have been so many great studio heads and producers who paved the way in Hollywood like Jack Warner, Adolph Zukor, Darryl F. Zanuck and many others. Are there any real studio heads working in Hollywood today?

There are very few studio heads that have any experience as a filmmaker. The days of the Jack Warners are gone. He was a mean son of a bitch, but he loved film. The only one who is in that professional category today is Harvey Weinstein. He is a throwback. Again, I am not talking about him, personally, I am talking about him, professionally. He is knowledgeable. I think he is gifted. I think Harvey Weinstein cares about film.

You discovered one of our greatest living actors on an off–Broadway stage in Al Pacino. You managed many other very well-known acting talents. What do you look for in an actor or actress?

They must have precisely that — talent. There are many talented and gifted people waiting for a stroke of good fortune. Luck plays a major role in this business. First of all, an actor or actress has to be gifted to begin with, and then that gift can be finely honed. It is honed by working in school and taking classes. They can't teach you acting, but they can help you hone your skills. You can be taught the technical information. Can acting school make you more talented? No. Every college and university in this country has acting, film and literary departments. Everybody who wants to be an actor or actress must realize that you can't teach an untalented person how to create talent. It has to be inside of you. As a writer, no one can teach you how to write. They may be able to teach you how to spell, but not how to write. You can't teach somebody how to sing. These gifts have to be inside you.

What advice can you give to a prospective filmmaker who wants to pitch you an original idea for a movie?

Well, pitches are hard. I guess it depends on who is pitching me. If it were a very talented writer, then it would interest me because he or she is a gifted writer. You can pitch me a wonderful story idea, but who is going to write it? So, there has to be a combination there. As a producer, you are not going to buy a pitch, a concept. I have never bought a pitched idea in my career as a producer.

Do you feel movie producers are, in fact, "unsung heroes"?

Absolutely. They are unsung heroes for two reasons. There aren't many of them left. There are a lot of people with a list of credits, but God knows what they have done to earn them. There are many people walking around and claiming they are film producers and have no idea how to produce. Sometimes, they use the title for their own selfish reasons. Very few producers in this business are experienced and are gifted.

Do you consider filmmaking more an art form or more a business?

Filmmaking is not a business. It is a popular art form. Films have to be made by artists. We must never lose sight of that. Do I consider myself an artist? Yes, I do. It doesn't make me richer and it doesn't make me smarter. In the future, I am going to keep producing, and keep doing what I do best. But, one thing is for sure. Filmmaking is a tough, tough world.

Martin Bregman Filmography

Carolina (Julia Stiles, Shirley MacLaine) 2003 — producer; *The Adventures of Pluto Nash* (Eddie Murphy, Rosario Dawson) 2002 — producer; *The Bone Collector* (Denzel Washington, Angelina Jolie) 1999 — producer; *One Tough Cop* (Stephen Baldwin, Gina Gershon) 1998 — producer; *Nothing to Lose* (Tim Robbins, Martin Lawrence) 1997 — producer; *Matilda* (Danny De Vito, Rhea Perlman) 1996 — executive producer; *Gold Diggers: The Secret of Bear Mountain* (Christina Ricci) 1995 — producer; *The Shadow* (Alec Baldwin, Penelope Anne Miller) 1994 — producer; *Carlito's Way* (Al Pacino, Sean Penn) 1993 — producer; *The Real McCoy* (Kim Basinger, Val Kilmer) 1993 — producer; *Blue Ice* (Michael Caine) 1992 — producer; *Whispers in the Dark* (Annabella Sciorra, John Leguizamo) 1992 — producer; *Betsy's Wedding* (Alan Alda, Molly Ringwald) 1990 — producer; *Sea of Love* (Al Pacino, Ellen Barkin) 1989 — producer; *A New Life* (Alan Alda, Ann-Margret) 1988 — producer; *Real Men* (James Belushi, John Ritter) 1987 — producer; *Sweet Liberty* (Alan Alda, Michael Caine) 1986 — producer; *The Four Seasons* (Joanna Kerns, Tony Roberts) 1984, TV Series — executive producer; *Scarface* (Al Pacino, Michelle Pfeiffer) 1983 — producer; *Eddie Macon's Run* (Kirk Douglas) 1983 — producer; *Venom* (Klaus Kinski) 1982 — producer; *The Four Seasons* (Alan Alda, Carol Burnett) 1981 — producer; *S*H*E* (Omar Shariff, Cornelia Sharpe) 1980, TV — producer; *Simon* (Alan Arkin, Madeline Kahn) 1980 — producer; *The Seduction of Joe Tynan* (Alan Alda, Meryl Streep) 1979 — producer; *The Next Man* (Sean Connery) 1976 — producer; *Dog Day Afternoon* (Al Pacino, John Cazale) 1975 — producer; *Serpico* (Al Pacino) 1973 — producer

Christine Vachon

Christine Vachon was born in New York City in 1962. After graduating Brown University, she worked as a proofreader at night, while during the day she worked for no pay as an assistant on independent films in New York City. After being inspired by unique independent filmmakers like Spike Lee, Jim Jarmush and Bill Sherwood who were directing their first movies at that time, she decided to open a not-for-profit short film production company called Apparatus with Todd Haynes and Barry Ellsworth. She went on produce Haynes' feature film directorial debut, Poison, *which won the Grand Jury Prize at Sundance. At her production company,* Killer Films, *she has gone to produce such hits as* Boys Don't Cry, I Shot Andy Warhol, Go Fish, Safe, Kids, Velvet Goldmine, Swoon *and many others. For years, she has continually produced feature films that helped expand and defy the expectations of Hollywood. Vachon has been known for helping many first-time directors get their films made. One of her recent films,* Far from Heaven, *directed by Todd Haynes, and starring Julianne Moore, was nominated for four Academy Awards.*

I was born in 1962, so I think the first movie that I, and many people of my generation, saw was *Mary Poppins*. I grew up in New York City next to a theater on 106th Street called the Olympia . I was able to go to the movies on my own from a very young age. It was the local $1 theater. I saw many great movies there that influenced me during my youth. Unfortunately, the Olympia Theatre was recently torn down.

Do you remember the first film that affected you and made you think about going into the movie industry?

I admire people that can come up with that kind of recollection, but I don't always believe it. For me, it was an amalgam of many different things. I had a stunning experience when I saw, for the first time, the Francois Truffaut film, *The 400 Blows*. I was 12 years old and this type of film was something I had never seen before on screen. I was about the same age as the main character in the movie, so I felt I could relate. The Parisian boy skips school to go to the movies and discovers his mother has a lover. It was an amazing movie. I was also impressed with *The Poseidon Adventure*. In some ways, *The Poseidon Adventure* was the granddaddy for all the real special effects–type movies today. It got nominated for an Academy Award for Best Picture, which was fabulous. So, I think it was those two films that got me thinking about movies. Then, I was off to Brown University, where I got a good solid education. Many people ask me why I did not go to film school and my answer is, it did not occur to me back then that there even *was* such a thing. I wasn't even interested in film as a business.

How did you support yourself financially right after graduating from college?

Everyone I knew was taking jobs to pay their rent while they pursued their artistic goals. I was not a good waitress, which many of my friends did. So, I became a proofreader. You have to understand this was the early mid–80s and I was getting paid $25 an hour. It was very decent money. I was working on independent films while I was a proofreader, but the films didn't pay. The first film I worked on was *Far from Poland*. It was a docudrama about Solidarity and its effects on America and the Solidarity movement in Poland. Then, I worked on a film called *Parting Glances*, the directorial debut of Bill Sherwood. This film was the first sort of taste of a burgeoning movement where there were a number of filmmakers making their first films. Jim Jarmusch, Spike Lee and Bill Sherwood's work gave the notion that there was an alternative to this Hollywood fare. These movies, like *Stranger Than Paradise*, *She's Gotta Have It* and *Parting Glances*, were movies that were being made independently, but were going to go to your local cinema. They weren't just going to be shown in someone's basement. One had a bohemian sensibility, one had a very black sensibility and one had a very gay sensibility — all stories that were not being told in any other way, but to entertain. So, it was an interesting time in film.

So you felt with this new breed of filmmakers there was a light at the end of the independent filmmaking tunnel?

I wasn't that smart. I was just interested in the fact there were movies being made in my neighborhood that I could work on. I always thought that if you wanted to work in movies, you had to go to LA. The idea that you could do it at a garage level in New York City was very exciting to me.

Could you tell me about your first film production company, Apparatus?

Christine Vachon. Photograph by Joyce George.

At Apparatus, we only did short films. We got an endowment from a rich relative of one of my partners. I formed the company with Todd Haynes and Barry Ellsworth. It was the '80s and a very different time. There was a lot of money around New York back then. Those were the years of what is popularly called "insane excess." We thought it would be a really interesting idea to set up a production company that was also a grant-giving organization. We would select people's scripts and fully produce their films with them. We were a genuine "not-for-profit" business. We were really just there to make movies and made seven short films over the course of two and a half years. Some of them worked. Some of them didn't. Some were certainly better than others. It was a really exciting way to learn production and learn how to produce.

How did you wind up producing your first feature-length film, *Poison*?

Todd Haynes had made a hit underground film, *Superstar: The Karen Carpenter Story*. It literally starred a bunch of "Barbie Dolls" and charted the rise of the pop group the Carpenters, with the lead female singer wasted away from anorexia nervosa. It was truly amazing. I felt it sort of epitomized all the things that I wanted to do as a filmmaker. It was incredibly funny, entertaining and smart, and at the end of the film, you really felt you went on a journey. It had a strong effect on me and I felt I wanted to make movies like that. I said to Todd, "I want to produce your next film." At that point in New York, there were two types of films being made. There was a real dividing line. You were either making movies that were being shown at the "Collection of Living Cinema," which were essentially films that were like watching paint dry, or you were making Hollywood-style movies. A lot of the movies that we were making were getting criticized for being too entertaining. Todd started applying for grants. At that time, you could get $100,000 from grants. That's how Spike Lee made *She's Gotta Have It*. Spike had investors, but he also had a lot of the same money I was getting for *Poison*. We had a lot of grants and we also got some investors to make *Poison*. I barely knew what a producer did. I assumed they were the ones who put it together. So that is, in fact, what I proceeded to do.

How was *Poison* received?

It won the Grand Jury Prize at Sundance. It also was at the center of a big controversy because it got some money from the National Endowment of the Arts. There had been a number of artists who had been criticized for getting money from the National Endowment of the Arts and doing what was termed "obscene art." For example, there was Karen Finley, who shoved a yam up her ass on stage. Well, this was performance art but, in reality, who is ever going to really see it? Then this movie *Poison*, *our* movie, got made. *Poison* was a compelling drama, weaving the story of a seven-year-old boy's murder of his father with two other tales of obsessive fringe behavior. We used money from the National Endowment of the Arts. The difference result-wise between the yam flick and our film, *Poison*, was that *Poison* was going to be seen on a much larger scale. Our movie got made on your tax dollars and it became a huge controversy, which couldn't have been better for the film. It got us a lot of attention. Todd and I did a number of radio shows as well as television shows like *Entertainment Tonight*. Now, I am an old pro at talking to reporters. I know how to say something without saying something. However, I didn't back then. The only downside was that people's interest in the film became prurient. They went to see it and it made a lot of money.

What attracted to you to producing the controversial hit *Kids*?

I thought it was a great script and a very exciting package, for lack of a better word. This young kid, Harmony Korine, had written a script that really rang true. *Kids* was a docudrama about 24 hours in the lives of some New York teenagers. Our lead character enjoys bragging about his skill in deflowering virgins, but results in Jenny testing HIV positive. It contained a vividness of life around us at that time. The director, Larry Clark, was quite an exciting character. Who he was and the stature he had achieved in his own career — was all a really good fit.

The use of non-actors in this film — was it a conscious decision to obtain realism?

Well, it was interesting because we were always going to use non-actors. However, Cary Woods, who was producing the film with me, became convinced that we had to use one pro. His concern was in terms of selling the movie, so he wanted us to cast Mia Kirshner in the role of Jenny, because she was very hot at that time. She was just in *Exotica*. We brought Mia in and Cary was reluctant, but saw her as a necessary evil. She hung out that weekend with the kids who were already cast and they got along well. So, we thought this was the direction we were going to go in. Honestly, it was immediately clear to me, and these things are always clearer in retrospect, that the other kids had a quality that Mia didn't have. They all hung out together and were a group and Mia clearly was not part of that group. Then, this issue came up that she did not want to take off any of her clothes. This was kind of odd because, in *Exotica*, Mia played a table dancer working in a Toronto strip club called Exotica. What does that tell you? It became a tough battle. She was holding firm and I am not criticizing her because an actress has the right to decide how far she will go. But, in some ways, in my mind, if you are going to hold a firm line like that, then what on Earth are you doing in this movie? The movie clearly is about sex, drugs and partying. Over the weekend, Mia went to Toronto to pack, say goodbye to her family and to come for the time being to live in New York City. I went home that weekend and on Sunday night, Larry called me. He said, "I have been thinking about it all weekend and I don't think it can be Mia. I think it has to be Chloe Sevigny. I don't know why I didn't see it before. She is perfect." Now, Chloe had totally been around, but this was about four years before her Oscar-nominated performance in *Boys Don't Cry* with Hillary Swank. Chloe tells the story now that she was saying, "Hello? Hello? I can be Jenny." Larry didn't see it. Then, Larry said, "Does Mia have a contract?" Larry had this overwhelming respect for a contract. If she had a contract, then we couldn't take her out. Well, she didn't have a contract because of her representative. I can't remember who it was. Anyway, he was treating us like we were some huge Hollywood production that was trying to take advantage of his client. So, I told Larry, "No, Larry, we don't have a contract. So, I think you should call Mia right now." I hung up and thought either Larry is going to call Mia and she will talk herself back into the part or Mia will hang up immediately and in two seconds I will get a call from her lawyer. So, it was like *ten, nine—ring*, and Mia's lawyer was on the line. He said, "Do you know who you are dealing with? Who do you think you are? Who does Larry Clark think he is? You better talk some sense into your director." Mia was represented by a major agency at the time, but we knew she was not going to work out for the role of Jenny. We then had the attitude, "It's over! Mia is not in the movie." Larry and I cast Chloe Sevigny for the part of Jenny. Then we went ahead with our cast of mostly kids from the hood.

Kids (1995, Miramax). The cast of kids in director Larry Clark's controversial film about sex, drugs and being young in downtown New York City.

What was the budget on *Kids*?

$1.2 million or $1.3 million.

How did you raise the financing for the film?

It was these two guys, Michael Chambers and Pat Panzerella, who were in the music industry and had some money and wanted to get into movies. Cary Woods had found them.

Another film I wanted to discuss was *Velvet Goldmine* starring Ewan McGregor. It had a lot of effects, music rights to be cleared, was a period piece and was shot overseas. Was this film a big learning experience for you?

Every film has been a learning experience for me. With *Velvet Goldmine*, we essentially produced a record album at the same time. The music was so complex and if I really knew how complicated it was going to be, I would have been too nervous to produce it. We were putting together all these different bands to actually play the music of the bands in the movie. People were writing songs for us. It was very crazy. We had many different bands involved; Radio Head, Placebo, the guy from Sonic Youth, another guy from Mudhoney. I was in London on location and I would call our music producer, Randy Poster, in New York at 5 A.M., waking him up. I would say, "Randy, the drum beat doesn't work for the song on this track. We need a new one right away!" It was crazy, just crazy! I love doing musicals. In fact, we are about to do *Urinetown*.

How did Ewan McGregor prepare for this role?

He lost weight. He studied tapes and modeled himself like Iggy Pop. That sort of thing.

How did the hit *Boys Don't Cry* come to your attention?

After we had done *Go Fish* a couple of years later, Rose Troshe called me up and said, "I met this girl. She is still a student at Columbia Film School and has this really cool script. Can I tell her she can call you?" I said, "Sure." Kimberly Pierce came in and I had already heard of the case, which was based on a true story of a girl who passes herself off as a boy in a small Midwestern town and the subsequent gender revelation leads to tragic consequences. Also, I think *Playboy* had written a big piece on it. Kim had shot about 20 minutes of footage for a student film that was languishing at Du Art because she couldn't pay the bill to get it out. So, I paid the bill to get it out of the

Velvet Goldmine (1998, Miramax). Ewan McGregor and Jonathan Rhys Meyers star in this story about the rise and fall of a pop legend.

lab, and we got it out and looked at the stuff. It was not bad. However, there was nothing in it that would give you any sense of the power the movie ultimately had. The actors were amateurish. It didn't have such an incredible breadth of style. It did show that she had a firm grasp of what this story was all about. She had a script that was called *Stone*, a totally fictionalized version of the trial. We started to develop that script with her and it, honestly, took years. Mostly, because, at first, I thought maybe we should raise money to finish the movie and use this footage. Then, I thought it wasn't good enough and she was getting smarter every day and she'll do it better. I then made a budget of $2 million for her script, *Take It Like a Man*. We had to change the title because Boy George had already written a known biography called *Take It Like a Man*. Then, I kept trying to get it financed and there were some roadblocks. Largely, because a lot of people felt there were competing projects and that the lead character of Brandon was just too unsympathetic. Gradually, as Kimberly kept working on it, she got drawn more and more to the real facts of the case. She went out to Nebraska and was at the murderers' trial. She also spent time with the real Lana, Chloe's part, and at a certain point, she felt, "Why can't it just be the real story of what happened? Why do we have to fictionalize it?" So, I said, "We don't." Finally we got the script into the best shape it was ever in. We had a "first look" deal with MGM, and we took it to them and they agreed to make it. They just wanted to have one meeting with the director. Kim went to LA to talk to MGM. I think we put her up at the Farmer's Daughter Motel. That's how tight our budget was. I wasn't there, but Pam was there and Kim wanted to talk about the story and its resonance. The executives kept asking her stuff like, "They really couldn't tell she was a guy? Was she a hermaphrodite?" Kim had to answer the questions. A few days later, they called and said, "This is a little too small for us. We don't want to do it." Then, across the hall from us, Art Sharpe had found financing for another movie and they had to wait on it. That movie was *You Can Count on Me*, ultimately starring Laura Linney, Mark Ruffalo and Matthew Broderick. They had more work to do on the script or maybe an actor was delayed. So, I knew they had the money, but no movie ready to roll.

That's a good neighbor to have!

(*Laughing*) Yes, it is. Well, they had originally passed on *Boys Don't Cry* like three times, and I just went over there and said, "You have to do it." And they did. The Independent Film Channel came in a few days into shooting and literally saw the first few days of dailies. They saw what Hillary Swank was doing and they said, "We are in. Where do we sign the check?"

Did Fox Searchlight make you cut anything?

Not for rating reasons, but just for length. Fox bought the movie for $5 million from just seeing the trailer. The movie hovered at two and a half hours for months. The problem was that Kim was a little paranoid, partially because at two and a half hours, it played very well. It was great at two and a half hours, but we knew it would be greater at two. It was really hard to cut the film down. It is a lot harder to convince a director to cut when it is good.

Anything you want to say about the casting of Hillary Swank in that role?

It was one of the great situations where we really got to cast the role. A lot of people came in to read for the part. I remember watching Hillary's tape with Kim and watching another potential actress' tape. However, that actress didn't have quite the stature that Hillary had. Kim thought Hillary was sexy and the perfect match of an actress to a part.

I read that Hillary convinced the doorman at an office building in LA that she was a boy.

(*Laughing*) Hillary can tell you her tales. We did have a Christmas party that Hillary came to in drag and nobody knew who she was. She successfully fooled everyone into believing that she was a nice little man coming to our holiday party.

Boys Don't Cry (1999, Fox Searchlight Pictures). The story of Teena Brandon (Hillary Swank, middle), a cross-dressing youth who preferred life in her male identity of Brandon Teena. Peter Saarsgard (left) and Brandon Sexton (right) portray John and Tom, friends who turn on Teena when her secret is revealed.

Your recent collaboration with director-writer Todd Haynes is *Far from Heaven*. Did you ever envision this film being so widely accepted, and getting nominated for four Academy Awards?

It sounds a little ungrateful, for lack of a better word, to complain about four Oscar nominations, but I feel that *Far from Heaven* is an absolutely extraordinary movie. Todd's work is, to me, so head and shoulders above so many directors. The meticulous touch and love he gave to each scene was incredible. I was disappointed he was not nominated for Best Director.

Do you feel *Far from Heaven* is a timeless tale?

Absolutely, and that is one of the reasons it has been so widely accepted.

Does the title of movie producer hold any credence today?

Well, I actually joined the Board of Directors of the Producers Guild not too long ago because I want to address this very issue. Why are there ten people listed as a producer at the end of a film when anyone who ever has made a movie knows that only one or two of them really had something to do with it? On the other hand, it's a chit that I often have to cash myself. For example, a guy writes a book that I am desperate to option because I feel it will make a great film. Guy says, "I'll let you produce it, but I want a producer credit." What am I going to say? Actors want it nowadays. They will say that the strength of their name brought in the financing. Investors want it. I am very into trying to regulate this producer credit. Studios do not finance my movies. Well, that is not entirely true. In part it is. It's rare that I have a film that is completely studio funded. *One Hour Photo* starring Robin Williams was. *Hedwig* was. *Storytelling* was. It happens. What often happens is, I am cobbling the financing from a number of different sources. I may have to deal with difficult material, often first-time directors, and I am not in a position to take a stance and tell somebody I will not take their money if I have to give them a producer credit. I can't do that. I don't like it and it does demean what I do. If you sit here for a half-hour, you see what I do all day long. It's things like figuring out an actor deal, calming down a director, arranging for another director to meet with an actor while he or she is still in LA. It is about pushing the movie incrementally forward. The title of "producer" has been horribly ill-treated, essentially watered down. If you try to mess with a writer's credit, maybe a degree in billing, the Writers Guild of America is all over you like white on rice. Directors are protected by the Directors Guild of America. The fact is the rights of those creative people, and how they are credited, are protected in a way that no one seems to feel they have to do for producers. Our Guild may actually make some strides.

What are your duties as a producer?

I am sure every producer has given you a version of the same answer. I basically provide the locomotion. I move it along. Whatever that entails, I do it. On every movie, it is different. When you came in to my office, you said, "I want to talk to producers who find the script, hire the director, raise the financing and are involved in their productions from soup to nuts." We do all of that to some extent. We also hire a lot of writer/directors. On the other hand, take the Robert Altman movie I recently produced. We brought him the script. It was developed over several years and I guess that is a more classic situation. Every movie has its own set of demands. Some are easier to finance than others. Some of them need to be financed in certain ways because of creative concerns. It is hard to define it in any other way than by saying, "We put it together and move it along."

Do you find yourself playing the role of an actor as a producer?

Yes, all the time. A producer constantly finds him or herself boxed into a "Catch 22" situation of, "I can't attach this actor until we are financed, and I can't get financing until I attach this actor. So what do I do?" Those are the kinds of things that put me in the mode to act. As a producer, I have to exude confidence all the time. We have to convince agents, managers, actors and other key creative personal that everything is going fine and moving ahead when we, the producers, may be the only ones who know the real deal — that the financing just fell apart.

You are quoted as saying, "A low-budget film is a crisis waiting to happen." Do you still feel that way?

Yes, I do. However, I also think you can say that about all filmmaking to a degree. It is constant crisis management. It is a whole bunch of people that you are moving from place to place. The odds are always against you in that something is going to go somewhat off-kilter. That is why filmmaking is so much fun. It is about serendipity,

Top: Far from Heaven (2002, Focus Features). Cathy Whitaker (Julianne Moore) jokes with her husband Frank Whitaker (Dennis Quaid) at a suburban Connecticut party where everything is not what it seems. *Bottom: Far from Heaven* (2002, Focus Features). Cathy Whitaker (Julianne Moore) confers with her gardener Raymond Deagan (Dennis Haysbert) about life in general outside of her picture-perfect Connecticut home.

working within your means and using what you've got. Even the most "planned" directors in the world have to think on their feet that way.

Since you are working independently, do you take points on your projects as a producer?

We try to take points on everything. That tends to be the only way we are ever compensated. Although, since the points hardly ever pay off, it is kind of a silly way to make a living, or not make a living.

What advice can you give to someone who is going to pitch you a project?

I guess the real advice is this: People who have a brand-new script call the office and ask to speak to me. That is just stupid because they are never going to get to speak to me. I am very, very busy. Why would I talk to them? It comes back to: Don't start at the top, start at the bottom. We have people here who are here specifically to take those calls. They're here to track those projects and to see who is new and interesting and exciting. If you call and ask to speak to Jocelyn, for instance, you'll probably get her. You might not get her right away, but you will get her eventually. Sell her on your project. She is the one who I listen to. She may come to me and say, "This guy came in and pitched me a really good project I think you might like. I need you to sit in with him on a pitch." I will. My peers in this business now were production assistants 15 years ago. That is the way of the world.

Do you find that the film business is recession-proof?

I feel that is a bit strong because I don't feel anything is truly recession-proof. But, at the same time, I think people will always respond to good stories.

Do you feel that investors are finding film a safer bet to invest in these days?

No. I think it is still wildly unprofitable. The thing about film is, I don't think profit is the only reason why people invest. They invest because they want to be part of the magic. That's why people stay in Hollywood and are attracted to it. Nobody is in any business not to make money. But in making a film, there are other types of return.

Do you ever start productions without all the financing in place?

I am not usually allowed to. We get bonded. In the old days I probably did more of that, but not today.

What advice can you give to an aspiring director?

Find a good producer.

What advice can you give to someone who is trying to become a producer and attempting to raise financing to start their own production company?

I am not good at the "giving advice" thing. No one ever gave me advice. I think there are a lot of different ways to find financing. You can't get too set in your ways. Great producers are people who can think on their feet, who do not terrify easily or at all, and have the ability to think "big picture" all the time. If you think you have those traits, then somehow you will get there. If you don't, you'll just be weeded out as you go along. People do it in different ways. I really worked my way up on film sets and really learned about the physical production of film. I know producers who have come from the world of exhibition and distribution. I know other producers who simply found some fantastic material and brought it to the attention of a terrific director. We have done that too, but what I also bring is the knowledge of physical production, which all producers get eventually. That is one way to start working your way up.

If you weren't working in the film business, what do you think you would be doing for a living?

I never really had to work for anyone so I don't know how good I would be at it. The trick is that if you start out without the steady paycheck when you are young, you don't miss it. Once you get it, you start getting terrified without it. Since I never had it, I don't know what it is like. I have only had health insurance as a constant for the past two years.

What do you want to accomplish in years to come?

More of the same. We are just going to keep making movies. I live very much in the moment, and at this moment, we are doing some really great films. I can promise that there will be more of the same in the future.

Christine Vachon Filmography

The Company (Neve Campbell, James Franco) 2003 — producer; *A Home at the End of the World* (Dallas Roberts) 2003 — producer; *Party Monster* (Macaulay Culkin, Seth Green) 2003 — producer; *Far from Heaven* (Julianne Moore, Dennis Quaid) 2002 — producer; *One Hour Photo* (Robin Williams) 2002 — producer; *Chelsea Walls* (Uma Thurman, Rosario Dawson) 2001 — producer; *The Grey Zone* (David Arquette, Harvey Keitel) 2001 — producer; *Storytelling* (Selma Blair) 2001 — producer; *The Safety of Objects* (Glenn Close) 2001 — producer; *Women in Film* (Beverly D'Angelo) 2001 — producer; *Hedwig and the Angry Inch* (John Cameron Mitchell) 2001 — producer; *Crime and Punishment in Suburbia* (Ellen Barkin) 2000 — producer; *Boys Don't Cry* (Hillary Swank, Chloe Sevigny) 1999 — producer; *Wildflowers* (Daryl Hannah, Eric Roberts) 1999 — executive producer; *I'm Losing You* (Rosanna Arquette, Andrew McCarthy) 1998 — producer; *Velvet Goldmine* (Ewan McGregor) 1998 — producer; *Happiness* (Philip Seymour Hoffman, Lara Flynn Boyle) 1998 — producer; *Office Killer* (Molly Ringwald) 1997 — producer; *Kiss Me Guido* (Nick Scotti, Anthony Barrile) 1997 — producer; *Plain Pleasures* (Frances McDormand) 1996 — producer; *I Shot Andy Warhol* (Lili Taylor, Jared Harris) 1996 — producer; *Stonewall* (Guillermo Diaz) 1995 — producer; *Safe* (Julianne Moore) 1995 — producer; *Kids* (Chloe Sevigny, Rosario Dawson) 1995 — co-producer; *Postcards from America* (James Lyons) 1994 — producer; *Go Fish* (Guinevere Turner) 1994 — executive producer; *Swoon* (Daniel Schlachet) 1992 — producer; *Poison* (Edith Meeks, Millie White) 1991 — producer

John Lyons

John Lyons moved to New York City from Michigan and started his career in theater. He eventually became a very successful casting director for theater at the Playwrights' Horizon. Lyons then advanced into the arena of casting for major motion pictures, working alongside directors like Frank Oz and the Coen Brothers. He cast top movies such as Raising Arizona, Striptease, City Hall, Cocktail *and many others. On the encouragement of a friend, John decided to make the transition to film producer when he hooked up with first-time director Paul Thomas Anderson on his low-budget* Hard Eight. *John raised the money and attached top talent to the picture like Samuel L. Jackson and Gwyneth Paltrow. John has gone on to produce mega-hit films like* Boogie Nights, Austin Powers: The Spy Who Shagged Me, Austin Powers in Goldmember *and, most recently, Peter Hedges' ultra-low budget directorial debut* Pieces of April.

When I was growing up, I watched a lot of movies on television. I do remember a British movie that affected me very vividly. It was a Michael Powell-Emeric Pressburger—directed film set in the Himalayas, *Black Narcissus*. I remember being ten or eleven and I watched it on CBC [Canadian Broadcasting Channel] and realized it was something different from anything I had ever seen before. Anglican nuns, led by the stern Sister Clodagh (Deborah Kerr), attempt to establish a hospital and a school in the Himalayas. They must battle not only suspicious locals and the elements, but their own demons as well. It was very disturbing and upsetting and was the first time that I realized how powerful a movie can be. The content of the film was far outside my little, complacent Midwestern world. I still remember it as something that shocked me.

Did you attend film school?

No. I went to the University of Michigan and majored in art history with a minor in theater. When I was close to graduating, I was fairly sure that I was going to move to New York City and work in theater. I had no desire to be an actor and equally little desire to be a director. When I graduated from school in 1977, I did an internship at a very thriving theater company in New York City called the Chelsea Theatre Center [now the West Side Arts Theatre]. They had just done a production with Hal Prince, so at the time, there were a lot of great people working there. Underneath it all, I think getting that internship was my excuse to move to New York City and for my parents to let me stay there. After that, I ended up becoming a stage manager at Playwrights'

141

Horizon just as Andre Bishop was taking over the theater company. It was Andre who gave me the job. In 1980, he made me the casting director there. I always thought I would be good in casting because I had the unique ability to remember everyone I ever met. I used to meet people, mentally store the image of what they looked like, then put it away and pull it out when needed. Since there was never a casting director before me at Playwrights' Horizon, and I was never formally trained in casting, I was always haunted by the idea that I might not be doing the job correctly, but, looking back, I think I did a good job there.

Why did you segue into casting for feature films?

I had a friend who was working at the Learning Corporation of America and, at this time, there were a lot of "After-School" TV specials being made in New York City. I quickly saw that I could make more money casting After-School specials, so I decided to make the switch from theater to television. Then, I eventually decided to segue into casting feature films, because I saw there was even more money and growth potential in that. Shortly after I entered casting for movies, I partnered up with another casting director named Donna Iverson, who is now the head of casting for features at 20th Century-Fox. Back then, we were both competing for a lot of the same jobs, so we thought it would be smart to partner up.

What was your first casting job on a major motion picture?

My first major film as a casting director was on *King Kong Lives*. The first casting job that had a really big impact on me and my career was *Raising Arizona,* which was directed by Joel and Ethan Coen. I had known Frances McDormand because she was temping at Playwrights' Horizons and then she left to act in the Coen Brothers' first film, *Blood Simple.* She suggested me as a casting director to Joel and Ethan because they were looking for people to work on *Raising Arizona.* They sent me the script and I loved it. I got the job and it was the beginning of a long relationship for me and the Coen Brothers. I cast all of their movies up till *The Big Lebowski.*

How was it to work for the Coen Brothers?

It was the best. They are a completely self-contained unit and they are so smart at the way they run their movies. They are a complete joy to work for. In most cases, they are working with the same people today that they started working with 15 years ago. Their productions have a really fun "family vibe."

Did you give any actor or actress that you cast for their first big break?

I had an impact on certain people's career, but I do not believe in that "first break" theory. When someone says, "I gave so and so their first job," it doesn't usually hold water with me. Maybe, if they saw someone randomly walking down the street and they picked them out of a crowd, approached them and said, "I want to cast you in a film" — then, maybe I can believe a casting director who says that they gave someone their first break. I did cast Macaulay Culkin in his first movie, but he he was not unknown at that point. He had done a stage show that literally every casting director in New York saw and it just so happened that I had a project that was right for him first. In Joel and Ethan's case, there were a lot of people who I cast that made a big splash for the first time in the Coen Brothers' movies. We cast John Goodman, John Turturro, Steve Buscemi and a number of other talented people who have gone on to have amazing careers. Directors like the Coen Brothers and Frank Oz are dedicated craftsmen and the type of talents I loved being a casting director for.

The first major film that you produced, *Hard Eight*, Paul Thomas Anderson's directorial debut, was amazing. You had such a great cast — Gwyneth Paltrow, Samuel L. Jackson and John C. Reilly. Did you cast that film as well as produce it?

Yes, I did. I had decided to enter producing at the urging of Michelle Satter, who runs the Writer and Director Labs at Sundance. Michelle is a very good friend and has been very influential in my life as she has been

Raising Arizona (1987, Twentieth Century–Fox). Hi (Nicolas Cage), an ex-con and the world's worst hold-up man, kidnaps a baby from furniture tycoon Nathan Arizona and a surreal comedy ensues.

in many other filmmakers' lives. She really was the person who convinced me that I should be producing and not just be casting. I had been the casting director at the June Directors' Lab for seven years. Every year, I would cast four of the film projects that were being done through the Lab. I had met writer/director Paul Thomas Anderson through the Sundance Lab because he was one of my projects in 1995. When it came to casting the movie, Paul and I had the same ideas. He had written the lead of Sydney for Philip Baker Hall, so I did not need to cast that part. Paul was still looking for an actor to play the other part of John Finnegan. I immediately suggested John C. Reilly and he said, "That was who I was thinking of as well." So, immediately, we were on the same page. Paul is really smart and has incredible taste when it comes to casting his films. It's almost as if he has psychic instincts when it comes to putting an actor or actress in a part. After the Sundance Lab ended, Paul had decided that *Hard Eight* would be his first movie. Paul called me and asked if I wanted to cast the film and I said, "No, but I will produce it if you let me." He told me to come to California to discuss the possibility of me producing *Hard Eight*. We met in person and we hit it off immediately. I said, "I will put the cast together and let's produce it."

I was able to get Gwyneth Paltrow attached. It took about a year and a half to get the whole picture put together, but when we first cast Gwyneth, she was on the rise. She was fantastically talented and she was not a star yet. About a year after we cast her, she became a huge star. At that time, Samuel L. Jackson was the star and the link to attach the money for the film. I had known Sam from when I was casting a TV series in New York called *Spenser: For Hire* for ABC. Every year I made sure Sam got a job acting on that show. Sam was very loyal and taking this low-budget role was sort of

Hard Eight (1997, Clementine (Gwyneth Paltrow) is the lead female character in this tale of love, revenge and redemption set against the seedy casinos of Reno, Nevada.

his gracious payback to me. When anyone met Paul Thomas Anderson face-to-face, they were really impressed by him and usually wanted to be in his films. This film turned out to be a very interesting first experience for me as a producer. At that point in time, many independent films were getting financed because of their pre-sales to foreign markets. Essentially, if you could find an actor who you could attract to a project, then you could pre-sell the film to foreign markets and generally have enough money to make the movie. You would make a domestic deal later and that was how many films got made. The people who put the financing together turned out to be a problematic group. Paul and I had a huge amount of trouble with them.

What was the budget on *Hard Eight*?
  I think it was about $3 million, which was really low.

Your second film as a producer was *Boogie Nights,* written and directed by Paul Thomas Anderson. Correct?
  Yes. That deal got set up at New Line Cinema and Paul asked me to produce it with him

What did you think of this controversial and very racy script about the porn industry?
  I thought it was amazing. Paul's scripts are like Joel and Ethan Coen's, to the extent that when you read them on paper, you can absolutely see the movie. The dia-

logue is fantastic and it tells you everything you need to know about the characters. Paul is so amazing because he was anywhere from four to eight years old when that movie takes place, and yet he had a far better grasp of what went on during that era then I did. He researches his movies so well. It definitely was a controversial script. There were many things filmed that did not make the final product. If you really look at the film, it is not that graphic. It is more suggestive. Even the nudity was rather brief. It was a struggle to secure talent for the movie because of the racy content. Either an actor really got the material quickly and wanted to be in right away — or they really had to be coaxed into it. Mark Wahlberg was very keen the minute he read the script. He loved it. The people who represented him thought it was career suicide. It took a lot of persuading all the way through.

Boogie Nights (1997, New Line Cinema). Rollergirl (Heather Graham) sits in class by day and acts in adult films by night.

Can you tell me about the casting of Burt Reynolds in the part of Jack Horner?

I had previously cast him in *Striptease* with Demi Moore. He was having his comeback moment. Burt was great in *Striptease* and everyone really liked working with him. I did look at a number of different guys. There was a brief flirtation with Warren Beatty, but that didn't work out. I said to Paul, "I really think you should talk to Burt about it." Burt is a really fascinating guy. He is a real film buff and is extremely literate in terms of filmography. I think Paul was very surprised about how thoughtful and literate Burt is about movies. I don't think he displays that side of himself publicly that often. Burt is sort of funny and jolly and loves to wisecrack. So, I think Paul was surprised by this other third-dimensional side of Burt. Anyway, in the end, he was perfect in the role. Burt won the Golden Globe and was also nominated for an Oscar.

I thought it was a shame that Burt Reynolds didn't win the Oscar for Best Actor, which he totally deserved for this daring and risky role that he played so well.

Burt wanted to win that Oscar very badly. It was such a pity that he didn't get it. He truly deserved to win and I am not just saying that because I was the producer of the film. I thought it was a brave performance and it took guts to say "yes" to that role

Boogie Nights (1997, New Line Cinema). Porn star Dirk Diggler (Mark Wahlberg) and porn producer Jack Horner (Burt Reynolds) share a laugh in the editing room of Jack's house.

of Jack Horner. I spoke to him the next day after the Oscars and it was heartbreaking for me that he didn't win because Burt is such a nice man.

Boogie Nights did well at the box office and over the years it has gone on to be a cult classic. Did you ever think it would become so widely accepted?

Yes, absolutely. Paul is an amazing storyteller and I think, over the long haul, Paul will be one of those directors who will have a huge effect on the film industry. He is an unusually talented guy. I am really proud of the fact that I produced his first two movies.

What were the major production obstacles on Boogie Nights for the cast, the crew and you?

Boogie Nights was a truly grueling shoot. It was made for basically no money, $12 million. It was a period piece and we shot a lot of it in the San Fernando Valley and West Covina. It was very hot and we shot so many days where it was 104 or 105 degrees. We shot a lot at night, which was really exhausting. When we made that movie, there was a lot of talk about workers in the sex industry and how it was a liberating thing. The reality was that I think we all got sort of depressed during the making of the film. It was intense and the reality of the lives that those people were leading are far from glamorous. I think what is great about Paul's script is that it is not judgmental at all. It really does sort of zero in on what is universally human in all of those characters as opposed to their emotionally damaged lives that has led them into the sex industry.

Part of the reality was that I remember Julianne Moore being so quiet during the filming of that movie. I think a lot of it was her professionalism, but I also think that she very wisely left her real self at home when she took on this role. I think that was the only way to get through it for an actor because it was a dark script and a dark experience. It was an uneasy mixture of the real actors and porn actors who were in the movie. I remember that everybody was just really exhausted at the wrap party. At the wrap party, people were drinking like crazy. There were many crazy things that happened on *Boogie Nights* because there was a very volatile mixture of nudity and sex. There were scenes shot that were very graphic and very volatile that did not make it in the movie. We all kind of moved into the house we used, Jack Warner's old house in West Covina. We also wondered if the owners who rented us the house really knew what was going on there. I was always freaked out when they came to visit during the shooting. The owners would come by for lunch and check on things periodically and I would always pray that they would not show up for a scene like the one where the character Lina Harley is getting raped in their laundry room and is about to be shot. They could never feel the same about doing their laundry in that laundry room again. (*Laughing*) Overall, it was a very intense shoot.

Did New Line Cinema give you and Paul Thomas Anderson a lot of freedom with *Boogie Nights*?

They gave us total freedom. I think the key player was Mike De Luca, who really championed the project. He knew what that film was about and really supported it. When we started previewing it, which was a mistake because you should never preview a film like this, people started saying, "What the hell is this?" De Luca was always very calm and he knew it would find an audience and be a success. The only problems between Paul Thomas Anderson and Mike De Luca were on cutting the film. De Luca thought it was too long. I remember there was one very tense meeting at New Line where I think Mike De Luca was half-kidding when he said, "Why don't we just leave it the length it is and we'll put an intermission in it?" Paul's eyes lit up and said, "God, yes, that would be great. It will be just like the 1960s when there were all those epics and we'll have an intermission and a curtain will come down at the end of Act One." We all know that never happened. Ultimately, the studio could not have been more supportive of *Boogie Nights*. A lot of times a studio reads the scripts or they don't, who really knows, and they freak out when they see a finished product. However, New Line knew what this film was about from the get-go and I have always found them to be very "filmmaker friendly." As long as the filmmaker is being responsible, then I've found that they will be respectful to the artistic vision.

How did you connect with Mike Myers and get the opportunity to produce *Austin Powers II* and *III*?

I did a little movie in Ireland called *Pete's Meteor* and that is where I first met Mike Myers. We got along really well and Mike then asked me to produce *Austin Powers II*. Since I worked with New Line Cinema already and I knew all the people there, Mike thought it would be a good mix.

Austin Powers: Goldmember (2002, New Line Cinema). Austin Powers (Mike Myers), the ultimate man of mystery, happily sits behind the wheel of his '70s pimpmobile.

**There is a string of producers listed on the lobby card for *Austin Powers*. Why is
that?**

In terms of your book, I think this is a very interesting and understandably puz-
zling point on who does what, producer-wise, and what producers get credit. I think
people are endlessly confused by what a producer actually does on a movie and that is
mainly because there is no set definition of what a producer does. There is no set billing
that corresponds to the specific job. So, there is enormous confusion about titles like
executive producer, producer, associate producer and who does what. The reality is
that in every single situation, it is different. In the *Austin Powers* situation, the Team
Todd producing team was involved in the first *Austin Powers* movie, but not involved
in the second or third. They were crucial in the development of the first *Austin Powers* film and they had a deal with the studio that they get billed on the second and third
installments. Eric McLeod got added as a producer on the second and the third movies,
because he is the completely invaluable line producer and, without him, these movies
would not go as smoothly as they do. He had asked on the second one to be billed as
a producer because he was trying to break out of that executive producer rut he was
in. He asked if that was fine with me and I asked Mike, who said, "yes" because Eric
was working as a producer on a daily basis. That is the genesis of the tortured producer
credits on that movie. Also, that was why Mike and I are billed as producers on the

second one, because we were actually the real day-to-day producers of *Austin Powers II* and *III.*

How did it feel to take over a series that was getting hotter and hotter in its after-life, with video, DVD and cable sales going through the roof?

It was great, largely because I love Mike Myers and got to work with him on a daily basis. I have a huge amount of respect for him. He is one of the smartest men I have ever encountered in any field, not just the movie industry. He is well-read and an extremely thoughtful guy. I then met the director, Jay Roach, who is unique too, and they made it really easy for me to get into the process of making an *Austin Powers* movie. I loved taking over the task of producing this amazing franchise.

On the first *Austin Powers*, how did the then unknown director, Jay Roach, hook up with Mike Myers?

Mike and Jay were friends and, on the first *Austin Powers,* he asked Jay to give him notes and help on the script for the initial film. Jay gave Mike script notes. Mike read them and was stunned at how good they were. Mike saw that Jay had a genuine understanding of the material. Then, Mike said to Jay, "You should direct the film." Jay said, "They would never let me direct this film." Mike said, "That's it. I want you to direct the film and I will convince them." The studio was not happy initially about Jay directing but, to Mike De Luca's credit, they came around. New Line allowed him to direct that film and right now he is probably the hottest comedy director in Hollywood.

Did you suggest the casting of Heather Graham in *Austin Powers II* since you cast her in *Boogie Nights* as Rollergirl?

Yes, I did. I genuinely thought that Jay, Mike and Heather would really get along because Heather is so much fun to work with. I also thought that audiences should see Heather's fun and bubbly side. I felt she would be a cool, swinging 1960s chick. As a producer, I stay hugely involved in the casting. I suggested Beyonce Knowles for the part of Foxxy Cleopatra for *Austin Powers III*. I told the casting directors, Jeanine McCarthy and Juel Bestrop, about her and they thought she was really good too. I really pushed for Beyonce to get the role.

Could you tell me about the casting of Mini Me, Verne Troyer?

When Mike came up with the character of Mini Me, it was so funny, but we all wondered where we would find the guy to play the part. I think on the first day that we started seeing people, the casting director had an actual tape of him. Verne was perfect. He is 32 inches tall, properly proportioned, and he also had done a lot of stunt work doubling for babies, so we knew he could be physical. He came in and he was just perfect. It was one of those casting challenges you think would be hard, but it was not at all. Verne is an inspired actor. I hope one day that he can get a part that he can really act in third-dimensionally because he is so talented. Verne and Mike have a great relationship and they have wonderful chemistry together.

How do the budgets compare on all three *Austin Powers* movies?

I am not exactly positive about the first *Austin Powers,* but I think it was budgeted at $16 million. *II* was $34 million and *III* was $76 million.

How did you get all those cameos like Tom Cruise, Steven Spielberg, Gwyneth Paltrow, Britney Spears and more, for the third installment?

I have to say it had to do mainly with Mike Myers being incredibly persistent and extremely smart about how to reach out to people and make big things happen. We brainstormed and made a list of the famous people we wanted. Every cameo we wound up having were the very first people we asked for. Mike is friendly with Steven Spielberg and that was sort of the catalyst to getting other cameos. Tom Cruise was the one that was the most difficult cameo to land. At that point, Tom was heavily promoting *Vanilla Sky,* involved in flying all over the world. I think the key to the whole thing was that we stayed extremely flexible with schedules. We figured that it would take four to six hours from the time they got on the set until they left. It was one very nerve-wracking day at Paramount. We successfully shot the cameos in only six hours.

The opening of *Goldmember* was one of the most surprising and exciting openings I have ever seen.

Yes, it was pretty amazing. We really tried to keep the cameos a secret. After the previews, the journalists actually bought into the fun and honored keeping it a secret, except one irritating columnist from *The Washington Post.* I called him and said, "Please don't print it. It is not news and just keep it quiet so people can enjoy these surprise cameos in the theater." Even though he didn't listen and leaked it out, nobody really picked it up over the wire. I remember when we hit that first preview and Tom Cruise dropped into the frame, the audience just screamed! All the cameo actors and actresses were fantastic to work with.

What were your biggest production obstacles during the production of *Goldmember*?

The thing that was hard about that movie was that even though the budget was over $70 million, it was so much bigger than the second movie. It is sort of a musical without conventional songs. There was a lot of dancing, especially with the Britney Spears section. The musical numbers all needed an enormous amount of rehearsal time before we actually shot the scenes. Another major challenge was that we knew when we started "prep" that there was a very tight schedule leading up to the release of the film. We were tightly locked into a release date. We had a 16–week post-production schedule and two preview deadlines to meet, which for a movie of that size and budget, is not a long time. Scheduling was tough, especially when Mike Myers was playing four different characters. You had to shoot many sides of those scenes separately. You had to have Mike as Austin Powers, then Mike as Dr. Evil and then Mike as Goldmember. It took an enormous amount of time to shoot those scenes. The make-up of Goldmember and Dr. Evil is so intense that you can't do two make-ups in a single day. So, if you are doing a Dr. Evil shooting day, you have to fully commit to a Dr. Evil day. If you are doing a Goldmember shooting day, then you have to commit to that.

We had to put the scenes together in an intense way, so you have a full day with that particular character.

Were you nervous for this opening weekend?

I think you are always nervous. On *Austin Powers II*, when the budget was $32 million, I knew we could do well opening weekend. Once you have a big budget like $76 million, I think people were absolutely staggered about how much money it made so quickly in the theater. Nobody expected it to do that well, that quick.

The budget of *Austin Powers III* was $76 million and your next film was *Pieces of April*, the directorial debut of Peter Hedges. This film was extremely low-budget, correct?

The budget on *Pieces of April* was a fraction of the price of *Goldmember*. We shot it on Digital Video.

Your choices of films to produce are so varied. How can you go from producing the high-budget *Goldmember*, which was the hottest movie of Summer 2002, to producing a Digital Video project for practically no money?

I don't think I am spoiled and I think that makes it easier for me. Believe me, during the *Pieces of April* shoot, when I was driving myself in my rental car with my associate, Lucy, at 5 AM and stopping to pick up the donuts, I was not thrilled. However, it was also a great group of actors and the director/writer Peter Hedges is a wonderful talent. We also had a truly fantastic crew. There were so many talented people who came forward and volunteered to work on this movie — people who were way overqualified. So, there was a fantastic atmosphere on the set.

What do you look for in a director?

You look for curiosity, inquisitiveness and someone who is really willing to collaborate. I am very actor-oriented as a producer and I want a director that communicates well with an actor. All the first-time directors I have worked with were all really great writers and it always starts with the script. If the script is good, and if they are able to communicate their ideas about the script, which not all writers can, then I think you are in really good shape.

What do you look for in an actor or actress?

You are always looking for that explosive connection to a part that will somehow lift the material and really make it "sing." It is the idea that the actor or actress is going to bring to the performance, something so very special and unique, that they are going to make the part memorable.

What is your goal as a producer on a movie?

My goal is to make it an easier atmosphere in which the creative people can collaborate. I want them to feel as free as possible while shooting. Whatever obstacles which are lurking out there, my role is to move them out the way so their path is clear to think. I want them to feel that they are in an environment that is comfortable to work and flourish in. I think it is also a holdover from my theater days to show how possible things are in rehearsal. If every day on a movie set can feel like a perfect rehearsal, then you are really lucky. As a producer, you want to make it as easy as possible to keep the cast and crew focused on the work.

Any advice you can give to an aspiring director?

Write a great script. The people who have the leg up in this business are the people who can write.

What does the future hold?

Early retirement! (*Laughing*) I have another film set up at New Line Cinema that I am hopefully starting soon. I would love to do another movie very soon with Peter Hedges. He is a great writing and directing talent and a great person. There is a lot of positive stuff in the offing!

John Lyons Filmography

Pieces of April (Katie Holmes, Oliver Platt) 2003 — producer; *Austin Powers in Goldmember* (Mike Myers, Beyonce Knowles) 2002 — producer; *The Opportunists* (Christopher Walken, Peter McDonald) 2000— producer; *Austin Powers: The Spy Who Shagged Me* (Mike Myers, Heather Graham) 1999 — producer; *Pete's Meteor* (Mike Myers, Brenda Fricker) 1998 — producer; *Boogie Nights* (Mark Whalberg, Burt Reynolds, Julianne Moore) 1997 — producer; *Sydney —(aka Hard Eight)* (Samuel L. Jackson, Gwyneth Paltrow) 1996 — producer

Mace Neufeld

Mace Neufeld is a true "Renaissance Man." He began his career as a photographer, taking a picture (at age 15) of a young soldier coming home after World War II that was syndicated all over the country. With that photo, he won first prize in an Eastman Kodak High School Photography Contest. After college, he began songwriting and sold numerous pieces. He then went into the management business, representing talent such as Don Knotts and Don Adams as well as musical acts like Herb Alpert and the Carpenters. Always wanting to go to sunny California, Neufeld left with his family and headed out to Los Angeles to start a career in movie producing. His first film was The Omen *(1976) starring Gregory Peck and Lee Remick. It was a major financial and critical hit. Neufeld has gone on to produce many other box office hits, most notably the film versions of best-selling author Tom Clancy's books, including* The Hunt for Red October, Clear and Present Danger, Patriot Games *and* The Sum of All Fears.

There was one movie that affected me when I was only five years old and I have since searched and searched for the title of the film, but I have, unfortunately, not come up with it. All I remember from this film of the 1930s was a disembodied head floating down a dark staircase, which really frightened me. This vivid memory may have subliminally influenced me to produce my first film in 1976, *The Omen*, starring Gregory Peck and Lee Remick. That '30s fright flick was my earliest memory of film. My second memory of a movie was seeing *Little Lord Fauntleroy* with Freddie Bartholomew and Mickey Rooney. I was taken to see it on my seventh birthday. Generally, I would go every Saturday to the movies with my first cousin, who is two years older than me. I remember that in those days they had a children's section of the theater with a matron in a white uniform who watched the children.

By the end of the day, I don't think her uniform was too white.

(*Laughing*) By the end of the day, her uniform looked more like a rainbow. Movies were a major part of my life growing up. During high school in New York, my friends and I would go to the Loew's State or the Capitol or the Paramount Theater to see movies and also to see Benny Goodman or Frank Sinatra or any of the other musical artists who performed between the movies. Or, as the *artists* thought, they ran movies in between their performances. (*Laughing*) I was always fascinated by movies that dealt with California youth. You know what I'm talking about — the kind of movies with the station wagons and the pretty girls on the beach. I had never been to California and my perceptions were built entirely on what I saw in the movies. My dream as a youth was not necessarily to make movies, but to go to California and see those beautiful blonde girls and sunny beaches.

Then why did you attend Yale University instead of going to school in California?
I attended Yale in protest. When I was in high school, I did a lot of photography and I was actually working for a women's clothing store, getting paid a substantial amount of money to take pictures of their dresses. Then, Eastman Kodak had their first High School Photography Contest and I entered a group of my pictures and won six prizes. I got a lot of attention for one particular picture that I took when I was 15 of a young soldier coming home from World War II in 1944. It was taken on the East Side of Manhattan, was published on a full page in the *New York Daily News* and was syndicated all over the country. I began to get inquiries from colleges that had photography departments. At the time, I decided I wanted to be a film cinematographer. I spoke to USC, but since I was very young, my parents did not want me to go to California. As far as they were concerned, California was as far away as Tokyo. They wanted me to go local and I decided on Yale. One thing that was great for me during college was that the Shubert Theater was in New Haven and it was the number one stop for out of town previews of Broadway-bound shows. I saw Marlon Brando in Tennessee William's *Streetcar Named Desire* and I saw two legendary Arthur Miller plays, *All My Sons* and *Death of a Salesman*.

What did you do about your dreams of becoming a cinematographer?
When I graduated from Yale, my dreams of becoming a cinematographer began to dissipate. I decided to do some songwriting with a friend of mine who had just graduated from Colgate. We wrote from late afternoon to late evening and then we went to the Brill Building to try to sell our songs.

Did you have much success?
Yes, I got songs published and I started writing special material for certain singers. Actually, this is how I slid into the management business, because there was a singer by the name of Dorothy Loudon who had just gotten out of Syracuse, who we heard singing at club called Jimmy Ryan's on 52nd Street. We talked and she asked if I could get her a record contract. I figured if I got her a record contract, then she would record *our* songs. So, I got her a record contract and she asked if I would be her manager.

Well, it seems you were doing the job of being a good manager thus far, anyway.
(*Laughing*) Yes, I was. I then called a lawyer friend and he sent me over a sample contract and I was in business as a talent manager with this one client. My partner in the management business was the son of a very talented musical conductor by the name of Ray Block. We developed the most important management company in the 1960s and '70s. I started the careers of musical acts like Herb Alpert and the Carpenters. Actually, A&M Records started their business with our clients. We went on to manage comedians like Don Adams [*Get Smart*] and Don Knotts [*The Andy Griffith Show*]. I

also began to put my clients on *The Steve Allen Show*. Then *The Steve Allen Show* moved from New York to Los Angeles, so I decided to move out here in 1961 and I thought California was prettier than in the movies. I moved my family to California on June 10, 1962, and I never looked back.

Did going from talent manager to movie producer seem like the natural progression for you in your career?

I really didn't enjoy the management business. It was something I never really wanted to do. My approach to management at that time was that the manager was the invisible person and the talent was the important one. It was basically a service business. I felt it was time to try something different.

Mace Neufeld

In 1976, you produced your first film, *The Omen*, starring Gregory Peck. Earlier you said that maybe the head you saw floating down the stairs in the old 1930s thriller might have somehow influenced you to produce this film. But can you tell me how this project came about?

A friend of mine, Harvey Bernhard, came to me with an idea to develop a script about the Anti-Christ. So, we hired a writer and developed a script called *The Anti-Christ* and I took it to the head of production at Warner Brothers and he decided to option the script. Then, we attached a director by the name of Chuck Bail and, over the next year, we tried to get this project off the ground. Unfortunately, we couldn't. Through my contacts in the music business, I was invited to a party by Joan Collins, whose then husband was running Apple Records for the Beatles. I didn't know anyone at the party except for one person standing at the bar, Richard Donner, who I knew because he directed many of the first season's episodes of *Get Smart*. We began to talk and he said he was looking for a really good script because his ex-agent Alan Ladd, Jr., was now running 20th Century–Fox and he thought Alan could set him up with a deal. I sent Donner the script and within three or four days we had a meeting with 20th. They agreed to do the picture. I got Warner Brothers to turn around the rights to Fox and I was now producing my first feature film.

Did you find the skills that you picked up from management helped you in movie producing?

All of the skills that I picked up in the management business have been extremely helpful in all facets of my producing career. For instance, my music background was helpful in dealing with composers on my films. My photography background has been helpful when I deal with the cinematographers on my films. My basic management

The Omen (1976, Twentieth Century–Fox) American diplomat Robert Thorn (Gregory Peck) grimaces at a bizarre turn of events.

skills have been helpful when I deal with stars on my movies. These skills that I obtained helped me become what I like to call an "old school" producer — a producer who is involved in his films from soup to nuts.

In 1989, you teamed up with Robert Rehme to form Rehme/Neufeld productions. Could you tell me about your partnership?

I optioned the book *The Hunt for Red October* in 1985 and it took me almost four years to get a studio to do it. Over that period of time, I started a company in 1989 with Bob Rehme. Bob, who had been an executive at many companies, teamed up with me and we decided to start an independent film company under the Paramount Pictures banner. We produced movies like *Patriot Games, Clear and Present Danger, Necessary Roughness* and *Beverly Hills Cop III*. About six or seven years ago, we ended our partnership and I'm now producing under Sony Pictures by myself.

When you optioned the rights to Tom Clancy's book, *The Hunt for Red October*, what did you see in it that made you feel it was a great movie and ultimately the basis for one of the most successful characters, Jack Ryan, in film history?

There was a young AFI film school graduate working for me who I sent down to the Dallas Book Fair to see what was coming up. He came back with a book called *The Hunt for Red October*. It was the first work of fiction published by the Naval Institute

Press. He urged me to read it and it sat on my night table for three or four weeks. Finally, one night, I could not sleep and I decided to pick it up. Once I began reading it, I couldn't put it down. I loved it and wanted to make it into a major motion picture. I found out that there was a local agent representing the Naval Institute Press, so I contacted him and began negotiations to option the book. No one had ever heard of the book, but two weeks into the negotiations there was an article in *Time* magazine that said it was President Reagan's favorite book. It quickly began selling heavily in the Washington, DC, area. I then thought to myself, "Here goes the price. It's now going to go way up!" I immediately got on the phone with the agent and said, "I want to close the deal right now." He said, "Okay, what was your last offer?" I told him and then he said, "Fine, send over the contract." Two or three days later, he called me and said, "When you called me the other day, I did not see that article in *Time* magazine. This is not a fair deal." I replied, "Yes, it is a fair deal. The book is only selling in Washington and is not a best-seller yet." The agent agreed and we went forward with the original agreement.

Did you meet Clancy prior to the signing of the option to talk about the book and where you wanted to go with making it into a feature film?

No, I did not meet him prior to the option. Tom did write me a note immediately that stated, in short, "Mr. Neufeld, thank you for having the confidence in my book to put some money on the line. I do not know too much about the movie business. But, I do know a lot about submarines, so if I can be helpful to you, please let me know," etc, etc, etc. After that, I met with him many times. We had a great relationship during the making of the film. Tom brought his family out while we were shooting and was introduced to Sean Connery and Alec Baldwin. We also showed him the dailies. In the end, the film was an enormous hit. Interestingly enough, it was released in March, which is considered to be a dead month in the movie business. This was a very important lesson to me, that if you make it well and sell it well, customers will come to the theaters.

What was the budget on the film?

The budget was $47 million and it pulled in $126 million opening weekend.

How does it feel to produce a movie and wake up Monday morning after the opening weekend and see those types of numbers?

This was not the first time this kind of big opening had happened to me. It happened with my first film, *The Omen*. That movie cost me slightly over $2 million and since it was done under the British tax plan, there was a rebate. So in the end, the film cost about $1.8 million. The opening weekend, we pulled in $4.4 million. This meant that it was in net profits in just four days. That was the first and last time that happened in my career.

You got spoiled quickly.

(*Laughing*) I began to think this happens on every film. Friends of mine advised me to quit while I was ahead. But, *The Hunt for Red October* was very, very exciting. I

Top: The Hunt for Red October (1990, Paramount Pictures). Marko Alexandrovich Ramius (Sean Connery), captain of the Soviet Typhoon submarine *Red October*, radios plans to terminate the rogue sub heading for U.S. waters. *Bottom: The Hunt for Red October* (1990, Paramount Pictures). Jack Ryan (Alec Baldwin) stalks a KGB agent in the missile bay of the Soviet nuclear submarine *Red October.*

remember standing in the lobby of the theater where it premiered with Frank Mancuso,
who was the chairman of Paramount Pictures. Frank said, "Enjoy it, Mace, because
it never gets any better than this."

**Has it ever gotten better than *The Hunt for
Red October* in your career?**

Sure, it has gotten better. But, when it
doesn't get at least as good, then that will be
the time I quit.

**How did you decide which film, *Patriot
Games* or *Clear and Present Danger*, to
produce next?**

Well, *Patriot Games* and *Clear and Present Danger* were very connected. We premiered *The Hunt for Red October* in
Washington, DC, and there was actually a

The Hunt for Red October (1990, Paramount
Pictures). Best-selling author Tom Clancy
visited the sound stages at Paramount Studios as his novel was turned into a movie.

party at Tom Clancy's house afterwards. On the plane going back to California, Frank
Mancuso said, "Tell me about the other Clancy books." I said, "Well, there is *Patriot
Games* and *Clear and Present Danger*." He then said, "We should option both of them
immediately." I agreed. He then asked, "Which do you want to produce first?" I said,
"I think *Patriot Games* deals more with Jack Ryan the person. I think we should do
both movies, but *Clear and Present Danger* should be first." I went back to California
and set Don Stewart to work writing *Clear and Present Danger*. He had written the
script for *The Hunt for Red October*. Along the way, I had expected that John McTiernan should direct *Patriot Games*. He did not want to do it. McTiernan felt it would
not be a success and it would kill the franchise. He was then out of the picture. Alec
Baldwin was soon out of the picture as well.

**As the producer on this project, what were your next steps to keep this multi-mil-
lion dollar franchise alive?**

I was in a very tough place. I not only needed a director who understood the
script, but I also needed a star to play the lead. I eventually decided on Phillip Noyce
to direct the film. I had seen a film he directed called *Dead Calm* and I really liked it.
Many years before I had seen a film called *Newsfront* that Phillip had also done. That
was a little motion picture that I really liked, too. We then sent the script to Harrison
Ford. Harrison immediately responded, overnight. Harrison had just left a film and he
was eager to do *Clear and Present Danger*. He called me and said, "Who do you have
in mind for a director?" I thought, "Oh my God, Harrison never goes to the movies
and he would have not heard of Phillip Noyce." I said, "Well, it is a fine director by
the name of Phillip Noyce. He did a great film with Nicole Kidman called *Dead Calm*."
He replied, "I have never seen it. What else has he done?" I then said, "Well, he directed
a smaller film called *Newsfront* that did a film festival run." He surprised me by say-

ing, "I saw that film at a festival and I loved it." Then, Phillip Noyce and I flew down to Harrison's house in Jackson Hole and the next thing I knew, we had Harrison Ford to play Jack Ryan and Phillip Noyce directing.

Even though Harrison Ford is a major star, was the studio a little nervous using another actor in this key part?

They got the confidence back when I attached Harrison Ford to the project. He is a huge star, a multi-talented actor and he understood Jack Ryan.

You launched the careers of many top actors and directors. You cast Kevin Costner in his first film, *No Way Out*, and Alec Baldwin in his first starring role in *Hunt for Red October*. You also launched the careers of directors like Noyce. Do you think it is important as a producer to not only have the ability to recognize talent but to be a mentor as well?

Alec and Kevin are extremely talented actors. Look how great their careers have gone on to be. Kevin is now directing movies. Phillip Noyce has just been a pleasure to work with. I don't think it is important to be a mentor as much as it is to be a partner. I always want to be a true collaborator with everyone I work with. What I need to know from a director is what he needs from me in order to do his job right. Up until the moment he says, "Action," all the things around him are basically what I had instituted and set up as a producer. Once he says, "Action," my director is in total command and once he says, "Cut," we can talk. I have heard producers being described as "expeditors," but I also think it is important for a producer to know when to move in and when to fade into the background during a production. A movie production is the most difficult collaborative commercial art form that exists. You have 200 or more artists in their own right trying to pull together and team up to make a movie, which is, in essence, a unique art form. Getting a good movie made, no less a great movie, is a miracle. My job as a producer is to get everyone working together harmoniously.

Do you consider yourself a creative producer?

You bet! That is why I left the management business. The management business was far too uncreative for me. I spend a lot of time looking at and listening to many, many pitches. I read many, many books. I very rarely get a "spec" screenplay that I like. So, since I almost always develop my own projects, I have to think creatively on every aspect of the film. I have to talk to the writer of a book and try to figure out what from the 600–page book will appear in the 140–page script. I then have to figure out who the director is going to be, and if we will get along and if he will understand the material. Then, I have to think, "Will the studio buy it?" Then, I have to go through the budgeting process. Creatively, I try to be on the set most of the time because I will watch a director shoot ten takes and perhaps hear him ask to print takes 1, 5 and 7. However, if I think take number 8 is a better one, I will ask them to print take 8. With a new director on a big movie, I'll be asked what I think and I will help it along the way with my opinions. Directing is one of the most difficult jobs in the world. They have every department head asking them questions. Directors keep very long hours and do not get enough sleep and so on. Part of my job is making the director feel comfortable and supporting him as much as possible on the film. I want to have my own creative touch on each of my movies.

Is the studio usually breathing down your neck, making sure you stay on budget during your movies?

I have found it to be the opposite during my career. Once the studios "green light" a film with me, we go off and make the picture. As a matter of fact, when we were shooting part of *Patriot Games* in London, I didn't hear from the studio for five days. We had been sending the studio the dailies and since I did not hear from them, I finally called. I said, "The shoot is going very well." The studio replied, "Yes, it is. We have been watching the dailies." I then said, "I think it would be smart to pick up the phone and call Harrison Ford and Phillip Noyce and say, Hey fellas, the movie looks great.'" They said, "Sure, that is a great idea." So, I think it has been the opposite. I think the studio really trusts me to deliver the film that they want based on the budget that I sign. The director and the producer sign the budget with the studio, but if you go over, it is not like they throw you in "film jail." (*Laughing*) It is still a major responsibility and I never consider a studio to be the enemy when I am making a film. After all, it is their money.

Do you think the title of "producer" holds any credence today?

No. It means something to me and it means something to some studio heads, but I think the public is in total confusion about the function of the producer. Some people get confused and think the producer is the director. I always explain the term at length when I meet people outside of the business. I think that since the Motion Picture Academy gives the award for Best Picture to the producer, they still acknowledge what the producer function is. Over the last six years, the title of producer has truly been diluted, disgraced and desecrated.

Why do you think the "producer" title has become so tarnished and misunderstood?

I think people have gotten involved with the film business who use their position as either a lawyer, an accountant, a friend of a star, a wife or a husband to get a credit on screen. I have rarely shared a producer credit on any of my films, except when I was partners with Bob Rehme. We were a partnership in the sense that I was the hands-on producer while Bob ran the company when I was on location. I am hard-pressed now to share a producer credit because I do not need any help producing a film. I know how to produce a film and produce it well. I think the producer title has fallen on bad times and I think a lot of it is because of the studios. The studios feel it is easier to give a credit to someone rather than give them money. It has become a joke in the movie business and I think that is the fault of the producers. The producers should have gotten together early in the game and formed a union, which they are trying to do now with the Producers Guild, and said, "No, I am the only producer on this project and that is final!" If we stood up, maybe we would have gotten some results. True, some may have lost their jobs, but you have to be willing to say *no* to get what you want.

Clear and Present Danger (1994, Paramount Pictures). With the Cold War over, CIA agent Jack Ryan (Harrison Ford, *right*) discovers a link between a presidental advisor and a South American drug cartel.

What in your career have you not accomplished that you want to?

I have gotten Golden Globes, but I have never gotten an Academy Award. I would really love to receive an Academy Award before my career is over.

I know that you recently received a star on the Hollywood Walk of Fame. I had also heard that you might be one of the last producers to receive one, mainly because people from foreign countries and the more provincial areas of America do not know enough about producers. Hence, it does not attract attention. How do you feel about that?

You mean my star has ruined it for all other producers? (*Laughing*) I feel that producers deserve to be on the Hollywood Walk of Fame if their work during their career warrants it. I think it would be a major mistake to drop them off. I do know that if there were not many producers, then there would be many fewer movies. The studio system is not geared up that way any more. The producer is the one that starts the film and stays with it all the way through to approving the trailer and publicity. So, it is very hard to make a film without a producer.

Is making movies your biggest passion?

My biggest passion is my family. I love to spend time with them. I also love to fly airplanes and I would like to bring photography back into my life. I was thinking of doing a photography book of my latest film production. One of my biggest passions is a good story. I have a lot of great scripts with great stories that I would like to do, but I do not know if I am going to live long enough to do all of them. However, I am sure going to try.

Mace Neufeld Filmography

Gods and Generals (Jeff Daniels, Robert Duvall) 2003 — executive producer; *The Sum of All Fears* (Ben Affleck, Morgan Freeman) 2002 — producer; *Love and Treason* (Timothy Carhart, Kim Delaney) 2001 TV — executive producer; *Bless the Child* (Kim Basinger, Jimmy Smits) 2000 — producer; *The General's Daughter* (John Travolta, Madeleine Stowe) 1999 — producer; *Black Dog* (Patrick Swayze, Meat Loaf, Randy Travis) 1998 — executive producer; *Lost in Space* (William Hurt, Mimi Rogers, Heather Graham) 1998 — executive producer; *Blind Faith* (Charles Dutton, Courtney B. Vance) 1998 — executive producer; *The Saint* (Val Kilmer, Elisabeth Shue) 1997 — producer; *Gridlock* (David Hasselhoff, Kathy Ireland) 1996 TV — producer; *Clear and Present Danger* (Harrison Ford, Willem Dafoe, Anne Archer) 1994 — producer; *Beverly Hills Cop III* (Eddie Murphy) 1994 — producer; *Patriot Games* (Harrison Ford, Anne Archer, Patrick Bergin) 1992 — producer; *Necessary Roughness* (Scott Bakula, Hector Elizondo, Robert Loggia) 1991 — producer; *Omen IV: The Awakening* (Faye Grant, Michael Woods) 1991 TV — executive producer; *Flight of the Intruder* (Danny Glover, Willem Dafoe) 1991 — producer; *The Hunt for Red October* (Sean Connery, Alec Baldwin) 1990 — producer; *No Way Out* (Kevin Costner, Gene Hackman) 1987 — executive producer; *Transylvania 6-5000* (Jeff Goldblum, Joseph Bologna) 1985 — producer; *A Death in California* (Cheryl Ladd, Sam Elliott) 1985 TV — executive producer; *The Aviator* (Christopher Reeve, Rosanna Arquette) 1985 — producer; *The Final Conflict* (Sam Neill, Rossano Brazzi, Don Gordon) 1981 — associate producer; *The Funhouse* (Elizabeth Berridge, Cooper Huckabee) 1981 — executive producer; *East of Eden* (Timothy Buttoms, Jane Seymour) 1981 TV — executive producer; *Angel on My Shoulder* (Peter Strauss, Richard Kiley) 1980 TV — executive producer; *The Frisco Kid* (Gene Wilder, Harrison Ford, Ramon Bieri) 1979 — producer; *Damien: Omen II* (William Holden, Lee Grant) 1978 — associate producer; *Quark* (Richard Benjamin, Richard Kelton) 1978 — TV Series co-executive producer; *The Omen* (Gregory Peck, Lee Remick) 1976– executive producer

Barbara De Fina

Barbara De Fina grew up in West New York, New Jersey, directly across the Hudson River from New York City. Drawn to the city because of its creative influence, Barbara found herself leaving Barnard College and making the daring decision to enter the film industry. She proceeded to work her way up on various feature film projects, going from a production assistant on The Taking of Pelham One Two Three, *to a production coordinator on* Interiors, *directed by Woody Allen, to an associate producer position on* Spring Break. *De Fina's first producing job came on the hit film* The Color of Money, *starring Paul Newman and Tom Cruise and directed by Martin Scorsese. Barbara became Scorsese's producing partner and went on to produce his* The Last Temptation of Christ, GoodFellas, Cape Fear *and* Casino.

I don't think I ever had the moment where I looked up at a movie screen and a film affected me so much that I knew I was going to work in the movie industry for the rest of my life. I think the thing that had influenced me the most, which I have heard a lot of other people say, is *Million Dollar Movie*, which was on a local New York area television station. They played the same movie every day for a week. You would come home, turn on the television and sometimes you would see the whole movie. Sometimes you would turn on the television and the movie would be halfway over. The station would air every kind of classic film from *King Kong* with Fay Wrey, to *Gunga Din* with Cary Grant and Douglas Fairbanks, Jr., to *Rebecca* with Laurence Olivier and Joan Fontaine — something for everyone, great variety. Through this program, I was able to study and analyze movies. Some movies I would watch five times, five days in a row. Through the repetition of the same movie, I really studied film and learned how movies worked. That's my first recollection of film.

Did you have any creative influences in your childhood?
I was born in West New York, New Jersey, just across the river from Manhattan. Growing up so close to New York City is very helpful in your growth as a creative person. By taking a quick trip across the Hudson, I got to explore one of the most artistic cities in the world. I think the thing that influenced my creative side the most during my childhood was my high school. I attended a small private school with only 13 students in a class. I had this really great English teacher who took us to see "live" theater. She took us to see *Cabaret* and it really affected me in a positive way. If that teacher

did that today, I think she would get fired, probably because the show was a little risqué to provincial, small minds. She was a true individual with conviction. My parents were not creative people at all. They were very blue collar. My mother worked as an executive secretary and my father worked for Allied Chemical for many years. My mother did take me to the movies all the time and my father was a very avid reader. After he finished his daily shift at work, he would come home and read for hours. My father would read the newspaper from front to back. He would also read a lot of novels. My father does not read as much now, but through my work he has grown to love movies.

Barbara De Fina

Did you attend film school to get educated on the process of filmmaking?

No. I did go to college for a year and then I decided to quit school and join "the circus"—by that, of course, I mean "the circus" that I like to call the film industry. Honestly speaking, I was really bored in college and when I discovered working in movies, I knew that was the career for me. I think if I were enrolled in a theater school like Carnegie Tech, I would have stayed. I felt I was studying the same courses like math, science and English all over again, just as I had done in high school. I wish I had studied drama in college. I probably would have stayed and found it rewarding.

How did you wind up working in the film business?

I stumbled upon a job in a television commercial production company. They hired me to work in their studio. Through this job, I met a lot of talented crew people who worked not only on commercials, but on feature films as well. Through these contacts at the commercial company, I got introduced to working on feature films. At that point in time, there was a lot of film work in New York City. I entered the business at a very opportune time, and once I started working in it, I quickly fell in love with it. The first movie I ever worked on was called *Blood Kin*, directed by Sidney Lumet. It was originally a play by Tennessee Williams. The film had an incredible cast. It starred James Coburn and Lynn Redgrave. We had a great director of photography by the name of James Wong Howe who was in his seventies then and a true master of cinematography. He, unfortunately, has since passed away. I was so lucky to have the opportunity to work with such experienced professionals on my first film and be able to sit back and watch it all happen. I worked my way up the ranks of the feature film business. I worked on *The Taking of Pelham One Two Three* starring Walter Malthan. I was a production coordinator on *The Gambler*, which was directed by Karel Reisz and starred James Caan. So, I worked on various films in various capacities.

When did you first meet director Martin Scorsese?

I worked as a production coordinator on feature films for many years. The last one I worked on was *Interiors*, directed by Woody Allen, in the late 1970s. At that point in time, I decided I didn't want to production coordinate anymore. Then, I did some associate producer work on a couple of movies with director Sean Cunningham, who directed the first *Friday the 13th*. We did this teen movie together called *Spring Break* that wound up making a lot of money. During this time, Marty Scorsese was editing a film he directed called *The King of Comedy* starring Robert De Niro, Jerry Lewis and Sandra Bernhard. I had just come back from Florida after working on *Spring Break* and a friend of mine called me, wondering if I could work in her place during the additional photography for *The King of Comedy*. So, I took the job and that was when I first met Marty. This job turned out to be very important because it led to my first film as a producer, *Color of Money*. Marty directed and it starred Paul Newman and Tom Cruise. Paul, of course, was excellent and won the Oscar for Best Actor for it in 1986.

Was it a difficult process producing your first film?

The Color of Money was a fairly self-contained movie. Originally, we were asked to shoot in Canada. However, the problem was that all the tables in Canada were snooker tables, not pool tables. So, in the end, we decided on shooting in Chicago. I hired a great production manager named Dodie Foster, who I had a previous relationship with from working together on other films. Dodie was very important to have on that shoot because she was originally from Chicago and knew the ins and outs of shooting there. I found that Chicago is an easier place to work in than New York City because it is not as congested and there was a lot more cooperation from the city. *The Color of Money* was a fairly simple movie and we had to build maybe one set. It was all practical locations. The transition to producer wasn't too difficult for me because I had a great physical production background. Since I prepped the movie properly, instead of 50 days of shooting, we completed the film in 49 days; and instead of a $14.5 million budget, we came in $1.5 million under at $13 million.

What I did have to start learning as a producer on *The Color of Money* was about script development. The development process for this film was tough. Paul Newman, who was a big fan of *Raging Bull*, called Marty and was wondering if he would be interested in directing *The Color of Money*, a kind of sequel to *The Hustler*. Paul sent him a script, but Marty didn't like it. Marty then developed it further with Paul Newman and brought in a writer by the name of Richard Price, who was a novelist who had written *The Wanderers*. They struggled with the script for nine months. It was hard trying to figure out what to do with the character of Minnesota Fats. I think there was a draft where he was in the script but, ultimately, he wasn't in the movie. The development process was not easy. So, I learned a very good lesson as a first-time producer. The script is everything. I also learned how to deal more with the actors. So, on *The Color of Money* I learned about these other aspects of producing.

For a first-time producer, it must have been a dream to work with a cast of actors like Paul Newman and Tom Cruise. Did you see it that way?

It was an easy production for me because I had the wonderful opportunity to pro-

The Color of Money (1986, Touchstone Pictures). Pool hustler Fast Eddie Felson (Paul Newman) stares down his next opponent.

duce my first film with such professional actors. Paul Newman was a fabulous actor to work with because he cares so much about the script. If you look at his long and successful career, he only does movies that are story-driven. Tom Cruise was not a big star yet. He had done *Top Gun*, but it hadn't come out yet. When *The Color of Money* was released, he was truly a big star. Paul Newman and Tom Cruise were total professionals throughout the production. They were great with Marty and treated him with so much respect. Looking back, it was the perfect movie for me to be provided with the best transition into producing.

The next project that you produced was a Michael Jackson *Bad* video. After big screen success, why would you produce a music video? Also, why would Scorsese direct it, because aren't videos something a director does to help him or her break into film directing?

When you produce for a talented director like Martin Scorsese, unusual offers like this arise. Marty's directing skills are revered by people in all professions, from film to music, to fashion. Michael Jackson was a big fan of *Mean Streets* and earnestly wanted Marty to direct his stylish and gritty video concept for *Bad*. It was a truly dynamic song. Marty knew that because Michael is such a talented dancer that he could have a lot of fun shooting this music video. Actually, it didn't really feel like a music video. It felt more like a small movie because there was a very significant story there. There are two parts to the video of *Bad*. One was the music part that everyone sees on MTV, but the other part, that Marty applied his forte to, were the gang scenes. This 16–minute film cost $2 million to make. It is amazing to think that *Taxi Driver* only cost $1.3 million to make. I guess the difference here was that Jackson paid for the video out of his own pocket. It was a great opportunity; a lot of fun, and Marty hasn't done a music video since. Today, the videos are much more music-driven, so, personally, I don't know if I would be able to produce them.

The next film that you produced was *The Last Temptation of Christ*. Was it hard for you to secure financing for this very risky and controversial film?

The original financing for that film was something Marty had started before I even met him. He had a pretty substantial budget and had gotten pretty far down the road with Michael Eisner and Jeffrey Katzenberg of (back then) Paramount. It had been developed and started as a major studio movie adapted from a fine novel by Nikos Kazantzakis. Then, at one point, everyone realized what trouble they were in with the Moral Majority and the far right. Frank Mancuso, head of distribution at Paramount, got a phone call from the head of the United Artists Theater Chain who told him he would not show *The Last Temptation of Christ* in his theaters. United Artists would not show the movie because they were afraid that their theaters would be destroyed. They felt they would be fire bombed. Well, that was the beginning of the end. They were in the middle of building sets in Israel and had already spent $5 million when Paramount decided to pull the plug and end the production. Paramount felt that they would never get their investment back. Even though film making is a creative medium, you quickly learn from working in this business that it is, in fact, a business and for studios it is about making a profit.

Then, nobody did anything with *The Last Temptation of Christ* project for a while. I knew that, deep down inside for Marty, this film was his dream film to make. Marty told me that he had always wanted to make a film portraying Christ. So, I said "No studio, Marty. Let's do *The Last Temptation of Christ* like an independent movie." So I then designed a $7 million budget. It had been originally budgeted at $30 million. I thought that if we got the budget down really low, somebody might be interested. After *The Color of Money,* Marty got a deal at Disney, pitched it to them and they rejected him. Tom Pollack, who was just made the head of Universal, was told about *The Last Temptation of Christ* by Mike Ovitz, who at that time was Paul Newman's agent and soon Marty's agent as well. Pollack said that for $7 million he'd do it as long as he could be assured that there was a theater chain that would be willing to show it. Then Garth Drabinsky, the head of Cineplex Odeon, said he would put it in the theaters. In fact, he actually wound up partially financing the picture as well. So that is how we got *The Last Temptation of Christ* financed and Marty got his Oscar nomination for Best Director in 1998. This also made us move over to Universal, where we stayed for a long time and made a lot of great movies.

The Last Temptation of Christ (1988, Universal). Martin Scorsese's controversial adaptation of the Nikos Kazantzakis novel portrayed Christ (Willem Dafoe) in the last year of his life.

As a producer, how did you handle the protests during production?

We went off to Morocco to make the movie. Since it was a movie about Jesus and not Mohammed, we were allowed to shoot in Morocco. To shoot in Israel was way too expensive and was going to be quite difficult. Morocco turned out to be a lot cheaper. We successfully made *The Last Temptation of Christ* with no protests at all. That was because we were outside of the United States.

How did you think the protests affected the film monetarily at the box office?

The Last Temptation of Christ wasn't treated as a movie. It was treated as an issue. I have seen this happen with other films. We got a lot of press. It was on the front cover of *Time* magazine. The film was talked about all over television. So, the awareness with the public was not about going to see the movie, but it was more centered around the controversy involving the movie. In retrospect, I believe *The Last Temptation of Christ* didn't do well because it was like a symptom of the disease. Protesters picketed Universal and even picketed outside the home of Lou Wasserman, the chairman of MCA. There were protests in Europe as well. Sadly, some turned violent. After *The Last Temptation of Christ* left the theaters, it was not allowed to be shown on TV for a long time. Even cable TV stations didn't want to show it. No airlines would show it to their passengers. Today *The Last Temptation of Christ* is shown everywhere, but at that point in time, it was extremely hard to make money with it. However, it was Marty's dream to make this film and it stands as an exceptional statement of artistic vision.

The next feature film that you produced and collaborated with Scorsese on was *GoodFellas*. This movie was a very long period piece with many, many characters and many, many locations. Was this a difficult film to produce?

It was very difficult to produce. The budget was $25 million, which was not that big considering the cast — Robert De Niro, Joe Pesci, Ray Liotta and so many great actors and actresses — and size of the film. During production, we were a little over-schedule and the studio was constantly complaining. I was dealing with all the studio problems so that Marty could solely concentrate on the film. I think underneath it all, the studio was nervous because they were not sure what was going to ultimately happen with the movie. It was a different type of film for them. It was violent and it was funny. Due to the fact that the film did not fit into a particular genre, I think they were extremely nervous about it. To the studio's credit, neither did the public. The previews did not go well. In fact, they went horrible, which made the studio even more nervous. The audience would get very agitated. Remember, when people come into a movie preview, they don't know anything about the movie. They haven't seen an ad, trailer or a review. So, the audience, during the previews, had absolutely no idea what to expect. During the previews, a lot of women walked out. I remember a preview card with just the words, "Fuck You." People got really emotional. Ironically, they were often using on the preview cards the same gritty language that they objected to on the screen. The studio had no idea how to market the film and couldn't figure out who was going to see it. It was a very tough time, because Marty and I felt it was a very good film.

Goodfellas (1990, Warner Brothers). Martin Scorsese joins the cast of his epic Mafia movie. From left to right: Henry Hill (Ray Liotta), Jimmy Conway (Robert De Niro), Paul Cicero (Paul Sorvino), Scorsese and Tommy De Vito (Joe Pesci).

Many fans say that Martin Scorsese's mother, Catherine, who played the part of Joe Pesci's mother, was one of the best and most convincing actresses in *Good-Fellas.*

It is a funny story behind the scene in *GoodFellas* when Liotta, De Niro and Pesci stop by the mother's house in the middle of the night to pick up a shovel so they can go bury the body that's in the trunk of the car. In the scene, Catherine is awakened by them and she convinces the boys to stay for a meal of pasta. Then, during the meal, we hear banging coming from the trunk outside. The character that she plays does not know there is a body in the car. The real reason she comes off so convincingly is that she really didn't know there was a body in the car. Marty and the cast and crew didn't tell her the total background of the scene. She thought it was just a scene where she makes dinner for the boys. Catherine acted wonderfully in Marty's movies. Scorsese's father, Charles, was in the movie too. His voice is on the other end of the pay phone saying, "He's gone," when De Niro is told that Tommy was killed. There are many little stories like that during the filming of *GoodFellas*, such as the Joe Pesci "You think I'm funny" scene with Ray Liotta. That scene was not in the script. Some guy actually did that to Joe in a bar and scared him to death. So, that was all Joe's idea, his contribution, and the effect was chilling.

I've read that Scorsese hates to do remakes. Why did you and Scorsese decide to remake the movie *Cape Fear*?

Steven Spielberg was developing the remake to *Cape Fear*. He had also been developing *Schindler's List* for years and somehow couldn't quite crack it. So, he had given Marty *Schindler's List* and he wrote it. After writing it, Marty decided he shouldn't direct the film. He felt Spielberg should direct it. Marty is not Jewish and he felt it wasn't his heritage. He felt it was a story Spielberg genuinely wanted to tell, so he should clearly tell it with his own directorial style. Spielberg took it back and, in return, gave Marty the script for *Cape Fear*.

How did you, personally, feel about producing a remake?

Actually, it was probably the movie that I had the most fun producing. It wasn't intense emotionally for me. You can say it was a great exercise in producing. We needed to shoot some place in the South. We also wanted to be in a place where we could not only bring in people, but also use the local crew so we could stay on budget. So, we decided that Fort Lauderdale, Florida, would be a good place to film *Cape Fear*. The city was happy to have us there and they really cooperated. It didn't really feel like I was producing a remake because it was so updated with a vast array of special effects. I had dealt with special effects before, but never at the sophisticated level of *Cape Fear*. To achieve the concluding water sequence, the city of Fort Lauderdale gave us a huge property where we built a tank that was really like an enormous swimming pool. It was very contained and controlled, which was exactly what we needed. It was quite involved, but this was not like *Titanic*. We were just using small houseboats. Then, we did some more finite miniature work in London to deliver the ending sequence and the boats. I had never done that before, so this was, as I said earlier, a great exercise in producing. It was very stimulating and satisfying.

Were the cameos of Gregory Peck and Robert Mitchum, the original Max Cady and Sam Bodin, cast in you film for the added publicity use?

Yes, I think it was motivated a little bit for the publicity. However, I also think it was just a nice touch of cinematic history to have these two actors that were so important in the original *Cape Fear,* made in 1962, in our new film. Marty values and adores them as actors and, in a sense, wanted them in his movie to pass down the torch to Bob and to Nick Nolte. I think they really enjoyed doing the cameo roles and they're extremely effective on screen, displaying more depth as actors than so-called "cameo" roles traditionally reflect. They were consummate professionals, brilliant.

What was Robert De Niro's prep like for the demanding role of Max Cady?

De Niro had a man by the name of Alan Greenberg go to maximum security prisons and interview a lot of guys who were in jail for life for extremely violent crimes against women. This is what Max Cady was originally put in jail for. The tapes were extremely twisted and scary. De Niro closely listened to those tapes and then he and Marty worked on the script with screenwriter, Wesley Strick. It was Bob's idea for the tattoos on Max Cady. He had seen many pictures of prisoners covered with tattoos. De Niro also had a physical trainer who got his body into top condition for the scenes where he takes his shirt off. It was a very demanding role. Bob was dedicated from Day One and it shows. He was ultimately nominated for an Academy Award in 1992 for Best Actor and deservedly so.

***Casino* must have been a challenging film to produce. It is a legendary fact that it's almost impossible to shoot a movie in a working casino. Was that the hardest phase of your shoot?**

Yes, absolutely. The hardest part of the whole shoot was finding a casino to film in. We had budgetary issues and considerations. It was very difficult to find a casino that we could work in. In *The Color of Money,* we had a small scene in a casino. The difference was that we shot it in New Jersey, in Atlantic City, and they do close. In Vegas, all the casinos are open 24 hours a day. They are making so much money that they don't need publicity. So, it was really hard for me to make a deal on that project. True, there were some closed-down casinos that we looked into. Ultimately, after I figured out the numbers, it was way too expensive to refurbish and redress them. Also, it was very hard to trace the owners of the closed casinos. We finally found a casino called the Riviera that would let us shoot at their place. We had to shoot during the graveyard shift, midnight to eight. The hard part was that we had to clear everything out — cameras, lights, props — at the end of the day so they could open for business. We shot on location at the Riviera for three weeks, a real challenge.

The script is adopted from another novel by Nicholas Pileggi, who wrote *Good-Fellas*. How involved was he during the production of *Casino*?

Very involved, because he published the novel after the movie was shot. They were actually writing the script from his notes and research. *GoodFellas* is a much tighter film, because he wrote the book first and the script second. *Casino* is much looser. The constant rewrites made it hard for me on this shoot. The budget was the biggest out of all of my collaborations with Marty and most of it was going to the above-the-line costs. This was a very long shoot and a long editing process for Marty and our long-time editor, Thelma Schoonmaker.

In *Kundun*, you and Scorsese gambled on using authentic Tibetan refugees, instead of professional actors, and it paid off. How big of a consideration was that?

We didn't have a big choice, actually, because there are no trained Tibetan actors. We were in Morocco and the hardest part was getting the extras. We had to bring all the extras and we couldn't bring anyone out of Tibet. Actually, most of the actors and extras came from India because there is a big Tibetan community there. In a country like India, not only do you need a passport, but you need an exit visa and then you need a piece of paper that says you have permission to go back. So, we had to get all the extras' papers and most didn't even have passports. A lot of them were refugees that didn't have papers at all because they had just crossed the border. I personally handled the paperwork. We brought them in by planeloads. The Moroccan government was great about it. They said they would give them all entry into Morocco as long as we would guarantee they all would be sent back home. They didn't want a Tibetan refugee community or a potential problem started there. So, everybody had to get their exit visas out of India, papers into Morocco and, finally, papers from Morocco to be allowed to go back into India after the shoot. It was a huge immigration challenge. I had a lot of paperwork and red tape to be concerned with because India is not easy to deal with. This movie was a lot like a Western because there were many people on horseback and only one car. Unfortunately, there was no Tibetan John Wayne.

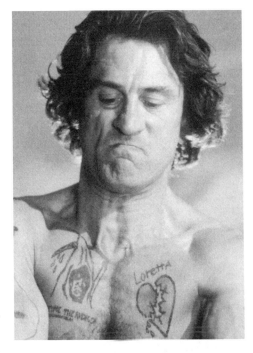

Cape Fear (1991, Universal Pictures). A psychotic and tattooed Max Cady (Robert De Niro) wrestles with his victim.

Was it hard for you to find financing for a picture like this due to our sensitive relations with the People's Republic of China, a major trading partner of the U.S., but an erratic political entity?

I think it was a major consideration. We tried to be fair and tried not to take any side. The film primarily was about the Dalai Lama. Secondarily, it was about the issues with China. Really, it was about his life, so we tried to be sensitive towards those issues and still tell the true story. The fact that Disney financed it was really courageous. Halfway through the production, a French company came in with a lot of foreign money. They bought all the foreign markets, so Disney was able to cut its financial exposure and didn't take as big a risk, ultimately.

An independent film you produced called *You Can Count on Me* with Laura Linney won the Sundance Film Festival and was nominated for numerous Academy Awards. How did this great script come to your attention?

Kenneth Lonergan wrote and directed it. We actually met him, because years ago we read *Analyze This*. His original version is different from what was eventually made on film. We really liked *Analyze This* and tried to buy it twice and, unfortunately, didn't get it. That was how Marty and I first met Kenny. *Analyze This* was held back for a few years. So, in between this time, he wrote several plays and he also wrote *You Can Count on Me,* which was his directorial debut. He made a deal, and Marty and I were brought on as a creative team more than anything else.

What did you do creatively as producers for Lonergan?

I think that evolved because he was a first-time director and he really had a definite idea of what he wanted to do with the movie and wanted to keep his vision protected. He wanted some sort of insulation. So that he could feel comfortable enough to deliver the movie that he wanted to make, Marty and I became his "insulation." We gave him creative and emotional support so he could keep his vision intact.

Casino (1995, Universal Pictures). Martin Scorsese discusses a scene with his lead actor Robert De Niro poolside at a Las Vegas hotel.

Casino (1995, Universal Pictures). Sam "Ace" Rothstein (Robert De Niro) and his lady Ginger (Sharon Stone) prepare to take off in their private jet.

Do you prefer producing big-budget or low-budget movies?

I like low-budget films because everyone is genuinely there because they want to be there. They are not there for the paycheck because they are not making that much money. They usually do films of this nature because they are only in an "assistant" capacity on other films. On low-budget productions, they can be the head of a department. So it is nice to go on a set and not have people come up to me and complain about their lunch money and how much their paycheck is. They are doing it because they love film and they want to be there. It is refreshing and fun to see people want to work and want to make movies. It also proves that you do not need $40 million or more to make a movie. You can make a movie for $2 million. You don't need a fleet of trucks and a ton of crew members. I might do an "Indigent Movie." There are basics to doing an indigent movie. The approach to the shoot is that you can have whatever you want to film with, as long as it fits into one van. Everyone gets paid the same amount of money a day, even the actors. You just go and make a movie for a low sum of money like $300,000. I guess it is the "extreme sport" of making movies. Some really great movies have come out of this approach.

These days, how do you feel about the title of producer?

The title of producer has become a big controversy. In fact, it has gotten out of control! You see a movie today and there are seven executive producers and five producers listed on a credit frame or printed lobby card. I think it is getting ridiculous and I think it is an important issue that needs to be addressed. In my eyes, the producer is really the person who developes and nurtures the material. They also package the movie. They get the actors, secure the director and get the script together. They obtain the financing. Sometimes, a producer will be a physical producer — that means the producer will be on the set. Then, the creative producer will take over in post-production to guide the editing process. Executive producers are sometimes line producers and production managers. It has gotten to the point today that most of the executive producers are the ones who write the checks. Now, managers have decided that since they manage an actor, they should also get an executive producer credit. Sometimes, they get extremely bold and say they are producers too. Now, the Academy of Motion Picture Arts and Sciences has decided if a film gets nominated for Best Picture, they will only allow three producers to receive the Oscar. Producers have to work it out amongst themselves or the Academy will determine who made the movie. They will not give out five Oscar statues, only three. So, this producer battle has gotten ugly. It doesn't take seven procedures to make a movie and it is highly unlikely that all seven have contributed traditional services.

The definition of the title of producer has become one of the big mysteries in Hollywood. Can you define what you do as a producer?

As a producer, I am very involved with the scripts and casting. I can read a script and find out what is wrong with it, but I can't rewrite it. I think all producers can pick up continuity mistakes, but the key to a successful producer is to pick up the emotions. Also, I put together the budget. I scout all the locations and help put the crew together. When I hire people, I always look to see if they have repeatedly worked with the same people. It shows me that they were good and were asked back. "Repeaters" are great to hire. During the physical production, I am generally on the set. Occasionally, like on the film *Grifters,* I wasn't involved on the set. There is a friend of mine who may direct this little movie in Toronto — a film that he developed, cast and is directing. He said, "If it gets made and if you're not busy, I would like you to produce it."

He is a friend and I told him that I would love to produce it. So, that would be something that I wouldn't have developed, but I will be on the set, producing. He knows I will help in keeping his mind clear and focused. As a producer, it is extremely important to take care of all the problems, so the director can keep his mind totally clear. I truly feel that the finished product will come out better.

When you are producing a film, what is the most important part to concentrate on during production?

The pre-production phase is the most important part, because if you don't set a movie up right at the start, you are scrambling every day. Also, if you are not honest with yourself, then you are in trouble. If you budget or schedule less days than you know you need, you are just setting yourself up to fail. Not only are you going to fall behind, but that deal you made for that specific location for precise dates and so forth means you are never going to get there in time. So, it just snowballs and gets worse and worse. You then have to try to fix something that you already knew up front. So, you are only cheating yourself and your reputation as an effective producer suffers. Sometimes people do it because, in the heat of the moment, they just want to get the movie going. You always pay for it later and it could wind up costing a lot more. There is a simple reality. You have to keep paying extra to fix your mistakes.

What is it like to produce for one of the most talented directors of all time, Martin Scorsese?

It has been truly rewarding. We have done some great films together. Marty really knows what he is doing. You always hear nightmare stories of films drastically going over-budget. As a producer, Marty makes your job of budgeting so much easier because he is so organized and plans everything out so thoroughly. My job of producing for someone the stature of Marty is to create a supportive atmosphere and keep his energy focused on making the movie. He doesn't need someone to watch over him to make sure he gets his coverage. He knows exactly what needs to be done at all times. I have really enjoyed the experience of producing for him.

After closely working for so many years with Scorsese, do you have any advice for aspiring directors?

You have to learn your craft. You have to pay your dues. I think many aspiring directors feel that Marty just arrives on the set. It is as if he was just born with all of his talent and that talent is all that gets him through a film. No it is not. Sure, he is one of the most talented directors in the business, but he worked very hard at honing his craft. You have to keep working at it. It is a position that I feel reflects the adage "practice makes perfect." Organization and preparation is the key. I think it is a little scary that, today, with the digital video age, anybody can now pick up a camera and direct and make a movie.

How do you feel about the medium of digital video?

Most of the time, I do not like how it looks. Many people say that if you shoot using digital video, you have to light it less. The answer to that is clearly, "no." In a small budget, using digital video is a big savings. However, in a big movie, the price of raw film stock and lab work is not, percentage-wise, an overwhelming savings. So, if you are spending $100,000 less on a $40 million movie, so what? I don't understand the benefit. If you are spending $100,000 less on a $1 million movie, then it is huge. I don't know if digital will translate to mainstream movies in the long term.

Which of your movies can you watch and see your creative touch on the screen?

Creatively, *GoodFellas.* I have always been a real supporter of that film. As I mentioned earlier, not many people liked or understood *GoodFellas* at the beginning. It was a rocky road but I was firm in my belief and never lost my faith. On the other hand, in the case of *Cape Fear,* I do not feel close to it creatively, but I feel close in the sense of being so involved in the physical production of the film. In a totally different sense, I still see my touch on the screen in that film, too. I do see a little of me in all of the films I have worked on.

How do you react being a woman producer in what many say is a male-dominated business?

I think it is tough, but getting better. Even though there is still a male bent on things, I think that if you look at the studios today, there are more women running the show. This is kind of odd, but one still has the feeling that the men are in charge. Now, you have Nina Jacobson, Mary Parent, Amy Pascal, Sherry Lansing and a lot of other women making big decisions. Yet, I think in some ways, overall it has to do with the big audience that is still perceived to be primarily male 18 to 25. I think a lot of things are aimed at making that audience happy. It is still hard today to produce a film and try to get a studio to back it with a female star as your lead. Sure, there are some exceptions like Julia Roberts and Nicole Kidman. But, it is still hard to get a female-driven movie script made. So, I think that the thing that is driving the train is the thought that Hollywood still has to make movies that men essentially like.

What advice can you give to women who want to enter the film business?

I think it is the same with anybody who wants to be in this business. A large part of success has to do with persistence. There are a lot of really talented people who are phenomenal at what they do and never go anywhere. Then, there are people with above-average talent and aren't gifted by any means, but do get to the top. It comes down to the fact that they are persistent. For actors and actresses, there is so much rejection. I don't know how they deal with it. I feel, in any business, it has to do with working hard, staying focused and hanging in there.

Barbara De Fina Filmography

.45 (Heather Graham, Haile Chesnut) 2003–producer; *The Mesmerist* (Neil Patrick Harris, Jessica Capshaw) 2002–executive producer; *You Can Count on Me* (Amy Ryan, Mark Ruffalo, Matthew Broderick) 2000–producer; *Bringing Out the Dead* (Nicolas Cage, Patricia Arquette, John Goodman) 1999–producer; *The Hi-Lo Country* (Woody Harrelson, Billy Crudup, Cole

Hauser) 1998–producer; ***Kundun*** (Tenzin Thuthob Tsarong, Tencho Gyalpo) 1997–producer; ***Kicked in the Head*** (Kevin Corrigan, Linda Fiorentino, James Woods) 1997–producer; ***Casino*** (Robert De Niro, Sharon Stone, Joe Pesci, James Woods) 1995–producer; ***The Age of Innocence*** (Daniel Day-Lewis, Michelle Pfeiffer, Winona Ryder) 1993–producer; ***Mad Dog and Glory*** (Robert De Niro, Uma Thurman, Bill Murray) 1993–producer; ***Cape Fear*** (Robert De Niro, Nick Nolte, Jessica Lange, Juliette Lewis) 1991–producer; ***Made in Milan*** (Giorgio Armani) 1990–producer; ***The Grifters*** (Anjelica Huston, John Cusack, Annette Bening) 1990–executive producer; ***GoodFellas*** (Robert De Niro, Joe Pesci, Ray Liotta, Lorraine Bracco) 1990–executive producer; ***New York Stories*** (Nick Nolte, Woody Allen) 1989–producer segment 1; ***The Last Temptation of Christ*** (Willem Dafoe, Harvey Keitel) 1988–producer; ***Bad*** (Michael Jackson) 1987–producer; ***The Color of Money*** (Paul Newman, Tom Cruise, Mary Elizabeth Mastrantonio) 1986–producer

Alex Kitman Ho

Born in Hong Kong, Alex Kitman Ho migrated to the United States with his family when he was five years old. After attending Richmond College and New York University, Ho worked his way up through the ranks of the film business. He rose from an assistant to a location manager to being one of the most sought-after production managers on the New York City movie scene. After working as a production manager for several years for legendary film producers like Dino De Laurentiis, Ho produced his first film, The Loveless *(1983), directed by Kathryn Bigelow and starring Willem Dafoe. His second producing effort, the hit film* Platoon, *started his long partnership with controversial director Oliver Stone. He went on to produce key films for Stone such as* Wall Street, Talk Radio, The Doors *and* Born on the Fourth of July. *He has also produced* Ali, *starring Will Smith and Jon Voight, for director Michael Mann.*

Alex Kitman Ho was nominated twice for Academy Awards, once in 1989 for Born on the 4th of July *and, again, in 1991 for* JFK. *He is busy in development with his company Miracle Pictures, located in Santa Monica.*

I was educated in New York City and grew up in Chinatown. I wanted to be in the film business after I saw a picture called *Rodan*. It's a Japanese horror movie about a prehistoric flying monster. It was right then and there that I realized I wanted to make films. Honestly, I didn't know what role I wanted to play in the film industry, because I was only 13 at the time and didn't know anything about it. I had absolutely no heritage related to it. I didn't have an uncle in the business. My parents were struggling immigrants who originally came here because of their fear of the Chinese Commies. In 1949, the Communists took over China so my folks had to leave or else they would get their hands cut off or something else horrible like that. Although Westerners aren't fully aware of it, this sadly happened to many people. When we moved to New York City, my father was a waiter in a restaurant and my mother was a seamstress. Over time, they both learned the restaurant business and, eventually, my father opened one across from Carnegie Hall. However, I knew I did not want to work in the restaurant business. I wanted to be involved in movies.

Where did you attend college to obtain your education in film?

I went to Richmond College on Staten Island. Then, I went to NYU. My major at Richmond was Cinema Studies. I never studied film production. That was the place

I learned how to write and where I wrote my first screenplay. I went to graduate school at NYU. The primary reason I went to school was because it helped me pay the rent, since you could readily get loans and grants. Unfortunately, in the summer you starved to death! However, it was great fun. At NYU, I got exposed to a lot of experimental film. The film *Scorpio Rising* directed by Kenneth Anger had a huge effect on me. I got to see the classics and these films were really helpful to me and I even refer back to them today. That's basically how I got started.

My first film gig was in college. I met a cameraman who I worked with and I was his sound man. We used to do various industrials with subjects like, "How to Be a Toll Taker for the Triboro Bridge." During these shoots, I learned a lot about the technical side of the business, like lighting and sound. The most interesting part of this experience was that I met a cameraman named Bruce Torbet. He shot one of director Robert Downey, Sr.'s movies. Bruce was a great director of photography. So, Bruce and I made these little films for Channel 13 on a series called *Fifty First State*. They paid you $200 per minute and you had to come up with little ideas about New York. We soon realized you don't make any money doing this. In retrospect, even though it didn't pay well, it was fun to do odd things about New York and you learned a lot. Essentially, that's how I started, just making little films.

How did the experience of creating these little films translate into you producing major motion pictures?

I did a lot of scouting locations for commercials. First, I did the locations for companies that produced commercials. Then, I scouted on my own. After that, I production managed a lot of big industrials. Some industrial films had the budget of $100,000 for companies like Kodak and Pepsi. I liked locations, because you're out on your own, doing your own thing. You get to talk to the director and contribute to the look of the film. Also, you learn about production in a businesslike management style. You have to go out there and make sure you come up with a practical and workable location. Back then, it usually was only you and maybe an assistant taking care of all the locations. Now there is a staff of 12 people. I really enjoyed doing location work and it eventually led me into doing it for feature films.

I heard that at one point, you were one of the most sought-after production managers in New York City. Is there any truth in that?

Well, I don't know about that, but I did work a lot. I production managed a lot of TV movies of the week and miniseries. They were tough to do, but they were good. One of the keys to my success is that I knew Manhattan very well. When you grow up there and you know the film crew guys, they try to protect you. I can remember walking on the set as a production manager and the Teamsters coming over to me and saying, "Come over here, kid, and we'll clue you in." They would tell me exactly what was going on before I spoke to the director or producers. This was truly invaluable because I was always ahead of the game. I learned so many great things from the crew guys because they had been around for so long. In New York City, the film business goes back generations. They really know their craft. Of course, I wasn't as seasoned as the crew. But, they knew I had enough knowledge to understand what they needed to do, because I had done a number of those jobs, lighting, gaffing and so forth, on those numerous documentaries. So, that was helpful and I earned their respect. I just love the crew people, especially on the East Coast. Over the years, I learned a lot from them.

Your first movie as a producer was *The Loveless* in 1983. Can you tell me about your transition from production manager to producer?

At that time, I was working for Fred Caruso as a production manager. Fred called me up and said, "I know these people who want to do this little film called *The Loveless*. Why don't you produce it?" I said, "Okay." The person who financed it was Monty Montgomery. He was later a partner for Propaganda Films, then headed into independent films. Many great directors came out of Propaganda Films like Spike Jonze who went on to direct *Being John Malkovich* and *Adaptation* and Antoine Fuqua who directed *Training Day*. They had a great concept in that they created a TV commercial company, hired a stable of directors, trained them through the commercial ranks and then they eventually directed their feature films. However, this movie, *The Loveless*, was financed by Monty Montgomery and co-directed by both he and Kathryn Bigelow. We cast Willem Dafoe for the lead role of Vance. I learned a lot from *Loveless* because I never actually produced a movie before. I put this whole film together. I also learned how to relate to directors as a producer. We all got along very well. *Loveless* won some awards and that created a buzz for everyone involved. I had a lot of fun on this picture.

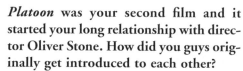

***Platoon* was your second film and it started your long relationship with director Oliver Stone. How did you guys originally get introduced to each other?**

I was working for the legendary producer Dino De Laurentiis quite a bit. Dino is an amazing guy. He is a true genius and produced classic films like *La Strada*, directed by Federico Fellini. This is a guy who put together the first major foreign movie deals. I learned a lot from him. Actually, I wish I learned more. Anyway, I had an idea about doing a picture about gangsters in Chinatown. That was my home turf. I grew up in Chinatown and it was a very typical story in the press. I pitched it to Dino, who thought it was a great idea. So, he hired some writers to help me with a script. We went around Chinatown and interviewed people. We wrote the script and it turned out terrible. So, we decided to let it rest for a while. One day, Dino

A. Kitman Ho

called me up and said, "Alex, I bought a book entitled *Year of the Dragon*." He sent me the book. I read it and loved it. I called Dino and said, "I love the book. What do you want to do next?" The next call I got from him was to meet at his office at 6 A.M. That's when he likes to have meetings. He's up early and then he takes a nap in the afternoon. Dino is a really hard worker. At the meeting, Dino told me he hired director Michael Cimino. I thought, "Oh, no!" Michael had a horrible reputation as being very tough to work with. He did have a good plan, though, and wanted to hire Oliver Stone as the writer. Michael's concept was that Oliver had this fabulous script called *Platoon* that he wanted to do. He thought maybe we could offer Oliver half the going price as a writing salary if Dino would promise to produce *Platoon*.

To make a long story short, they cut the deal. Oliver, Michael and myself spent six months writing the screenplay. I was the low man on the totem pole in the writing process, but I learned and helped a lot. I grew up in Chinatown. I knew where all the gangs hung out. I knew where all the gambling houses were. One night Cimino and Oliver wanted to see this gambling house that was restricted to only Chinese people. This police officer who knew us was extremely nice and busted one of the gambling joints so we could see what went on inside. The writing process was wild! After doing the screenplay, we unfortunately had a budget disagreement for *The Year of the Dragon*. Dino gave us $11 million to do the movie and I budgeted it at $23 million. In those days, that was a killer budget, probably equivalent to $100 million today. Well, Michael wouldn't talk to me after that. He felt I budgeted it way too high. Now, if you look at the bottom line of *Year of the Dragon*, in the end that is basically what it came out to be. So, I realized I couldn't deal with this project because I couldn't talk to the director. Dino said to me, "All right, then you produce *Platoon*." I said, "I don't really want to do *Platoon*. I hate war movies." However, Oliver and I got along really well and he persuaded me. I read the script and made some notes of my own. Oliver thought I had some great ideas and did a rewrite on the script for *Platoon*. I thought I really made a contribution. I liked working with Oliver because he has an amazing passion to do a movie. To top it off, he is a fantastic writer too. We budgeted *Platoon* at $7.5 million. We did a very thorough job scouting locations for *Platoon*. We went to Mexico and the Philippines. I always wanted to shoot in the Philippines because financially it worked. However, at the last minute, after we scouted it, Dino De Laurentiis pulled the plug on the project.

After Dino De Laurentiis bailed, how did you ultimately get *Platoon* on the big screen?

Oliver and I continued to talk and we still wanted to make *Platoon*. I adjusted the budget and came up with several options — budgets between $4 million and $7.5 million. We came out to LA with the budgets and we shopped the movie. This process took us a year and a half. In between this time, while shopping *Platoon*, Oliver had an idea. We were in New York one day and he said, "I have this manuscript in the back of my car in Los Angeles that the photo journalist Richard Boyle gave me about his book called *Salvador*. Do you want to produce it?" I said, "Sure, let's do it." So, we sat down and talked about the story and where it should go. Oliver used to write 25 pages every week and send it to me. I would read it, give him comments and send it back. Then, I put a budget together for $1.3 million. Eventually what happened was that I wanted to do it at $1.3 million but Gerald Green came on board and told us he could get more money from Mexico and do it for $3 million. I didn't want to get involved with that. I felt the financing was kind of wacky and I smelled trouble. I also wasn't going to make any real money on it. When something doesn't feel right, I just don't do it. Then, I came back to New York to do some "movies of the week" and to basically make some cash. In the meantime, I did promise Oliver that I would produce *Platoon*. In the whole line of the story, that's how *Salvador* got done. After *Salvador* came out and was hot, it was a lot easier to get the finishing funds to do *Platoon*. After Hemdale came on board to produce, we got someone to come in and put up $1.3 million for the foreign rights. In negotiating my deal for *Platoon*, I was dumb and took a co-producer credit. That film was an important learning lesson for me in many ways. In the end, we finally put *Platoon* together for about $5 million and shot the film. Production turned out to be a total nightmare. However, it was a great film.

Why was it a nightmare? What were the production obstacles on *Platoon*?

Well, the basic problem was that it was a war movie involving equipment, weapons and vehicles — all military and authentic. The reason I wanted to go to the Philippines is that they had American armor there. I made a deal with the Marcos government for the armor. The deal was a payoff of $40,000 to the general. Unfortunately, two weeks before we started prep for the movie, the Marcos government fell. I remember being in the hotel and I got a call from my head of production there and he said, "We've got a crisis. Don't leave the hotel." Through heavy negotiations, we finally got the new general, Ramon, to agree to let us film there for the same deal. If we didn't secure that deal with Ramon, we would have been screwed. At that point, we could never have done *Platoon* anywhere else because we were already totally set up and involved there. Everything finally calmed down and we shot the movie in the Philippines.

Was your casting of the platoon for the movie a very strategic and carefully planned process?

Here is another great aspect of the *Platoon* story. I remember that during the casting, Oliver came in early because we had two weeks for the actors to go through basic training. It was basically a military boot camp training process. Right before the training, five actors that we had cast from New York got together and had a meeting. It was a non–Screen Actors Guild movie and they decided they did not want to act in the film. Oliver and I then had to cast the movie by just looking at headshots. We needed a whole entire platoon and we did that by just using headshots, which is unheard of. Ironically, we wound up with a great cast of then-unknown actors like Forest Whitaker, Johnny Depp, Kevin Dillon and John McGinley. We always wanted Willem to be in the movie because I liked him and I felt he would be perfect in the part of Sgt. Elias. And he was. Charlie Sheen was great in the role of Chris Taylor as was Tom Berenger as Sgt. Barnes. Those were some of the most rewarding high points from the casting process of *Platoon*.

Platoon (1985, MGM). Sgt. Barnes (Tom Berenger) prepares to attack in this dark view of the Vietnam War in all of its horrific detail.

Wall Street was your next film. With Platoon you were in the jungle and now you're in a totally different jungle, Manhattan. Your locations were plush executive suites, the restaurant "21," the River Café and East Hampton. Was this a welcome transition?

I loved it. I loved scouting the locations. I was very happy to be back in New York. Oliver always wanted to do a picture about Wall Street because his father was a former stockbroker. When we did the film back in the 1980s, Wall Street was a hot topic. Oliver got Ed Pressman involved to pay a screenwriter named Stanley Wiser. Ed Pressman is a producer who has been successful at finding financing for motion pictures. He has been doing it a long time and is still good at it. After Pressman paid the screenwriter and we had a script that we all liked, he made the deal with 20th Century–Fox. I remember having a meeting with Leonard Goldberg and Gene Levy, who were the heads of production at Fox back then, and I gave them the budget of $17 million. They said, "No, we want to give you $15 million." Then I said, "I'll tell you what. If you give me $17 million, I promise I will bring it in under budget." Well, in the end, we brought it in $2 million under budget.

You worked with Charlie Sheen again, on Wall Street. In those days, he had quite the reputation as a "party animal." As a producer, how did you keep him under control and out of trouble?

Well, we almost did have a problem with him. However, I moved ahead cautiously and actually had a handler to keep an eye on him. As a producer, you always want to troubleshoot problems with actors or actresses so the director can concentrate on the film. On *Wall Street* he was a challenge, but we dealt with it. Ultimately he did a super job.

What did the hardcore Wall Street businessmen think of your portrayal of them in the film?

They all loved it. We worked really hard on that film all the way through. We captured the tempo of Wall Street in the movie and that was very important. Ken Lipper, managing director of Solomon Brothers and a former Deputy Mayor of New York, was the overall technical advisor. He gave us a lot of technical input to make sure it was right and realistic. Ken took a special interest and is still a close friend of mine.

How did *Born on the 4th of July* come about?

Oliver always had the script and wanted to direct it. Originally, it was optioned by producer Martin Bregman and he wanted Al Pacino to play the lead role of Ron Kovic. That fell through. So, while we were shooting *Wall Street*, we met with Tom Cruise. Tom read the script and really wanted to do it. Tom was young and he was having a bit of a slump back then. He had just done *Cocktail*, and Oliver and I both thought he was a great actor. The only problem was, we had to wait for Tom because he wasn't going to be available until the Fall. So Oliver said to me, "What do you want to do for the next eight months?" We talked about it and decided we could do a small movie. This is how the film *Talk Radio* got made. The idea was that we could prep *Born on the 4th of July* in Dallas while we shot *Talk Radio*. This way, I had two crews and I could use the same office for both movies. For *Talk Radio* we only had one set and two exteriors. It took five weeks to shoot. It cost $5 million to make and we sold it for $10 million.

How did Tom Cruise prepare for the role of the real-life character Ron Kovic?

Tom spent a lot of time with Ron Kovic who wrote the book and lived *Born on the 4th of July*. He studied him and really got his character down perfectly. Tom also went to all the veteran's hospitals and did a lot of wheelchair practice. Tom Cruise is such a great actor because, when he agrees to do a part, he really commits himself to the role. I was impressed at how diligent and completely involved he was during the entire movie.

You won a Golden Globe and were nominated for an Academy Award for this film. Can you tell me about the emotions you felt with these nominations?

Awards of this magnitude are so overwhelming for me. It is something I don't think about when I'm producing a movie. For me the nominations were a surprise, let alone actually winning the Golden Globe. In my eyes, I thought *Platoon* was a superior film and more emotional. I felt that *Platoon* should have been nominated. But, don't get me wrong. I do feel that *Born on the 4th of July* is a great film too, just not quite on the same level. To be honest, I don't feel that comfortable with press attention, but I was extremely happy when I won the award.

Wall Street (1987, Twentieth Century–Fox). Sleek entrepreneur Gordan Gecco (Michael Douglas) indoctrinates naïve stockbroker Bud Fox (Charlie Sheen) into insider trading.

The next film that you produced was *The Doors*. How was it to deal with an actor that many producers and directors claim is troublesome, Val Kilmer?

The hardest part of *The Doors* was to find someone who really worked and fit the lead role of Jim Morrison. The process was a nightmare. At that time, Paula Wagner of Creative Arts Agency was Val Kilmer's agent and she told us he really wanted the role. Oliver and I knew Val had a reputation. Then, Paula called again and said that Val had done a little video imitating Jim Morrison and that we should watch it. Oliver and I looked at the video and it was purely stunning. Val looked like him and, most importantly, *sounded* like him. He was absolutely great. From watching that video, we were quickly convinced that Val Kilmer was perfect for the role of Jim Morrison.

As a producer, how did you assemble the large-scale concert scenes that can easily propel a film way over-budget?

We just did it. We had great casting people on *The Doors*. To be honest, we hardly paid background people anything. For the big concert shoots, we basically just fed everyone in the crowd. We tried our hardest to shoot outside of Los Angeles. Shooting in Los Angeles was extremely difficult.

Since almost all movies are shot in California, why was shooting outdoors is Los Angeles difficult?

Well, we had to shoot on Sunset Boulevard. I remember negotiating with the City of West Hollywood and that was a nightmare. For one week, we got use of Sunset Boule-

Born on the 4th of July (1989, Universal Pictures). Ron Kovic (Tom Cruise) develops from a naïve recruit to an angry, wheelchair-bound paraplegic, to an active antiwar protestor.

vard from Monday through Thursday from 11 P.M. to 4 A.M. and it cost us a fortune. The City of West Hollywood wanted us to buy a piece of property on Sunset so they could build a garage and then they would give us the permits. I remember arguing with them and it was one of the toughest negotiations of my producing career. In the end, we had to pay the salary of two policemen for a year. It was like blackmail, in order to get the permits. But, to portray The Doors correctly, you need Sunset Boulevard. It was exhilarating to produce a musical. It was something I never had done. I think we captured the '60s and '70s successfully.

Can you tell me how the film *JFK* came about?

We started developing *JFK* during the production of *Born on the 4th of July*. Oliver gave me the outlines. I prepped the budget and then we figured out where to shoot it. That was the approach and how we came out with so many movies so quickly. We used to prep the movie way ahead and, then when it came time to shoot it, we were already in sync. I know exactly what Oliver wants, so all he has to do is focus on the preparation to direct it. Making the movie was not that tough. Once you set up and prep a movie correctly during pre-production, the actual production will go smoothly. The biggest problem for us on *JFK* was the bad publicity. We had to deal with negative publicity all the way through the production. That was the most time-consuming part of the movie.

Do you have any stories about your continual publicity problems during *JFK*?

Yes. One day I got a call from the CIA publicity department. My first reaction was, "Are you serious? You guys have a publicity department? Get out of here!" They said, "We are highly concerned about this film. We feel you are defaming us." I told them, "It simply is not true." As the producer, I had to keep the script away from many organizations. We had writers checking into hotels under assumed names. It was wild. Aside from that, as far as the production aspect of *JFK*, it was pretty simple.

Do you feel that the tremendous controversy helped the box office success of *JFK*, and ultimately helped secured your Oscar nomination for Best Picture?

The controversy definitely propelled it. It is also a subject that Americans and the world are interested in. I thought we took a very neutral stand in it. I think that other people thought we took a radical stand. The only thing we said is that you can't kill anyone with that shitty rifle. It isn't possible in 3.5 seconds. Which is true. People keep arguing with me about it. Who knows who did it? However, the Warren Report is wrong. If anyone takes that rifle and shoots three shots off in the same amount of time, you get a completely objective picture. If you think that makes sense, then fine. That's your subjective right.

How about the irony of Jim Garrison playing the part of Chief Justice Earl Warren? Was that a conscious decision by you and Oliver Stone?

We liked Jim Garrison a lot and got along with him extremely well. He was very sick at that point in his life. One thing that Oliver is really great at is spending time with people, especially people that he is writing about. We both wound up spending a lot of time with Jim so we could really know the character. Oliver and I really wanted Jim to be involved at all times. We thought him playing the part put a great twist on things.

How did the studio react to your finished cut of *JFK*?

All the executives at Warner Brothers thought it was very controversial. At the first screening, you could sense the nervousness. One of the executives actually hated it. However, there was nothing they could really do about it because they "green-lighted" the script and that was what the movie was about. One of the executives had some words with Oliver and they don't speak any more. As a producer, I generally deal with the studio execs. However, if there is a big problem, then Oliver steps in. I always try to protect my directors on all my productions.

You had such a great cast in that film — Kevin Costner, Kevin Bacon, Tommy Lee Jones, Sissy Spacek, Joe Pesci, Jack Lemmon and more. Did most of your budget go to above-the-line costs?

At the time of *JFK*, we were truly on a roll, working at a fast clip. Oliver was just casting as he saw fit. At one point, we couldn't afford it and then I had to fight with New Regency and Warners for more money. Overall the budget was $23 million. We got the entire cast, except for Kevin Costner, for a total of $2 million. As a producer, my job is to get the cast cheap, and when you have a hot director, you can do that. If you don't have a hot director like Oliver Stone, then you can't do that. As a producer, that makes my job fun. The other way, you have to continuously fight and negotiate dollar figures. You also have to create situations as a producer. For instance, you tell

Left: The Doors (1991, Carolco). Jim Morrison (Val Kilmer) is a drug-abusing hippie rock star whose life is stormy. *Right: JFK* (1992, Warner Brothers). New Orleans district attorney Jim Garrison (Kevin Costner) is busy at his desk attempting to crack the case of President John F. Kennedy's assassination.

one actor you have *another* actor signed on when you don't in order to get the other one to commit. There are a lot of things you can do when you're packaging a movie.

You produced *On Deadly Ground*. What was it like going from working with a true director like Oliver Stone to working with actor Steven Seagal in his directorial debut?

I was working on *Heaven and Earth* and then Oliver and I decided we didn't want to work together any more, which is a very long and involved story. Warner Brothers called and told me about this deal they had with Steven Seagal and that the picture was to be done for $55 million. They didn't actually have a budget, cast or a script. They made a four-picture deal with Seagal and this was the film, contractually, he was going to direct. I went in there and started working with the writer and Steven, and we just did it. I eventually produced *On Deadly Ground* for the $55 million I mentioned before, although it was budgeted at $65 million.

It seems like you never go over budget and you always stay on your mark.

As a producer, you have to carefully think the movie out in the beginning. If you don't think it out in the beginning, you are in deep trouble. It's similar to how a director has a plan for the creative part of the movie. It goes the same for the production side. You must have a solid game plan that goes all the way through the production process. For example, when they did *Anna and the King* with Jodie Foster at Fox, they told me they wanted to go to Malaysia. I said it was a very bad idea because we had to import everyone in there, crew, extras, etc., and it is a Muslim country. Plain and simple, it is a tough place to work. They went in there and went $40 million over budget. It's all a matter of a precise game plan. For me, the physical production part of a movie is easy. It is putting your mind to what it is you want to deliver. As long as you get the director to verbalize and let everyone understand what he wants to do, you can pull it off. For me, the hard part isn't following the budget, the hard part is doing the film creatively right.

How did you hook up with director Michael Mann to produce his film *Ali*?

Michael Mann called me because he had a real problem with *Ali*. I initially turned him down for over a month because I did not want to deal with it. Then, I began to think about it as a challenge. I had shot in Africa before. I liked the story of Muhammad Ali. I thought the script was very good. In the end, I did it because it was a challenge. I thought I would learn something, which I did. What I learned was what *not* to do. I think I chose a lot of projects during my career because I felt I could learn something from them. If you don't learn something, then what's the point?

What is the major difference between Oliver Stone and Michael Mann in their directorial approach?

Michael is a one-man band. Oliver is a great writer. Both are great with actors. Both are tough.

When you produce a film on subjects like Jim Morrison, John F. Kennedy and Muhammad Ali, is it harder because there is a fan base anticipating the film?

Yes and no. If you tap into that fan base, which is fascinating with those famous icons, then it is easy and you can make a lot of money at the box office. There is a thin line between whether the script on one of those subjects is a winner or a loser. There is more of a challenge to doing it successfully, but I love challenges.

You have worked with what many people say is one of the best writers in Hollywood, Oliver Stone. What do you personally look for in a script?

I have to really like it. I have to really connect to it. The script has to be resonate. It gives you something that when you turn back, you have a chuckle. You have to be moved. It has to stay with you. Somehow after you're done reading it, you are still thinking about it. *JFK*, *The Doors*, *Platoon* were all fabulous scripts. Oliver is such a talented writer. He is so gifted. Our relationship was so rewarding at that time in our lives. I got introduced to great writing by reading his scripts.

Would you define what you do as a producer?

In a nutshell, basically you are the shepherd. You have to start the film, deliver the picture, and make sure it opens up properly. Every single step of the way affects the movie. As a producer, I play the role of a trouble-shooter. I also am a fix-it man. From a problem with a studio, to an actor who walks off the set, to the makeup women who throw a hissy fit, I need to handle all the situations. In the old days, the production manager could handle it. Now, the job of making movies has gotten to be more specialized. Today, most of the movies have three production managers and three producer supervisors. Producing a big movie is like having a $150 million company spend all their money and close it up within a year. To be a good producer, you have to be prepared. There is no such thing as too much preparation. However, most of the time, producers do not prepare.

As a producer, are you involved with the creative aspects and budget more than the financing and raising of funds?

I am not good at the financing. I really wish I were better at raising money. That's my weakest point. I am great at the budget. Production for me is a piece of cake. I also think I am very good at the creative side. I am great with analytic notes, with advising writers and directors. Financing is something I need to get better at.

What producers have influenced you in this business?

I think Dino De Laurentiis is an amazing producer. I worked for him early in my career and I learned a great deal from him. He was a true mentor for me. Today, I think Scott Rudin is incredible. I have known Scott for years and he is a wonderful producer. I think these two guys are extremely talented and really know their craft. They define "producer" in the truest sense.

Have you ever had the burning desire to direct a film?

I never wanted to direct. It is too much work. You have 90 million people asking you questions simultaneously on set. I do appreciate and respect great directors. I had a chance to work with one of the best for a long time in Oliver Stone. As a producer, you oversee the director and make sure they don't fall down. I give them multiple choices so they can make their decisions. I would give them my recommendation and then they make the choices. I don't have a confrontational relationship with directors. I try to have a relationship that consists of teamwork because, basically, they are the creators. I like directors who listen and respect my opinion because together we can come up with better ideas. In the end, I think that a truly collaborative relationship makes for a better movie.

Could you see yourself doing anything else as a career?

I think about that question once in a while. But, producing has been so much fun. I have had a great career. I do feel that if you want to stay fresh in this business, you have to fine-tune your skills over time. The landscape changes around you. I am currently taking some CGI (computer generated image) classes. So much of the movie business these days is based on effectively using computer images. There are many directors and producers who do not know the first thing about CGI. It is a whole new world and it is here to stay. Even though it is actually 10 to 15 years old, it's still a mystery to many in the industry. If you don't learn about it, I don't think you can survive in the film business in the future. You are never really great at what you do unless you keep practicing it and keep up with the techniques that can enhance the creative product.

What does the future hold for you?

Right now I am producing a film called *Hotel Rwanda*, written and directed by Terry George. My company, Miracle Pictures, is currently in development with several projects. I love the development process because that is really where you see the movie happen. I am currently working with writers a lot more and I am trying to expand my horizons. In general, I have some children's books I would like to produce as well as an action-adventure franchise. I am also looking into doing a big biography film. As I reflect back on my career, I never once regretted becoming a producer. I have had a really great life.

Alex Kitman Ho Filmography

Ali (Will Smith, Jon Voight) 2001—producer; *The Weight of Water* (Sean Penn. Elizabeth Hurley) 2000—producer; *Brokedown Palace* (Claire Danes, Kate Beckinsale) 1999—executive producer; *The Ghost and the Darkness* (Michael Douglas, Val Kilmer) 1996—producer; *On Deadly Ground* (Steven Seagal, Michael Caine) 1994—producer; *Heaven & Earth* (Haing S. Ngor) 1993—producer; *JFK* (Kevin Costner, Kevin Bacon, Tommy Lee Jones) 1991—producer; *The Doors* (Val Kilmer, Meg Ryan) 1991—producer; *Born on the Fourth of July* (Tom Cruise) 1989—producer; *Talk Radio* (Alec Baldwin, Leslie Hope) 1988—producer; *Wall Street* (Michael Douglas, Charlie Sheen) 1987—co-producer; *Platoon* (Tom Berenger, Charlie Sheen) 1986—co-producer; *The Loveless* (Willem Dafoe) 1982—producer

Marianne Maddalena

While attending the University of Michigan, with a language major of both Italian and French, Marianne Maddalena knew she was going to be a movie producer one day. So, she headed to Cannes to use her French to make it in the film industry. After meeting writer Harold Robbins there, she was invited to Los Angeles to be his assistant. Not long after that, she went on to be the assistant for acclaimed horror director Wes Craven. She transitioned from assistant to producer on the cult horror flick, Shocker. *From that point on, she hasn't stopped producing hit films like* Scream, *its two sequels, and the critically acclaimed* Music of the Heart *starring Meryl Streep. She became partners with Wes Craven and, at their company, Craven/Maddalena Films, they have numerous projects in development.*

One thing that my whole family had in common was that we were all obsessed with movies. Whenever we would take long drives, we would always play our movie guessing game. What we would do is give the initials of a movie, with a brief description of the plot, and you would have to guess the name. We'd play for hours and hours and it feels just like yesterday that I was struggling for one of those names. I grew up in Lansing, Michigan. I was one of five children — our family consisted of one sister, three brothers and myself. My mother was a schoolteacher and my father owned a family business, selling carpet, tile and marble. My father would take me to movies all the time. That was what we would do together. We used to go to the drive-ins and see all the James Bond movies. The Bond movie that really affected me was *On Her Majesty's Secret Service.* When James Bond's wife Tracy died, I was just crying and crying and crying. However, I guess the first movie that I was really affected by was *Papillon* with Dustin Hoffman and Steve McQueen. I went to the theater, watched the movie, left the theater, went back into the car and just burst into tears. I was sitting in the car, just bawling my eyes out in the parking lot. I always loved the really sad movies. As I got older, my tastes changed and I became a big Woody Allen fan. I love *Annie Hall* and *Manhattan.* I truly feel that the film *Manhattan* is a perfect movie. It is very rare when you find a truly perfect movie. When you become a producer, you can even have more admiration for an accomplishment like that.

You have produced some of the top-grossing thriller movies of all time. What is your first memory of a scary movie?

I remember seeing *The Stepford Wives* and I was scared to death! I had to literally

194

walk out of the theater because I was so frightened. It was the part when they went to get Katharine Ross' character, Joanna Eberhart, that made me get up and leave. When I watch it now it isn't even that scary, but back then I was totally affected by it.

What is your educational background in film, and the inspiration for you to enter the entertainment industry?

After high school, I attended Michigan State University. I had a language major of both Italian and French. I took no film classes, but knew all along I was going to make movies. I also knew I wanted to travel. I spoke French better than Italian, so I took one look at France and decided on Cannes because of the Cannes Film Festival. So, I moved there after college. I literally arrived in Cannes with my Samsonite luggage in hand and I had never even eaten an artichoke before. My first job there was as an au pair. During that time, I started hanging out at the certain bars that au pairs would go to and I began meeting a whole bunch of people who worked on yachts, which is very much a subculture in Cannes. I got a job as a chef on Harold Robbins' yacht. He was one of the most successful and famous pulp fiction writers of his era. He invited many and entertained movie industry people on the boat, stars like Margaux Hemingway, hot writers like Allan Carr of *Grease* fame and others. It was so much fun and we would travel around the South of France. It was wonderful absorbing the French lifestyle and the culture, especially since I came from Lansing, Michigan. So, I got a major education, especially working as a chef. I had no idea how to really cook. Sure, I had a flair for it, but not enough experience to cook for millionaires and movie stars. I eventually learned and had a lot of fun. I was there for three Cannes film festivals. I fell in love with French cinema and really admired Francois Truffaut's work. Eventually, though, Harold Robbins offered me a job in LA. So I took it. He had a little film company on the West Coast.

It must have been a major culture shock for you, going from France to Los Angeles.

No kidding! (*Laughing*) Unfortunately, not much went on in LA until I started working for Mort Viner, who was an established Hollywood agent. He represented Dean Martin, Shirley MacLaine, Gene Kelly and others. It was a lot of fun because the agency was in the mainstream and represented a lot of great talent. I even got the opportunity to meet the legendary Alfred Hitchcock, which was a huge thrill for me. So here I was living in LA and in the film business, but I knew I wanted something more. I wanted to become a film producer. So, then I took any job I could get. I did a lot of script reading. I worked at an editorial company, syncing dailies. After that, I started working as a production coordinator on various independent films. Then, finally, I began working as Wes Craven's assistant.

How did you get connected with Craven?

It was basically word of mouth. Wes was looking for an assistant and I was looking for a job. Before I started working for Wes, I had no idea about his movies. Come to think of it, I hadn't even seen *Nightmare on Elm Street*. I wasn't a scary movie buff at all. However, I met with Wes and I really liked him. It was a "He needed me" and

"I needed him" kind of situation. I actually didn't want to become an assistant. I wanted to produce. Wes was a really nice guy and so open. Before he became a director, he had many different jobs. He mainly was a professor, but he had a side job as a cab driver. He was even a sound editor for a post-production company in New York City. Anyway, Wes decided to take a chance and chuck it all in and become a film director. I really admire that. Wes also took a chance on me, gave me a job and it was clearly endearing for him to do at the time.

Can you tell me about your experiences in Haiti as an assistant on *The Serpent and the Rainbow*?

That was kind of when we realized we could get through anything, basically. We had a blast down there because it was so crazy and insane and you just had to throw yourself into it. From the beginning, we were all excited about the project. Haiti is a beautiful country with beautiful people even though it has an element of danger. The culture and the art is so beautiful. People actually have an amazing spirit for a place that practically has no trees. From a production standpoint, it was just one of those situations where at the time, the production team didn't really understand how Third World this was going to be. It was a very violent and dangerous country. The people were very poor and we had money. So it was a very dangerous situation for us to be in because they were not shy about asking for that money.

Did the locals attack any of the crew physically during the shooting of the film?

We were in the middle of shooting and had thousands of extras and all of a sudden they wanted us to double their fee. When we didn't agree, they decided to pick up rocks. The whole crew ran to take cover inside the church. We left the equipment sitting outside. The camera, the footage, the lights. Can you imagine that? Then, producer David Ladd got up on top of a bus and talked everyone into putting the rocks down and they finally agreed on a price. That was very brave of David Ladd. Our other producer, Doug Claybourne, was a gun-runner in Vietnam and he said he never felt as scared as he did in Haiti. It was so wild! As hard as that shoot had been, it was a blast. It was such an amazing experience, never to be duplicated, because you really had to be 26 years old and ready for anything.

How did you move up from assistant to producer on *Shocker*?

Wes Craven said to me, "Do you want to produce? Here's a movie, produce it."

Was it a smooth transition, going from assistant to producer on this film?

Well, it kind of reminded me of when I agreed to be a chef in the South of France. I was cooking for millionaires and I had no idea what I was doing. So, I read cookbooks all night. When I went from assistant to producer, it was basically the same thing. I was scared to death, but yet willing and kind of ignorant. I feel it was my ignorance that got me through my first experience producing. I didn't know any better, but I was very good at organizing. I had a really good line producer on *Shocker* who taught me so much. His name was Barin Kumar and, sadly, he suffered a heart attack and died during post-production. It was so horrible. He was only 37 years old, he was getting a

The Serpent and the Rainbow (1987, Universal Pictures). In this serious speculation on the pos-sibility of zombies in Haiti, Marielle (Cathy Tyson) performs a voodoo dance for Harvard anthropologist Dennis Alan (Bill Pullman).

massage and dropped dead right on the massage table. He had a wife and baby and that was a blow. Barth was genuinely talented and helped me through the production. In *People Under the Stairs* we had a great line producer in Stuart Bessel, who I have now worked with for 16 years. The budget was only $4 million and it took in $20 million. So, that was a big help in making my transition as a producer look smooth.

Shocker (1989, Universal Pictures). Mass murderer Horace Pinker (Mitch Pileggi) wreaks havoc upon a prison doctor (Janine Peters) after his unsuccessful electrocution.

As a producer, do you feel with a lower budget you are more creative than with a higher budget where you can just throw money at a problem?

It is amazing how much money does get thrown at a problem. Back in the day of *Shocker,* I didn't really know any better because I never produced a movie before. The film was non-union and we had names like Peter Berg and Mitch Pileggi. So, it didn't seem at all like we were doing a low-budget movie. I didn't know any better. The creative angle was that because it was so cheap, on a daily basis you could go over-budget without killing yourself. If you go over on a union movie, it's $150,000 to $200,000 a day. In those days it was $35,000 and it was usually findable if you really needed it.

Your next movie was *New Nightmare.* After *not* directing installments 3, 4, 5 and 6, why did Wes Craven decide to direct this installment?

Because he came up with a brilliant idea which was to have Freddy attack Heather Langenkamp and to come into the real world of the actress. Freddy attempts to murder the actors and creators from his previous films. I, personally, thought that was a brilliant idea because, how *else* do you re-tell Freddy? There have been hundreds of stories but when Wes pitched me the idea, I said, 'We have to do this movie!" Heather was really willing to play herself. This was a unique idea and a great way to end the series.

The film that you produced, *Vampire in Brooklyn,* starring Eddie Murphy, did not do well at the box office. Do you learn from your failures as much as your successes?

That is a very good question. I definitely learn from my failures as much as my hit films. That particular project was kind of a strange film because of the comedy-horror aspect of it. I thought the script was pretty funny and cute, but I think the audience was expecting something different. I think the film didn't deliver to Eddie Murphy's audience what they were looking for.

After this failed venture, were you extremely cautious about what your next film would be?

Wes and I were really cautious. We were looking for something out of the genre, so when *Scream* landed on our desk, our first reaction was, "Oh no!" Basically, it was because it was the same genre, which was very bloody and violent. However, Bob Weinstein of Dimension Films made a great offer that included Drew Barrymore already signed on as the star. So, we moved ahead and probably had the most fun on a movie. *Scream* was such a blast because we didn't know that we had a hit on our hands. We were in beautiful Napa Valley. We felt we had plenty of money and we didn't feel like we were skimping. We had a great cast and a fabulous crew. It felt like the same thing as *Serpeant and the Rainbow*, but we were older. Here we were in Napa Valley on location. I mean, what's more fun? So we had exactly that — fun. We had fabulous dinners, parties and unlimited wine. There were pool parties, throwing people in with their clothes on and a lot of fun. It was wild! Then, to make it even greater, the movie was a hit.

How did writer Kevin Williamson's script for *Scream* first strike you when you read it?

I thought it was really funny, scary and clever. Although, I did think the opening was a little too violent with regard to Drew Barrymore's character's guts hanging out. Just as scripted, it was shot with Drew's character hanging from a tree with her guts falling out of her body. There is no denying it was beautifully written and smart. The ending was fabulous. Thinking back, the script was exceptionally well-done.

Have your thriller projects ever had trouble getting ratings?

Always. Wes gets mad and says, "I want to put out an NC 17 movie." I tell him, "You really can't do that." Then, it just takes a couple of days to cut a little here and cut a little there, but it is always a horrible experience. As a producer, I act as the intermediary in that situation. So it is very hard. A filmmaker does not want to cut an inch of the film and I don't blame him. Somebody is dictating what to do and that is not what the filmmaker wants to hear. It is not an easy part of the job. One incident that became an ongoing battle happened with *Scream*. The ending, when Billy and Stew were stabbing themselves, is what I'm referring to. We had to trim that a lot, but I think it was still very effective. In retrospect, I don't know if Wes would say it really hurt the movie or not. That would be a good question.

At that time, your lead actors were lesser-knowns. Can you tell me about the casting process you went through?

We went down to the wire when picking the part of Sidney. There were many talented actresses up for the role. I don't think it would be fair if I named them. Wes and I looked forever. We decided to cast Neve Campbell and she was obviously wonderful. Same situation with the part of Tatum. There were a lot of actresses up for it and we finally got down to Rose McGowan. She was obviously fabulous. Also, who could be better than Skeet Ulrich? No one has ever walked into my office with that kind of danger and seductive handsomeness. He was the perfect Billy. David Arquette was so great with his creation of Dewey. The rest of the cast, Matthew Lillard, Jamie Kennedy, Courteney Cox, and Henry Winkler were all fantastic. That's what happens when a movie really works. You look back and you realize that you assembled the perfect people. It was a great script, great director, great cast and a great crew.

Did you ever expect such a monetary and commercial success with *Scream* and that kids would be wearing that costume for the next 30 Halloweens?

Never. Every Halloween brings back great memories. Already, a month previously *Variety* had listed us as DOA, dead on arrival, because *One Fine Day* starring Michelle Pfeiffer and George Clooney was going to be the big one. I will never forget reading the headlines, "*Scream* DOA." It was like "oh God." Plus, we were also opening up against *Beavis and Butt-Head* the same night. Wes and I went to Universal for an eight o'clock showing of *Scream* and it was half-empty. No one was getting the jokes. We felt very down. We wondered what happened? We went to *Beavis and Butt-Head* and people were screaming and yelling and throwing things at the screen. We thought, "Oh well, too bad our film didn't do it. It's not going to make any money. We had a great

New Nightmare (1994, New Line Cinema). Freddy Krueger (Robert Englund), the scarred maniac with fedora and razor finger gloves, once again wreaks havoc on his unsuspecting victims.

time, but what a drag." The next day I went up to Carmel for Christmas and I got a call from Bob Weinstein. He said, "Congratulations, this is fabulous." And I thought, "Really? You are happy about a $6 million opening?" I just didn't fully comprehend at first that the exit polls from the audience were so high and strong.

Did you learn a valuable lesson about the importance of audience exit polls?

I learned a very important lesson that day as a producer. Always look at the exit polls. The next weekend, it made $9 million and the next $12 million. It was so exciting and what could be better than that? Wes and I originally thought it was going to be a total bomb.

For your next film, *Scream 2*, did the budget go up substantially?

It went up from $12 million to $25 million, and it mostly went to above-the-line costs. We wanted the same surviving cast members back and had to pay for it. So, we had Neve Campbell, Courteney Cox, Jamie

Scream (1996, Dimension Films). Sidney Prescott (Neve Campbell) and Tatum Riley (Rose McGowan) speak on the phone with the psychopathic killer who is stalking them.

Kennedy, and the others, but we even had cameos by Tori Spelling and Heather Graham.

Were you impressed with the script for *Scream 2* as much as you were impressed with Kevin Williamson's first installment?

I thought it was good. Unfortunately, it was written in kind of a hurry. Plus, there was no way you were going to top *Scream*. It was brilliant. However, I felt it worked well and I am still happy about it. Miramax gave us a lot of freedom with this project.

Why did Ehren Kruger write the third *Scream* installment instead of Kevin Williamson?

Kevin was unavailable. He was involved with *Wasteland* and just didn't have time. Kevin was attempting to do it, but he just ran out of time and we couldn't wait. We had committed that slot. Ehren Kruger came in and did a great job. He is so talented. Ehren has also written *The Ring*.

Ehren's last name is Kruger. Any correlation to Freddy Krueger?

Total coincidence. Then, subsequently, we worked with another talented writer, Mark Kruger. Isn't that funny? It was all a total coincidence.

***Scream* changed everything in Hollywood. Studios started a whole new push of teen thriller movies. As a producer, how does it feel to pioneer a trend?**

It feels great. It's totally exciting. The thing about a hit movie is that it's a "win-

win" for everybody involved. Your friends, your family, everybody is happy for you. Obviously, there are people who aren't, but that happens in any business. You go home at Christmas and everyone is thrilled. The studio is happy, the actors are happy, your agents are happy, their agents are happy, your lawyers are happy. It's just so much fun, a real high. Starting a trend is one of the most exciting things in the film business that can happen to a producer.

You guys were successful with the thriller genre projects, so, why in the midst of this success did you produce something like the drama, *Music of the Heart*?

Mainly because Wes had always wanted to do it. When *Scream* was such a hit, Harvey and Bob Weinstein of Miramax sat us down and said, "What do you want to do? If you do three more movies with us, we'll give you any movie you want from our slate." Wes chose *Music of the Heart* because he'd seen the 1996 documentary *Small Wonders*, which it was based on, and loved it. It was a real heart-tugger about the dream of a woman to teach violin to a group of Harlem kids that eventually leads to a performance at Carnegie Hall. They just said, "Okay." I thought it was a great idea. We got writer Pamela Gray, and the script was wonderful. They gave a green light and we were off.

Can you tell me about the initial casting of Madonna and then, subsequently, Meryl Streep for the lead role of Roberta Guaspari, the inner city violin teacher?

Harvey Weinstein really wanted Madonna. We didn't actually have a choice when it came to the casting of the lead role. So, we agreed and we worked with Madonna for a few months and in the end it was obvious it wasn't going to work with her. It came down to creative differences, with Madonna and Wes seeing the part differently. Then we parted ways with Madonna and shut down the movie after it was only two weeks into the filming. When we parted ways with Madonna, there was a small list, but not very many of the actresses were available. Originally, there were many women interested in this role, including Julia Roberts, but we never really had time to explore these other options because Harvey had wanted Madonna from very early on. Then, Wes wrote a very passionate letter to Meryl Streep about the role and she responded. Originally, Meryl passed because she was too busy. However, after the passionate letter from Wes' heart, she accepted.

In the end, it must have been bittersweet when Meryl Streep won the Golden Globe and was nominated for an Oscar.

No kidding! Meryl was genuinely committed from the day she accepted the role. She rehearsed and practiced so hard and was simply fabulous. The interesting thing is even though *Music of the Heart* wasn't a big commercial success, it was as exciting as *Scream*, because on another level we had so much fun making it. We shot in Carnegie Hall. We took the film to the White House. We showed it to the President. Everything about it was so wonderful, exciting and, most importantly, inspirational. It was a "win-win." You produce a movie like that, about that unique subject matter, with a Meryl Streep, and it was simply a privilege to be involved.

Scream (1996, Dimension Films). Billy Loomis (Skeet Ulrich), Randy Meeks (Jamie Kennedy) and Stuart Macher (Matthew Lillard) plan to attack the killer who is stalking them.

Since *Music of the Heart* was such a critical success and so much fun to work on, do you want to produce more films of this genre?

Oh, yes, definitely. We have plenty of movies like that in development already. However, we have a deal with Dimension Films and Bob Weinstein wants another thriller movie. So, we are going to do one more for him called *Cursed*. Then, our next movie after that will definitely be outside the thriller genre.

Can you describe your role as a producer?

A producer really needs to be someone who is a very good organizer and has to have a lot of empathy. You have to figure out what people need before they say it. It's kind of a very maternal job. I'm not saying men can't be maternal. Men can certainly be great producers. Most of it is intuitive and involves an extremely organized mind. As a producer, you tend to be an enabler for highly creative people. You have to be the kind of person to whom every detail is important. You have to possess a lot of energy and be a great communicator. I sometimes find that creative types are not the best communicators outside of their specialized area. They need someone else to communicate for them. You do a lot of talking and a lot of care-taking. Yet, the job is creative as well. My creative touch is all over the movie. Wes leaves a lot up to me. I am involved in every writing meeting, so this is a very creative job. We collaborate on the casting. I handle a lot of the wardrobe. I work closely with the production designers, so it's creative to the kind of third-dimensional person I am and that I always knew I was. As opposed to, say, me wanting to direct. I am not good at doing one thing at a time. So,

Music of the Heart (1999, Miramax). Roberta Guaspari (Meryl Streep) with her students in this story of a schoolteacher's struggle to teach violin to inner-city kids.

I probably would not be a good director or editor. However, I chose something that I was good at. Luckily, when you find something that you are good at and you want to do it as a career, that's the best of both worlds and you can achieve what you truly want.

What do you look for in a script when considering producing it into a major motion picture?

I look for a good story. When I read it, I say to myself, "I want to see that movie." There are stories you truly want to hear and stories you don't want to hear. I am always looking for that hook.

What is it like to be the main producer and partner of Wes Craven?

It is a total partnership. He is extremely generous with everything. In fact, he was that way from the beginning. Wes brought me into casting meetings, location scouts, writing meetings. From the very beginning, he opened the door for me because Wes knew what I wanted to do, which was produce. He let me come to any meeting, even though some people would raise their eyebrow wondering why I was there. As an assistant, I stayed late, sometimes 'til one in the morning. If Wes worked on Saturday from eight in the morning 'til midnight, as his assistant, I was there. Nothing was more important for me than learning. I think that is how you move up the ladder in any business.

Nowadays when assistants say "I have to be home by 5 PM," I'm totally shocked.

That is certainly not the way we did it when I started. To make it in this business, you have to be willing to work, work and work. It takes the passion, but it also takes a solid work ethic. In this business, there is no such thing as watching a "time clock."

You, obviously, have a very keen eye for young talent. What do you look for in an actor or actress?

It's always that certain magic. Like I said, when we were looking and looking to cast the role of Billy, all of a sudden Skeet Ulrich walked in. All the women in the office went crazy. They were saying he was so cute and charming. Skeet had this sexy, dangerous side that was definitely perfect for the role of Billy. As soon as he walked in, you just knew. As a producer during the casting process, you are always looking for that kind of magic.

Are you loyal to your crew members, hiring the same people for all of your productions?

Sure you can say we are loyal, but it's because we love those people and they make our business lives easier and it's fun to work with them. All our crew members are invaluable. Our first assistant director, Nick Mass, our production designer, Bruce Miller, our other producers, Stuart Besser and Daniel Arredondo, who we have worked with for years, are all gold. So, it's really that we are extremely lucky that they are free when we need them.

Can you offer any advice for aspiring producers and other filmmakers?

You have to speak your mind. Say out loud and tell everyone what you want to do. You always must just keep asking. You want to vocalize your intent all the time. You really have to want it and then work your butt off to achieve it. That's what makes it all worthwhile.

Marianne Maddalena Filmography

Cursed (Christina Ricci) 2004 — producer; *Dracula* **2000** (Jonny Lee Miller, Jennifer Esposito) 2000 — executive producer; *Scream 3* (Neve Cambell, David Arquette) 2000 — producer; *Music of the Heart* (Meryl Streep) 1999 — producer; *Scream 2* (Neve Campbell, Courtney Cox, Sarah Michelle Gellar) 1997 — producer; *Scream* (Neve Campbell, Skeet Ulrich, Rose McGowan) 1996 — executive producer; *Vampire in Brooklyn* (Eddie Murphy) 1995 — executive producer; *New Nightmare* (Heather Langenkamp) 1994 — producer; *The People Under the Stairs* (Ving Rhames) 1991 — producer; *Shocker* (Mitch Pileggi, Peter Berg) 1989 — producer

Scott Mosier

When Scott Mosier attended Vancouver Film School, he met Kevin Smith, a fellow student who aspired to be a film director. They teamed up and headed for New Jersey to film Smith's clever and well-written independent film, Clerks. *Mosier produced this ultra–low-budget film and it became a huge hit. Mosier and Smith formed their own company called View Askew Productions. They have gone on to make the hit films* Chasing Amy, Dogma, Jay and Silent Bob Strike Back *and more. Smith and Mosier have a great working relationship and a true friendship. They are one of the most successful director/producer teams working in Hollywood today.*

I wasn't the type of kid who shot High–8 movies in my backyard, but I always loved watching films growing up. I had a pretty normal childhood. I played sports, hung out with my friends, partook in underage drinking and spent the majority of my time trying to lose my virginity. (*Laughing*) All the normal kid stuff. I think the first film that had any effect on me was *Raiders of the Lost Ark.* That was the first time I actually thought about the process of making movies. However, when I was in college, my tastes in film began to become more sophisticated. I think the reason my grades were so bad in college was because I spent most of my time watching Federico Fellini, Ingmar Bergman and Francois Truffaut movies. I would skip class and watch three or four movies a day. I then began to watch a lot of independent movies like *Stranger in Paradise, Trust* and *Slacker.* I wanted to see what the world of independent filmmaking was all about. Don't get me wrong, I love watching a film like *The Matrix,* but I wouldn't want to make it. That is not my style, professionally. Also, today, if I was an aspiring filmmaker and I loved *The Matrix,* that would be great. However, you also have to think to yourself, "How am I going to make a movie like that on a $50,000 budget?" So, from watching all of those great independent films, I began thinking about making my own independent film. I was in LA taking some night classes at UCLA when I decided to go back to Vancouver, where I grew up, because there was a really good film school there. To be honest, I also wanted to get the hell out of LA. When I got to the Vancouver Film School, I met Kevin Smith, who had just arrived from New Jersey. I also met David Klein, who would be director of photography on our first three movies. Kevin and I became friends pretty quickly and he told me that he was planning on staying at the school for only four months out of the eight-month curriculum. Kevin had *Clerks* already in mind, so his plan was to go to school to learn how to make a movie and then go back to New Jersey and direct *Clerks*. The course consisted of four months of instruction and four months of practical moviemaking — actually doing a film, a short film.

Did you and Kevin wind up making a film at the school?

We did a High–8 documentary project. Everyone in the class had to pitch a documentary concept, so Kevin and I pitched an idea about a pre-op transsexual that Kevin had recently met. We were not well-liked in the class because the students thought we were not taking the course seriously. Anyway, there were 26 people in the class, 12 pitches were made and they only picked four. We had a really convincing pitch and we wound up being one of the four picked. To be honest, we didn't even want to do this documentary idea. We just wanted to be picked and to win. We got a crew together and things did not go very well. Finally, the pre-op transsexual bailed on us. In the end, we decided to make a documentary of how the documentary fell apart. It was really cool, because we mostly made fun of ourselves. Then, we came to the four-month mark and the short film part of the course. Kevin wanted to leave so he could save the $5,000 tuition. During the first four months, Kevin, Dave and myself all talked about the three of us getting together in New Jersey to make *Clerks*.

Did you find the knowledge you obtained in the film course helpful when you made *Clerks*?

Yes, because I learned about all the other positions on a film set. I think that, basically, everyone goes to film school to be a director. That's because you don't know about the other jobs on a film set, like the costume designer, director of photography, editor, etc., etc. I stayed at the school and did many short films and learned about all these different positions, which turned out to be very helpful in making *Clerks*. Toward the end of my eight-month course, I began to research about low-budget filmmaking. I graduated school in October of 1992 and we planned on shooting *Clerks* in December, but there was a big flood and we had to put it off until March. From Canada, I made phone calls to the New York area and I booked all the equipment. I also wanted Kevin to hire Dave Klein from school to be our director of photography. Kevin said, "Do you think he will do a good job?" I replied, "We have no money and no food and Dave doesn't care about that. He's like us." So, we agreed on Dave being our d.p. The key was not to hire anyone on the film with too much experience. We felt it could really mess things up because they will start telling us all the things we don't have that we need to make a movie properly. As far as we were concerned, to make a movie all you needed was a camera, film, a couple of lights and something to record sound on. We thought it was so simple, and our naivete is what got us through.

As the producer of *Clerks*, did you get heavily involved in trying to raise funds to make the movie?

I wasn't really a producer on *Clerks*, just Kevin's friend who had never been to the East Coast. In the end, I guess I *was* a producer, among many other positions. At that point in my life, I was only 22 years old and had no real aspirations. I think the only thing I was aspiring for was to not get a job. So, I sold all of my stuff to go make *Clerks*.

I sold my car, my clothes, whatever I could so I didn't have to work during the making of the film. As far as the budget, Kevin wanted to spend $25,000 on the movie. If he'd spent over $30,000, I think he would have freaked out big time. In the end, we wound up spending $27,000 on the whole movie. Kevin's parents loaned him $3,000 to get the camera equipment and my parents loaned us $3,000 to do the print of the film. All the rest was on Kevin's credit cards.

What were your job duties?

I organized the renting of all the equipment. I put together a budget. I talked to everyone and asked, "What is the bare minimum you need?" Kevin had a casting call and he cast everyone before I got there. I got to New Jersey three weeks before shooting. Once I got there, it was the process of going to all these places that I spoke to on the phone and picking up the equipment. Then, I made more calls to find a lab, to make mag transfers, etc., etc. There wasn't really a shooting schedule. There was a three-week window for all the rented equipment and we had to use it during that time frame. We worked seven days a week, all night long. Actually, that was the only time we could get to shoot in the convenience store where *Clerks* takes place.

Why did you choose black-and-white film? Was it better for budgetary reasons?

Our thought was that there were all fluorescent lights in the store and since that was our primary lighting source, we felt it would look best on black-and-white film. On a budget this low, you have to deal with the practical limitations that are available to you. We also knew that if we didn't shoot color, we wouldn't have to worry about color balancing. It was a little bit cheaper shooting it in black-and-white. In the end, I think the black-and-white lent itself perfectly to the film. The only reason we could think of to *not* do it on black-and-white film was because many people said it would be harder to sell. However, another reason we opted for black-and-white was that if it looked bad in color, we had no money to color-correct it. We did not have a seasoned crew. Our director of photography, Dave, was 20 years old and had only shot one short film prior to *Clerks*. So he didn't have a lot of answers to the questions we had, nor did we expect him to. In the end, black-and-white was the "safe" call for us.

They say the film stock is the most expensive part of making a movie. How did you afford the film stock?

We went to buy the film stock at Kodak because we heard they were offering a film student's rate of something like 30 percent off! We went there and found out that you needed to present a student ID to be given the discount. So, Kevin ingeniously decided to register for a class at the New School so he could get a student ID. Then, we could get the student discount on film. His foresight was that this whole ID escapade could make for a funny anecdote if the film ever got bought. We tried to find the most obscure, weird class possible. Kevin signed up for a cooking class in Roast Suckling Pig. We were actually going to pick "Understanding Your Homosexuality." (*Laughing*) Anyway, we got the school ID and we got the film student's discount at Kodak.

Clerks (1994, Miramax). Dante Hicks (Brian O'Halloran) and Randal Graves (Jeff Anderson) kick back with some candy bars while on break at the convenience store.

Tell me you cancelled the class and got your money back.

We did immediately after we got the film! (*Laughing*) The camera package was $1,000 per week. It was a 16mm Arriflex SR camera. Unfortunately, it was kind of loud so I threw my big leather jacket over the camera to keep the noise down. *Clerks* was that kind of cut-and-paste effort, a "figure it out as you go along" type of situation. We started the film in March and the print was done in August. We submitted it to the Independent Feature Film Market at the Angelica in downtown New York City.

Did anything happen for you at the Independent Feature Film Market?

There was a guy named Robert Hawk who was at the IFFM representing Sundance. He was the only person who saw the movie besides us because the theater was pretty empty. Robert started to tell many important people at the market about us like Peter Broderick, who wrote articles and worked for the IFC. He also told Amy Taubin, who wrote for *The Village Voice*. Every year, Amy wrote an article and picked out the films that she thought were good. One year she wrote about *Slacker*. The next year she wrote about Edward Burns' directorial debut, *The Brothers McMullen*. Amy sort of encapsulated the whole IFFM event through her article. She saw our film and we became the focus of that year's article, which was really great for us. We got enough juice and hype out of the IFFM event so that John Pierson, a producer's rep, and who had also written a book called *Spike, Mike, Slackers and Dykes*, contacted us. Anyway, John, as a producer's rep, takes finished or unfinished independent films and either sells them as a finished product or he gets the money to finish them. John had a long history of selling and finishing films like Spike Lee's first movie, *She's Gotta Have It*, and other productions like *Roger and Me* and *Slacker*. John watched our movie and decided to represent us right before we got into the Sundance Festival.

What was the Sundance Film Festival experience like for you?

It was pretty exciting to get in. When you finish an ultra–low-budget movie like *Clerks,* where there's so much uncertainty, the problem is that at any given moment it could all end. The end being that there is no distribution. We, fortunately, never had that problem. However, you have to remember, getting into Sundance is a great opportunity. Unfortunately, for many filmmakers, often the case is that nothing happens there. In fact, every company saw our movie, but Miramax was the only one who took a chance and bid on it. Had Miramax never bid, who knows whether we would had gotten distribution at all. So, fortunately for us, each moment was another door opening, with us all along hoping that the door wouldn't shut in our faces. I know a lot of people who have made good films that haven't gone anywhere. I was very thankful for what happened to us. Finally, at the end of the Sundance Film Festival, the deal was locked in with Miramax.

How much did you sell *Clerks* for?

They gave us $227,000 for the film. Of the total, $27,000 covered the production costs and $100,000 was for completion costs. That meant, after remixing it, blowing it up to 35mm and to basically create the other deliverables, we did have a profit! In the end, our profit was about $80,000, which we split amongst the cast and the crew, who originally worked for free. That $80,000 surely wasn't like winning the lottery, but it was winning the "career lottery," in a sense.

Have you ever seen any back end profits from *Clerks*?

Just recently, we have seen some profits, which is always great. *Clerks* was such a fun experience that none of us really cared about the money. We traveled all over the world. Naturally, we went to Utah for the Sundance Film Festival. We then went to a film event in Tokyo and then to Cannes. We just got swept up in all this crazy, fun, exciting stuff. It was a truly great time in my life.

How did your second film *Mall Rats* come about?

Kevin had a writing agent at CAA before we went to Sundance with *Clerks*. At this time, we started the process of *Mall Rats* at Universal. We went in and pitched it and they bought it. Over the course of us flying around the world, Kevin was actually writing *Mall Rats*. James Jacks and Shawn Daniels were the producers of *Mall Rats* and I was the co-producer. I met the line producer, Laura Greenlee, we hit it off and she really boosted my confidence. I was only 24 years old at the time and I was worried about what people would think of me being that young and that inexperienced. Laura was my mentor in a sense, because she told me what to do and what not to do. I knew nothing about unions and all the other important stuff that a producer should know on a picture. However, I quickly became useful because I became a voice on the set. In fact, I was such a solid voice that by the end of the movie, they changed my title from co-producer to producer. I didn't get paid a lot, but I was a producer and, once again, it was another win in the "career lottery." Then, the movie bombed at the box office. Before the movie came out, we smartly made an overall deal with Miramax. Kevin decided to write *Chasing Amy* because we felt we did not have the clout to do a controversial film like *Dogma* yet. Also, he wanted to do something low-budget because *Mall Rats* cost $6 million and $3.5 million was above the line.

How did it feel to go from a budget of $27,000 on *Clerks* to $6 million on *Mall Rats*?

It was a whole new world to me and I had trouble understanding it.

With the mentoring of Laura Greenlee, did you feel more comfortable producing *Chasing Amy*?

Yes. I was the main producer on *Chasing Amy*. I was 90 percent of the final word on that film. All of the decisions beyond the direction and the performances were all mine. On *Mall Rats,* I was truly watching things happen from the sidelines. However, on *Chasing Amy*, I was in control. I learned one very important thing about producing very early in my career: If you really do the job right as a producer on a film, all the way through from prep to release, then the picture will run smoothly. The prep on our latest picture, *Jersey Girl* starring Ben Affleck, was really tough.

Tell me a little bit about the casting of the then more or less unknown Ben Affleck and Jason Lee in *Chasing Amy*.

On *Chasing Amy,* we wanted a specific cast. The studio did not want Ben Affleck, Jason Lee or Joey Lauren Adams. Kevin and I fought for them. They were then, and still are, very talented actors. Joey Lauren Adams, who played the part of Gwen Turner, went on to win a Golden Globe as Best Actress. So, because of us pushing for this particular cast of lesser-known actors, we had a lot smaller budget to work with. We shot *Chasing Amy* on Super–16 film for $250,000. Ultimately, with all the music and blowing up to 35mm film, the final cost was almost $800,000. It was a great accomplishment to produce that film, but something I would never try again. I had the attitude that I didn't care if I slept on that shoot. I just smoked and drank coffee. Those were the years I could do that, but now I just can't. I had a line producer and a production manager and we just did everything. We shot it in 1996 and 1997. We premiered at Sundance and everyone loved it, including Miramax. Kevin was going to film *Dogma* before *Chasing Amy*. In retrospect, I think that it was really smart that Kevin decided to do *Chasing Amy* first because when other actors saw the film, they wanted to be in *Dogma*. That film really put us on the map and that allowed us to make *Dogma*. Miramax really wanted to make *Dogma*, but they were equally scared to make it. They did not want to put in a lot of money because of the risky story content.

Was getting *Dogma* made a true battle all the way through?

Yes, it was tough. We didn't have enough money and we were over-schedule and under-budget. However, it was one of those instances where if we didn't do *Dogma* right after *Chasing Amy*, we would have never been able to do it. I learned a huge les-

Chasing Amy (1997, Miramax). Holden McNeil (Ben Affleck) shares a laugh with Alyssa Jones (Joey Lauren Adams) over drinks at a local bar.

son on this film as a producer. I'd rather spend more time arguing during prep and say, "This is what we need to make the movie. I need this much time and I need this much money. Give it to me and I will do it and do it well. I won't come back to you unless there is a tornado." Anyway, *Dogma* was not like that for me. It was a total underestimation of what it would cost to pull this off. We went over budget by about $1 million.

Did you take a lot of heat from Miramax for going over budget?

No, because it wasn't really just because of me. It was a lot of outside factors, like actors' schedules, that was kicking the shit out of us. When you have a budget of only $7 million and you are using top name talent, things happen. Salma Hayek had to stop shooting in the middle of our film because of her schedule on *Wild Wild West*. Ben Affleck had to do *Shakespeare in Love* and *200 Cigarettes* in the middle of our shoot. It just went on and on and on. Chris Rock was a huge problem because of his schedule on *Lethal Weapon 4*. When we finally got into post-production, things settled down. *Chasing Amy* and *Dogma* were back-to-back films and they were just grueling.

What lessons did you learn about producing from those two movies?

The main lesson was to spend the time to get all the information you need before you enter into actually filming the movie. I now spend the necessary time in prep, arguing to the grave to make sure I have the right amount of money and the right

Chasing Amy (1997, Miramax). Kevin Smith discusses a scene between takes with star Ben Affleck.

amount of time to shoot the picture. I want to say to a studio, "Why are you arguing with me about this extra $1 million? Trust me, I don't want to use it on better catering. This extra money is about a song, a CGI shot, basically something that will bring up the production value of the movie which will, in turn, get more people into the theater. I am trying to add to the movie so we can add to the returns." Getting *Dogma* made was hard enough, but getting it put in the theaters was even harder. We got death threats. The Catholics freaked out. There were protests because of the issues of race, women and the Bible. Catholics felt that we were tearing their religion apart. When *Dogma* finally came out, we renewed our deal with Miramax and we decided to do a less stressful film with a more simplistic topic — something that was not controversial in the least. We wanted to just make some money and have some fun. So, that is how the film *Jay and Silent Bob Strike Back* came into being.

There were a lot of special effects in *Jay and Silent Bob Strike Back.*

We did have a lot of CGI on that film. We used light sabers and bong sabers. (*Laughing*) We used map paintings. What was the most pleasant thing for me on this project was that on all our prior films, we worked six-day weeks and on this film we did five-day weeks. To be home on a Saturday and not have to go back to work the next day was a revelation. When you work six-day weeks, on your one day off, you are just plagued with the fact you have to go back to work the next day. You're truly plagued by it. It felt good to be more relaxed and I think it contributed to the film. We started shooting in January and released the film in August. It was a quick production.

When you started out in this business and you made *Clerks*, did you ever say to yourselves, "Let's make a film like director/writer Robert Rodriguez did"?

Kevin did read an article focusing on Rodriguez before we made *Clerks*. It basically quoted him as saying, "You should make a movie built around what you have at your disposal." That is what Kevin essentially did. Kevin wrote a script about a convenience store because he worked in one and had access to shoot in it. As far as making a film like Rodriguez did for $7,000, that was not what we wanted to do. What Rodriguez was trying to do for $7,000 was to produce a finished product on a tape so he could get it to an agent. What we needed to do was to get a print and sell it to a distributor. I had to look at budgets that involved a lot more than Robert Rodriguez's first film, *El Mariachi*. *Slackers* was more money like what we were trying to accomplish. That was shot for $23,000 and we came in at $27,000 on *Clerks*.

I have heard many aspiring filmmakers say, "Let's make an independent film like *Clerks*." You have given some guys in a dorm room right now a glimmer of hope.

(*Laughing*) It is great to be part of a chain of people who made movies that are accessible for the aspiring filmmaker to attempt. In our own code, the films *Slackers* and *Trust* made us say to ourselves, "We can do this!" I am sure there are three guys in a dorm room who just finished watching *Clerks* and are saying, "We can do this." Certainly $27,000 is not that much money. Many kids get into a lot more debt than that in going to four years of film school. If you went to NYU for a year, with the tuition and living costs involved, I am sure it is more than $27,000. I guess I am sort of telling kids to quit school and go make a movie. But, you know what? Maybe they should. It feels really cool to be a part of our process. Now it is even less expensive because there is Digital Video and Final Cut Pro. The whole business has changed. However, I guess it basically remains the same premise—go out and try to do it yourself. If I was going to give advice to someone now, I would tell them to shoot Digital Video and buy Final Cut Pro to edit their movie. You can buy and own all the equipment today based on the price of our rentals for *Clerks*.

What do you do as a producer?

I am sure that this book will reflect that different producers do very different things. I am not a deal-maker at all. I came up learning the physical production on a film. I am the hands-on producer who is involved from soup to nuts. Kevin and I are partners and I do stick my head in about casting. However, I do not go to lunch with agents and shmooze. That is not really my game. Kevin and I have a true partnership. There is no "Scott Mosier Productions" where I am doing numerous movies at a time. I make sure Kevin has everything he needs to make the best movie he can. I also do whatever he is not doing. For a director, Kevin is extremely involved in the marketing of our films. I pick up the slack in other areas.

If I owned my own production company, I would be more involved in the marketing of my films because I would have to represent myself. Kevin and I are more about representing each other. Mostly, I spend the time figuring out how we are going to make the movie that everyone wants to make. That includes the studio as well. I say to the studio, "If you want to make a movie with two big stars, then this is the amount of

Top: Dogma (1999, Lions Gate Films). Friends, Rufus (Chris Rock), Jay (Jason Mewes) and Serendipity (Salma Hayek) join together in a scene directed by Kevin Smith. *Bottom: Dogma* (1999, Lions Gate Films). Loki (Matt Damon) and Bartleby (Ben Affleck) are two angels who are prevented from entering Heaven.

money I need to make the movie you want. If you want to shoot on Park Avenue in New York City, then this is the price to make that happen." As a producer, I also try to hear everyone out and then come to a conclusion with the budget. I hear what Kevin wants. I hear what the studio wants. Then, I will present my case to both parties. Sometimes, I have to convince Kevin not to shoot something so we can save money. I ask him, "Do you really feel we need this shot?" Many times he says, "You're right, Scott. It will not change the face of this movie. Let's get rid of it." On the other hand, many times I go to Miramax and say to them, "Please give me more money for this shot. Kevin and I think it will really make this movie. This is a big shot that we can put in the trailer." The way I generally work is that I will listen to everyone and if I feel they are making a mistake, I will voice my opinion. A producer has to voice his or her opinion when necessary.

Do you try to protect Kevin Smith on your films, so he stays as focused as possible?

Yes. I always tell Kevin that I will deal with the studio or anybody else and I will only come to him for his help if it is totally necessary.

Do you have any advice for struggling producers who are trying to find financing?

The best advice I have is to meet a Kevin Smith. I know that is kind of stupid advice, because it is like winning the lottery. However, you have to find a director or writer that is so talented that he or she will be noticed someday. Then, as a producer, you should help him or her so they can perform to their highest capability. Also, learn as much as you can about every aspect of a production. Learn about all the positions and functions. I am involved from soup to nuts with our productions. When other producers start exerting their opinions on things that they actually have no expertise or experience with, it drives me crazy.

What does the future hold for Scott Mosier?

Jersey Girl just ended and I need to take a break. I enjoyed the film and, for the first time in 11 years, I am finally going to take some time to relax. I just turned 32 and we shot *Clerks* in 1993. It is now 2003, the end of my first decade. It is time for me to take a break and smell the roses.

Scott Mosier Filmography

Jersey Girl (Liv Tyler, Ben Affleck) 2004 — producer; *Jay and Silent Bob Strike Back* (Kevin Smith, Jason Mewes) 2001— producer; *Clerks* (Brian O'Halloran, Kevin Smith) 2000 TV cartoon — executive producer; *Dogma* (Linda Fiorentino, Chris Rock, Matt Damon, Ben Affleck) 1999 — producer; *Good Will Hunting* (Ben Affleck, Matt Damon) 1997 — co-executive producer; *A Better Place* (Jerry Rosamilia, Jason Lee) 1997 — producer; *Chasing Amy* (Joey Lauren Adams, Ben Affleck, Jason Lee) 1997 — producer; *Drawing Flies* (Joey Lauren Adams, Jason Lee) 1996 — producer; *Mallrats* (Shannen Doherty, Jason Lee, Jeremy London) 1995 — producer; *Clerks* (Brian O'Halloran, Kevin Smith, Jason Mewes) 1994 — producer

Index